AF646679

FACETS OF SPIRITUALITY

Dialogues and Discourses of Swami Krishnananda

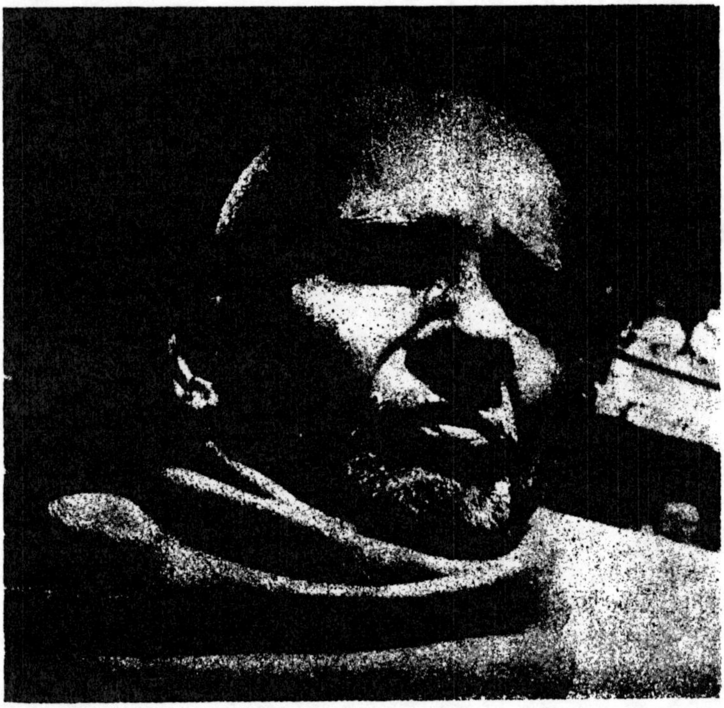

FACETS OF SPIRITUALITY

Dialogues and Discourses of
Swami Krishnananda

Compiled by
S. BHAGYALAKSHMI

MOTILAL BANARSIDASS
Delhi Varanasi Patna
Bangalore Madras

First Published: Delhi, 1986
Reprint: Delhi, 1987

MOTILAL BANARSIDASS
Bungalow Road, Jawahar Nagar, Delhi 110 007
Branches
Chowk, Varanasi 221 001
Ashok Rajpath, Patna 800 004
24 Race Course Road, Bangalore 560 001
120 Royapettah High Road, Mylapore, Madras 600 004

© MOTILAL BANARSIDASS. ALL RIGHTS RESERVED

ISBN: 81-208-0087-7 (Cloth)
ISBN: 81-208-0093-1 (Paper)

PRINTED IN INDIA

BY JAINENDRA PRAKASH JAIN AT SHRI JAINENDRA PRESS, A-45 NARAINA INDUSTRIAL AREA, PHASE I, NEW DELHI 110 028 AND PUBLISHED BY NARENDRA PRAKASH JAIN FOR MOTILAL BANARSIDASS, DELHI 110 007.

To

VIRAT

in whom reside my Guru Swami Sivananda
and Upaguru Swami Krishnananda

His Holiness founded the Divine Life Society in 1936 with the following aims in view:

1. To disseminate spiritual knowledge.
2. To establish and run educational institutions.
3. To help deserving orphans and destitutes.
4. To establish and run medical organisations.
5. To take similar other steps from time to time to further these aims.

The Society was registered in the year 1936 and has been functioning actively through a Board of Trustees, an elected body whose elected President is the head of the Society.

Foreword

Om Sri Sadguru Paramatmane Namah !

I deem it a spiritual privilege to have been asked to write a Foreword to this treasure house of spiritual inspiration, wisdom and practical instruction. This unique compilation of H.H. Revered Sri Swami Krishnanandaji's conversations, discourses, answers to the seekers' queries, writings, lectures, etc., testifies to the dedicated labour of love for which the author deserves not only our congratulations and deep appreciation but also our gratitude.

To modern man in quest of knowledge, the contents of this book come as answers to his deepest needs. Here in these pages is the quintessence of the highest Upanishadic revelations commingled with sound pragmatic common sense and humane understanding of the problems that vex the heart and mind of man today.

Sri Swami Krishnananda is at this moment one of the foremost thinkers and philosophers of the world. His writings like *The Realisation of the Absolute, The Philosophy of Life, The Ascent of the Spirit* have created a spiritual stir among the intelligent reading public. His wide-ranging knowledge of both Indian and Western philosophy, his almost intuitional grasp of the mysticisms of the East and the West combined with his own personal realisation have made him the spiritual teacher of eminence much sought after by seekers from all over the world. His illumined personality radiates spiritual light and wisdom to all those who draw near to him even for a brief period of time. He is both a sage and a saint at once. Sincere seekers receive from him deepest sympathy and love as well as highest insights, inspiration, and spiritual upliftment.

The author has done a great service to mankind by bringing out his personality and his hidden wisdom in this invaluable compendium of Swamiji's wisdom and wit and his practical spiritual teachings. I wish this publication fullest success and widest possible circulation throughout the world.

May the Divine Grace and the choicest blessings of the Almighty Universal Spirit be upon the author, the worthy publisher as also the fortunate readers!

Homage unto the Divine! Adorations at the feet of worshipful and beloved Gurudev Swami Sivananda!

Shivananda Nagar
May 30, 1983

SWAMI CHIDANANDA

Preface

Sri Swami Sivanandaji Maharaj may be considered as one of the major contributing forces in the building up of the edifice of India's spiritual renaissance in the modern era. Gurudev pulled out the soul of man that lay buried under the debris of religiosity, "isms" and clichés about a Sannyasi, a Sadhu and a Risi. He was the meeting point of the well-proven ancient Vedic traditions and those of the modern world. Addressing Sri Sivananda, a foreign visitor once said, "Swamiji, why do you wear so well-cut an over-coat? You are a Sannyasi, aren't you?" "Would I be a greater soul by draping round a blanket shoddily and with my hair un-kempt and in disarray? Does a clean-shaven head and face shed off the worth of man, the Divine in him?" was the repartee from him. He founded the Divine Life Society to bring home to modern man the Divinity he enshrines and the value he possesses as the temple of the soul within.

Dissemination of knowledge was his heart's desire. His ashram on the banks of the Himalayan Ganga distributes free books, hand-outs, pamphlets and spiritual literature of all varieties worth thousands of rupees. Gurudev alone has written over three hundred books, culling knowledge and wisdom from the ancient lore and also rendering into unforgettable words his own practical philosophy and personal experiences, without any inhibition or reserve as a guide, for everyone to follow. All knowledge, he held, was spiritual, for there is no distinction between the spiritual and the not-spiritual. And, in the ultimate analysis, nothing was "only" spiritual—of 'the other world'. The media through which Gurudev disseminated his wide-ranging knowledge included in his time such weeklies as *Health and Hygiene, Wit and Wisdom*, and numerous stories, quizzes and puzzles of all sorts for children. Since man has the Divine within him how can any knowledge be exclusive and profane? When knowledge is used to serve the Divine, does it not become spiritual?

Swami Krishnanandaji, one of Gurudev's most beloved disciples, has imbibed every 'aṁśa' (intimate part) of his Guru-in-God. The Absolute, the Supreme Being, is Sri Krishnanandaji's 'Ultimate Being'; and Sri Sivananda Maharaj is the incarnation of that same Supreme Being. Like his master he also disseminates knowledge either in the enclosed verandah or on the open terrace* in front of his *Kutir* "Guru-Kripa" (ground floor). Once he emphatically said that people did not go to the ashram to see the buildings and the scenery; someone must be available to them to impart spiritual knowledge.** And this spread of spiritual knowledge is carried out informally in the morning between 9 a.m. and 11.30 a.m. Anyone can put a question and get an answer to his particular problem, mundane or spiritual. His pen flows over just as his Guru's did. His writings and talks, discourses, lectures, etc. have caught the imagination of thinking men in all the different parts of the world.

This fact inspired in this humble self an urge to compile excerpts of all that Swamiji talked about, lectured or wrote. I decided that such outpourings of his knowledge of the ancient texts, particularly of the Vedas and Upanisads, as also the discussions on spirituality, science, philosophy and metaphysics should be brought to all those who had not had the opportunity of directly getting the benefit of such valuable and rare knowledge.

Yet another reason for my undertaking this compilation is Gurudev's exhortation: share knowledge with others as you should share your bread. In Gurudev's autobiography, there is a point worth repeating any number of times and on any occasion. Swami Sivananda says that when he replied to letters from people seeking his wisdom (on any matter whatsoever), he always exhorts the writer of the letter to share with his friends the knowledge that he has now acquired and to ask that friend to share it again with other friends, when the latter writes to them. It is this instruction that I have humbly tried to follow in this book. Nothing here is mine. In the course of editing, or while transcribing the tapes and compiling them, errors may have crept in. I beg the kind reader

*This has been converted into an 'enclosure' very recently.

**It is said of Swami Krishnananda that he moves out of the ashram next only to the bricks of the walls of the ashram. And this remark was made in response to an appeal from some devotees to join one of the annual celebrations of the All India Divine Life Society held in one of the big cities.

and the elders to bear with me for the errors, if any, found in these pages. Such shortcomings are obviously mine.

No work, however minor, gets done without travails and tribulations. This book too is no exception. Its editing, in one way or the other, has passed through the hands of more than one friend—of more than one Karma-yogi to be exact, so that I can but thank them all with all my heart only collectively and not by their individual names. Ashramites, friends and even nodding acquaintances or visiting Sannyasis such as the one from Trinidad, have rendered ungrudging help in typing the manuscript of over 600 pages, in proof-reading and in arranging the contents. My humble thanks to one and all. My Gurudev and God shower their blessings on one and all of these kind souls!

I am particularly thankful to the publishers, Motilal Banarsidass of Delhi, for their interest in bringing out this book. This firm is a very old friend of the ashram whose infinite variety of publications include H.H. Sri Sivananda's writings and other publications of the Sivananda Publication League, Rishikesh, U.P. May they prosper unendingly from generation to generation!

I am deeply beholden to the holy feet of Sri Swami Chidananda Maharajji the well-known global personality, who tirelessly spreads his master's message of hope in the Divinity of man and his salvation in the spirit of his Guru Swami Sivanandaji Maharaj's dictum: "Give. Serve. Meditate. Realise. Enquire who I am. Know thyself and be free." It is no mere empty phrase to say that Swami Chidanandaji's frail frame gets literally worn out in this task. Yet his loving heart has found time to write a foreword to such a minor book of mine. My tears of gratitude wash his holy feet!

S. BHAGYALAKSHMI

Introduction

This book is an attempt by this humble author to present H.H. Sri Swami Krishnananda, the renowned disciple of Sivananda Ashram, Rishikesh: the man, the mentor and the philosopher. A person with a far higher intelligence and wisdom than mine can adequately achieve this objective. But when it comes to talking about the fourth deeper level, the inner man, the true being of an individual, leave alone that of a sage-philosopher, no one can even attempt the task. For, a person such as Swami Krishnananda lives within the cocoon of spirituality invisibly transforming himself into the very Brahman he ever contemplates on, like the worm becoming the stinging wasp, to borrow a Vedic metaphor. This metaphor is a well-known cliché of the sacred texts. It is said that the worm in the stinging wasp's nest being constantly stung by the wasp, broods over its fear of pain until it is metamorphosed into a stinging wasp. The biological truth of this is a matter for the biologists. It is not a phenomenon known to everybody.

The division of this book into three parts, the man, the mentor and the philosopher, is, however, not made with a view to unfolding Swami Krishnananda's personality. It is, rather, like viewing the different patterns formed in a kaleidoscope by just rotating it. When the kaleidoscope is rotated, an equally interesting but a different pattern is formed within the strips of the mirrors by the coloured pieces in between them arranged at 60° to each other. The different aspects of Swamiji's personality viewed from different angles are presented in this volume. These pages do bring out the different potentialities in him like the coloured pieces in the kaleidoscope. The reader should not look for "continuity" in the dictionary sense but in a variety of moods. For, spirituality is the common ground wherein the varieties take root and grow into fruits of practical knowledge. This common ground is necessary for man to pass to the higher levels of his true being. For this purpose the Yoga-Vedanta Forest University was founded by Gurudev "over-night" in 1956. The term university is here used in the sense of an institution of higher learning. However when the meaning of the term "university" meant buildings and involvement in the steel-frame nature of it, it was changed to 'Academy'. And the classes were held every morning from 4.30—6 a.m. This period, the Vedic texts declare to be the *Brahma Muhurta*, when the waves of spirituality are at their height. Hence, it is at this time that yogis and seekers concentrate and direct their minds upon the Supreme Being. In these *Brahma Muhurta* classes senior monks of the ashram as also learned men from other universities lectured on all branches of spiritual texts. Swami Krishnananda was asked to lecture on Vedanta and philosophy. It is recorded that he excelled himself and thrilled his class. Swami Sivananda Maharaj was the first to arrive and himself the first student studiously taking down not only Swami Krishnananda's lectures but of all those professors of this "University". After Gurudev's times this University later known as the Yogavedanta Forest Academy was re-modelled to impart regular 'basic' courses of three month's duration at the end of which 'certificates' were awarded to the students who came from all parts of India and the world. Both at the *Brahma Muhurta* classes and the Academy of later years truths concerning the Eternal Being were argued out on the basis of all available sources. At the level of the average seeker the "aim of life" is God-realisation, all other duties being only contributory to this supreme duty. Swami Krishnananda can lucidly explain the deepest and most profound truths within any given time. This is possible for him because of his voracious reading, thorough studies and insatiable thirst for knowledge.

He learnt Sanskrit through his self-study, though he was initiated into it under the guidance of a Sanskrit teacher in his student days to enable him to read the ancient sacred texts in the original. He spared himself only three to four hours of sleep, spending the remaining hours of the night in deep study. His day was filled with all sorts of work entrusted to him by his Guru. Though only an undergraduate of the late twenties his erudition has brought him in line with the best English scholars of today. In August 1980, in the Ahmedabad University Hall, Swamiji gave discourses in the Hindi language for three successive days.

Though he hails from the districts of South Kannada and his mother-tongue is Kannada, his capacity to speak the Hindi language so fluently is just like his capacity to become proficient in anything he takes up.

The freshness and interest in everything he says or discourses upon is as much due to his high sense of humour and wit as to the fact that it is the assimilated knowledge of a seeker ripened into a sage who has read voraciously "all my life", to quote his own words. He had learnt the most difficult parts of the Vedas under the strict discipline of his father and learnt by heart more than 144 Upanishads, besides other ancient texts such as the Bhagavadgita and the Puranas in original Sanskrit. No wonder then that when he answers a question, he brings to bear upon his answers his own assimilated knowledge. No bookish sermon he delivers. Each answer is a complete pamphlet in itself, so that one does not have to read volumes to get at and understand the answer to a problem. This distinctive quality of his genius, this adaptability to every type of audience is easily seen. A very important and significant fact to note here is that nothing is noted down as a preparation for what is going to be said or written. Incidentally, Swamiji's handwriting is at once clear and beautiful. While reading through his writings and speeches for the purpose of this as also for other compilations, two things struck me: One was a growing sense of awe at the giant of knowledge and wisdom these writings revealed; the other was the question: when was he not a giant? Where is the point at which we can say that from now on Swami Krishnananda started growing into the stature of a giant of knowledge, wisdom and saintliness?

His lectures and discourses have been recorded on tapes, though their actual transcription began only in the seventies. Earlier, say during the period 1946-1960, they were taken down by the students of the Yoga-Vedanta Forest University and printed by the editors of the "University" weeklies, to which Swamiji regularly contributed articles as individual pieces or serials, even as he continues to do so in *The Divine Life Monthly* (Rishikesh). From around 1954 the articles in the "University" Weeklies of this period were re-printed in the form of a book to mark the birthdays of the several senior monks of the Asram. One such is *Essays on Upanishad* and other essays. That was in 1948-49. This has been re-edited for free distribution in 1984. A compilation of Swamiji's contributions to the world, the present volume was also meant to be a Diamond Jubilee gift as my homage to him on his sixty-first birthday, THE SHASHTYABDAPURTI. However, this has been possible only now: for his sixty-third birthday, perhaps!

The text has been divided into three parts. Part I portrays Swamiji talking as man to man without any of the formal atmosphere prevailing at lectures and discourses. It is, therefore, a pen-picture faithfully reflecting the informal morning darshan-hours, say between 9 a.m. and 11.30 a.m. In Part II these pen-pictures have been trimmed to present him as the mentor who provides guidance to seekers by answering their several questions on a variety of aspects of spiritual Sadhana, i.e. yoga, meditation, yoga-asanas, and the like. Mundane matters have also been discussed. Says J. Bronowski, an author of repute, in his book, *The Ascent of Man* (pp. 14-15): "Spoken argument is informal and heuristic; it singles out the heart of the matter and shows in what way it is cruciate, and new; and it gives the direction and line of solution; so that simplified as it is, still the logic is right....this philosophical argument is the foundation...of scientific thinking." And on p. 153 he says, "Ask an impertinent question and you are on the way to the pertinent answer." This is what Part II presents to the reader. A fact relevant to this part is the guidance even research scholars seek whether their research concerns the field of Vedanta and Philosophy or the world of science and technology. Such research scholars as Mr. Jim McMicheal and Sri T.K. Chatterjee, discuss the subject of their theses and get definite, valuable guidance from Swamiji. The subject of Mr. Jim McMicheal's thesis is "The Concept of Isvara in the Advaita Philosophy of Sankara,"* while that of the other is "Particles", a highly intricate subject of research in the field of sub-atomic science. The range of Swamiji's knowledge and his prodigious ability to guide scholars in any field are obvious and need no further emphasis.

Part III is a sampling of what he spoke or wrote and includes his individual articles in the Yoga-Vedanta University Weeklies. Excerpts of these are given here by way of reprints. These are simple in style, charming in appeal and hardly believable of one

*Mr. Jim McMicheal has been awarded Ph.D. by Banaras Hindu University and is back in his home University in the U.S.A.

who in 1980 wrote *The Ascent of the Spirit*. These pages in particular bring out his erudite scholarship and depth of learning and reveal how his mind absorbs into itself the subtleties of truths.

His major works are listed in the Appendix. The short notes in the brief biographical sketch in the succeeding pages provide the reader with the context in which these have been written and the purpose of their inclusion in this book. The list is by no means exhaustive, for Swamiji's pen and his thoughts flow like the Ganga waters. Thus, the whole exercise is to get a panoramic view of the "totality" of his personality in which no one part is developed at the cost of or in neglect of the other parts.

How it is that this deeper look into his personality is placed at the end when it has been admitted at the outset that this book does not attempt to take the reader from the superficial or lighter layer to the higher layer of his personality? Personally I have felt that during the morning Darshan hours what is given as answers, directions or solutions is, though simple and informal, still a key to the formal atmosphere in which the lectures, discourses etc. are given. Swami Krishnananda is often seen lost within himself communing with himself in a kind of loud thinking: his thought is not delivered as a doctrine or instruction; neither does he philosophise like an arm-chair thinker. With all the oratory and rhetoric and imagery marshalled in explaining the great truths found in philosophy and metaphysics, he naturally leaves nothing to be desired, whether at the Yoga-Vedanta Forest Academy, at formal lectures, or during the night Satsangas and other special events like religious festivals celebrated in traditions instituted by Gurudev Sivananda. He is attended to with fervour even by those who do not quite understand his high standard of English. When asked how it benefits them, they answer, "Though it may not be, I feel I understand him". Such is the attraction and appeal of his lectures. The earlier Parts I and II of this book provide basic foundation and a necessary background to get the most out of these discourses. So it is that the informal, effervescent and ebullient outpourings of Swamiji's inner personality have been placed as the last portion of this book though their contents deserve to be a book by itself to shine in their own pristine glory.

The effort involved in getting this book ready for publication has been a herculean task for one like me, an inexperienced author. It is all but a miracle that Swami Sivananda's grace has worked to accomplish this and put the manuscript in the hands of such a well known firm of publishers.

As a dedication to the 'Virat' (revealed to Arjuna by Lord Krishna) in whom reside my most beloved Guru Swami Sivananda and my Upa-Guru (Second Guru) Swami Krishnananda, I lay this book at the feet of the highest, the Supreme Being.

Innumerable are the friends who have helped me in all the crucial stages of this work from typing to editing and have selflessly worked on my MS which was originally full of imperfections due to my inexperience. The credit for all the merit that this book possesses is, therefore, entirely theirs. I beg their kind forgiveness for not mentioning them by their names, though in some cases it is their own request that this Karmayoga (selfless service) of theirs should not be mentioned in writing. With a heart overflowing with gratitude I can only pray that God and Gurudev shower their blessings on each and every one of them as they have showered their kindness upon me.

Sri Swami Krishnanandaji

A BRIEF BIOGRAPHICAL SKETCH

Born of parents highly orthodox and deeply religious, Swami Krishnananda inherits an illustrious tradition of Vedic learning and scholarship. On April 25, 1922 in the village of Keminje a child later named Subbaraya Putturaya, was born. He now lives at the Sivananda Ashram, Rishikesh, as His Holiness Swami Krishnananda Saraswati. The village Keminje is in South Kanara in the erstwhile Mysore State on the western coast of South India. His ancestors on both sides belonged to the high Brahman caste and enjoyed the respect and patronage of kings.

Swami Krishnananda's maternal grandfather belonged to a line of priests who were the highest authorities in all Vedic rituals and sastras, particularly the Tantra Sastra and also in the Vedantic philosophy. His paternal grandfather was a rare Bhakta of infinite faith, his devotion and dedication to God being unsurpassed. In addition, he was a truly magnanimous man by nature; he sold his own property to be able to help those in need. Thus, nobility, religion, and piety run in the blood of Sri Swami Krishnananda who is a Jnanayogi single-mindedly devoted to the *Brahman*, the Supreme Being of the Advaita Vedanta School of Philosophy.

In those (ancient) days, pilgrimages were undertaken on foot. Little toddlers or even the 5-7 year olds were carried on shoulders by the elders. Subbaraya Putturaya too was carried in this manner on pilgrimages by the members of his family. At the age of three, the child visited Talakkaveri, the source of the river Kaveri, held sacred in South India just as the river Ganga is held sacred all over India. On two more such pilgrimages during the fifth and seventh years of his childhood, Subbaraya Putturaya was taken to the very sacred temple at Tirupati on the northernmost border of South India. The philosophical bent in him was very strong even in the earlier years and inspired his trekking to holy places in search of deeper knowledge and richer experience; Badrinath, Kedarnath and Gangotri were the last in his pilgrimages undertaken as "Swami Krishnananda".

True to the Brahmanic tradition Subbaraya was initiated in the Vedas by his father and maternal grandfather. His grandfather had passed away when Subbaraya's father was hardly two or three years old. The grind that this required was strictly enforced on the young boy even at the early age of seven or so. Thus did this Brahman boy learn the Vedic lore in his childhood. But he played as many pranks in his school and with his playmates and brothers as any other boy did. Playing the story of the Ramayana was one of his favourites. He asked a puckish question of the missionary visiting his school, "Why was Jesus born in Jerusalem, Sir?" The priest taken by surprise replied, "Because, it is the centre of the earth". The boy accepted this statement sceptically.

His college education lasted only for two years. Subbaraya was only an undergraduate when he took up a petty Government job which in the early twenties of this century was a big honour. A Brahman by caste was allowed only a limited number of professions, such as would not in any way go against the code of the caste laid down in the scriptures.

However, Subbaraya was not interested in a career; even though he was employed to do a Government job at the age of eighteen or so, he conducted discourses on the Bhagavadgita in the evenings! His insatiable thirst for knowledge kept him absorbed in the library of an elderly lawyer in his home-town, during his student days. Today he is rated by all who hear him speak or read his books as one of the best scholars in English. He is also an authority on all schools of philosophy, particularly the Vedic Scriptures, Vedanta, Upanishads, Srutis and Smritis as also the Epics and Puranas besides books on History, Geography, Science and other branches of learning. Illness ended this very short period of Subbaraya's life as a Government employee. A chronic patient of asthma from childhood, he was now laid low with typhoid. Earlier, even at the age of thirteen, he had suffered in succession from bronchitis, jaundice and other ailments that sap one's energy and reduce the vitality of the body. Frail as his body was, his mind matured fast almost in an inverse proportion! His thoughts were centred on his inner 'being'. He kept telling his family who did not take him seriously that he would go away to Kashi—Varanasi as it is now called. This was regarded as the most sacred place by the Hindus. Lord Vishwanath, on the banks of the Ganga in Northern India, presides over this hoary city of great learned Pundits.

At the end of his illness, Subbaraya quietly left home, went to Pandaripur and then to Kashi. His parents and family came to know of this unbelievable event from a letter he wrote to them from Kashi. Here, this young man still in his teens won many a debate in Sanskrit held among the renowned Sanskrit Pundits. But soon he felt that this was not satisfying the urges within him: he must journey farther north—to the Himalayas—Haridwar and Rishikesh where the rising sun of Rishikesh, the sage who had already won the highest place of regard amongst the wise, Sri Swami Sivananda lived on the banks of the Ganga at Muni-ki-Reti, which literally means "The Sands of the Sages". Subbaraya had read all of Siva's books. There had been a feeling within him that he should reach Rishikesh, and he should meet this sage.

One day when he was only seven years old, he was sitting in his mother's lap and being petted he made a prim statement; "I am going to be a Sannyasi". "What"! said the stupefied mother, "Dare you say that again?" And thrice, with uplifted finger did the mother chide him. In reply the boy only giggled. And Subbaraya at the age of twenty stood before the great Master Swami Sivananda to surrender himself to this Godman of the twentieth century. At the very first meeting the inner contact was established; and it grew into an intimate Guru-Sishya (preceptor-disciple) relationship, the Sishya becoming a part of the 'being' of the Guru himself—a Guru-Amsa to shine as an eternal lamp of sagacity and Sannyasihood, in the Sivananda Ashram as Swami Krishnananda Saraswati.

Subbaraya took Sannyasa on the 14th January 1946, on the auspicious day of Makara Sankranti, when the Sun turns to the north and for all the six months traverses northwards before turning back towards the south and when starts the 'bright half of the year'. It was only two years since he had arrived at the Ashram from Varanasi. And even within this short period he earned encomiums from his Guru: "He is a Vedanta-Kesari (lion of Vedanta-philosophy)": "He is a Sankaracharya", crowning it all with the words, "I marvel at Swami Krishnananda!"

As Professor of Vedanta in the Brahmamuhurta classes of the Yoga-Vedanta Forest University in the forties of Gurudev's time, when Gurudev himself took down notes of the lectures, Swami

Krishnananda had expounded the Mundaka Upanishad—one of the Upanishads particularly meant for the "mundakas" or the shaven heads, the sannyasis.

As a young man of hardly 22 years he wrote the commentary to Gurudev's Moksha Gita. "It was my maiden attempt", blushingly he told us. "What is a maiden attempt?" laughed Swami Krishnananda. Belying the dictionary meaning of the word: "there has been no previous experience or achievements", to anyone who reads the Moksha Gita it is clear that the commentary reads as coming from the mature mind of a full blown *jnani*. And it is for this that he has earned Gurudev's encomium: many Sankaras are rolled into one Krishnananda.

The Isavasya Upanishad has been re-edited for a Diamond Jubilee Number by Swamiji. A special feature of it must be noted. The long-forgotten intimate atmosphere of the Gurukula tradition of the ancient times came alive in Swami Krishnanandaji's half-hour talks to novices, Brahmacharis and seekers waiting to be initiated into Sannyasa. In 1974-75, between 7 and 7.30 p.m. at Gokul Dham which at that time was Swamiji's residence, Kena, Katha, Mandukya, Munduka, Prasna and Isavasya Upanishads were expounded in simple Hindi. There was no difficulty whatever in understanding the eternal truths of the Upanishads nor in following the language of exposition. His spoken Hindi was so simple that even a non-Hindi disciple could understand it and even translate this Upanishad into English. Yet even his self-study did not include a formal learning of the Hindi language.

In 1978 or 1979, one of the Trustees of the Divine Life Society, the late Mr. Kapoor bemoaned: "We have discovered that Swami Krishnanandaji has been doing 98% of the work of the Ashram. It is a disgrace for us that we allow this of him who can so usefully devote his time for our spiritual uplift and guidance on the Blessed path". These words tell us that Swamiji was no mere Buddha sitting in deep meditation, nor Jesus spreading the gospel of love and mercy. He is a Karmayogi of the highest order in its fullest connotation.

Swami Chidanandaji records that even in the early years of his life as an Ashramite, as an initiate, Swami Krishnananda was recognised as an authority, and whenever any argument arose regarding any matter, Gurudev always said: "Swami Krishnanandaji is right. Do as Swami Krishnanandaji says." This I have heard again with my own ears from the highest sources. Work and wisdom are his second nature, whether at sixteen or at sixty. It seems to me that in looking for the greatness of Swami Krishnanandaji, the Philosopher and the Sage, we have missed the Jivanmukta in him.

No wonder, then, that when asked for a message for the materials such as those contained in this book he gave this: "The aim of life is God-realisation and every other duty is only contributory to this supreme duty." "Ask him anything, he will soon veer round to its philosophical implication", remarks Dr. David Miller, Ph.D. of Concordia University, Montreal, Canada.

Neither revered Swami Krishnanandaji's face nor his presence was registered in my recollection of my early visits to the Ashram in thirst for the Darshan of Master Sivanandaji Maharaj, though he was there together with revered Swami Chidanandaji Maharaj engaged in explaining at the night-Satsang the underlying principles and the key to the details of private ceremonial ritual: the investiture of the sacred thread. Nor did I come to live in the Ashram to be the disciple of that Swami Krishnananda who used to sit under the easy chair on which Gurudev reclined. Swamiji had been sent for. He came, sat literally in the shadow of his beloved Gurudev. In a while, when the Satsang passed on to other items of the schedule—where was that Swami, Krishnanandaji, that was sitting beside the Omniscient Master, Swami Sivananda's chair? "Must have gone back to his Kutir". "Really!" There were then the other night-Satsang when word went round, "Swami Krishnananda is going to speak!" This word was passed on and received with joy and wonder. "It was very nice", all remarked. Once I heard revered Swami Hridayananda Mataji, who in her own way like the global personality H.H. Sri Swami Chidananda is spreading Gurudev's message in Paris and Netherlands in particular, still a novice at that time, say: "After hearing Swami Krishnanandaji, I want to sit and meditate". And now as the Dean of the Yoga-Vedanta Forest Academy Swamiji gives lectures on Vedic and philosophical subjects. And his lectures are being edited and printed as books. "Don't use me like a book of reference", he remonstrates. He is so easy of approach that we do so and his protests are of no avail. The answers come so promptly and to the point, be it from a philosophical treatise, the mundane view of the world, or history, or the latest theories in sub-atomic science which is identifying itself slowly and surely with the Upanishadic Truth, or the controversial schools of thought, theistic or agnostic, or a moot point overlooked by the very questioner, no one resists the temptation to get this push-button service of a reference book-shelf from his most Revered Self!

Ill health assailed him more often than good health hailed him. But this has never been a hindrance to his utter self-abandonment as may be seen from the following incident. For two days (on 24th and 25th March 1981) Swamiji had been in the grip of a liver disorder, his blood pressure was erratic, all this being a sequel to the severe asthmatic attack he had suffered. On the third day, as usual he was in his chair blessing us with his holy presence and chatting too. The work-part of his morning hours had been strictly kept away from him. But the devotees gradually forgot that he had been ill mainly because Swamiji was smiling and joking. Spiritual guidance was sought, he himself volunteering to impart it to some visitors in the last hour of their stay in the Ashram. For one full hour and a half he carried on. The growing strain on him was now more visible. The Brahmachari in the service of his Guru made this request, "Swamiji, please you must listen to the Doctors, take rest now". "Please", he pleaded, turning to us with folded hands, "all of you come again tomorrow." When all of us got up to leave, Swamiji with a divine smile pleaded: "Please do not be angry with me." Who was apologizing to whom? Such is his loving concern for others and his incredible capacity for self-abnegation. The demonstration by monoacting of a point by way of illustrating his jokes and anecdotes is a unique technique, inimitably all his own, even while explaining philosophy or meditation. His chair in a moment becomes the stage for his self-propelled cinescreen. And the arms of the same chair become the desk to sign the "papers". A 'Satavadhanist' (performer of a hundred things simultaneously) that his Revered Self is, certainly no one feels left out of the centre of his interest. It is he who leads the laughter invoked by the story narrated or enacted, quite often continuing to giggle like a teenager, utterly uninhibited.

There are no spectacular dramatic events in the life of Swami Krishnanandaji but one is enthralled by sitting with him during the informal morning hours, not only for a "Darshan" of a Mahatma, but also for hearing him pun and joke and mono-act, bubbling with laughter and light-heartedness during all the activities, while simultaneously attending to diverse problems, mundane and metaphysical. "How do you manage it Swamiji?", asked a French priest. "Like the telephone operator, I switch off the one and attend to the other," he replied. And that is Swami Krishnanandaji—many splendoured aspects of whose personality are projected in the pages of this book.

Contents

PART II: *THE MENTOR*

PART I

Swami Krishnananda—The Man

22 June 1977

On this day, 22 June 1977, revered Swami Krishnanandaji Maharaj complied with the request by this humble disciple to give a message for starting a daily recording of the informal conversations in the mornings usually between 9 and 11 a.m. with all those that came for his holy *darsan*. This was the time when Swamiji also received visitors, sadhaks from outside the Sivananda Ashram, seekers from all over the East and the West, the Netherlands and Australia, the African continent, besides the ashramites themselves, the ashram Brahmacharis.

Simultaneously, he carried on the office work of the Sivananda Ashram. There is thus a constant demand on his attention from different directions and also from different angles especially when over a dozen departments, all managed by the Ashram or by the Board of Management of the Board of Trustees, seek Swamiji's guidance and decisions for their respective departments. Swamiji has been the Secretary from the very inception of the Ashram and is currently its General Secretary. In fact, he has not only been the one constant factor amid all the phases of change and growth of the establishment, but also the indwelling spirit of the Ashram. For, Swamiji, along with the President Swami Chidananda Maharaj and the Vice-President Swami Madhavananda Maharaj, is one of the first group of disciples of Gurudev Swami Sivananda Maharaj, close to the heart of their great and beloved Master-Guru. Though he is the youngest of the monks, he is the oldest of them all in Sannyashood.

To Swamiji, these diverse demands and constant interruptions in the midst of profound expositions of truth are hardly, if ever, capable of interrupting the thread of his thoughts. And he expressed his thoughts in a manner that did not let the listeners feel that they had been interrupted. These interruptions were often minutes long entirely unrelated to the question put or the exposition given, but even as one was giving up the hope of the continuity being kept up, Swamiji would pick up from the very last word of the sentence that had been interrupted by the messenger or the problem.

It was for a diary of the picture that presented itself in these morning *darshan* hours that I had requested for a message of blessings from Swami Krishnananda Maharaj. The message given in his own beautiful hand is this:

"The aim of life is God-realisation, and every other duty is only contributory to this supreme duty".

Thus began the Diary on 22nd June '77.

In the summer we gathered inside the verandah of Guru-kripa Kutir on the ground floor, where a few visitors, disciples and other ashramites sat around at revered Swamiji's feet to have his *darshan* as also to learn what he taught and chat informally. It was about 9.30 a.m. People walked in and out now and then with varied problems—personal, official or spiritual.

Dr. (Smt.) Nagaratnam from the Vivekananda Yoga Training Centre, Kanyakumari, the doctor incharge, with Smt Shailaja, a worker of the Vivekananda Kendra, was here for a couple of days to refresh her knowledge of Yoga as therapy and to get guidance and blessings from Swamiji. Swamiji questioned her on the resources of the Institution for starting this Yoga-therapy and about the work at the Institution, etc. When in the course of her replies the doctor made the remark "Economics is the best use of resources," Swamiji laughed and said: "The best answer ! You are a shrewd person!"

An office boy with a bag of bills stands at the door awaiting his turn to have them passed by Swamiji, while the man kneeling in the only space—an island in an ocean of files, books and papers, presents a series of cheques and "forms" to be signed or countersigned and to be otherwise disposed of and keeps Swamiji's attention rivetted to it all. Swamiji is simultaneously dealing with these and talking and discussing with those around him.

Smt. Shobha, a very old Ashram devotee and disciple of Gurudev Swami Sivananda, greets Swamiji with Pranams.

Swami Krishnandaji [*looking up from the papers he is dealing with*]: "Where are you coming from now?"

Shobha: I have been touring, rather going on pilgrimage—to Hastinapur, Ayodhya, Sukhtal and Vidur Kutir.

Sw. K.: Vidur Kutir as yet stands untouched by time as a monument to its ancient occupant. But Duryodhana's palace has gone to complete ruins and even the site of it is unrecognisable.

In comes the contractor who was constructing the buildings of the Yoga Vedanta Forest Academy. He discusses business and leaves. The boy at the door with the bag of bills steps in and presents them.

In between, as if business and interviews were in harmony with each other, Swamiji is guiding a lady research student from Garhwal writing a thesis on Patanjali Yoga Sutras in Hindi. That she hails from Tehri-Garhwal and is the daughter of a late scholar well known to Swamiji is apparent from their conversation. She has come to Swamiji with the specific purpose of getting his guidance. Having ascertained her reading, Swamiji recommends the following books useful for her thesis: (1) History of Patanjali Yoga Sutras, by Dr. Kenge (English); (2) Patanjali Yoga-Pradipika, by Omanandaji (Hindi); (3) Vyasa-Bhashya-per Tattwa Vaisharadi by Vachaspati Misra (Sanskrit); (4) Vyasa-Bhashya-per Yoga Vartik by Vigyan Bhikshu; (5) Vivaranaprameya Sangraha ki Hindi Tika by Lalita Prasadji Dabhrall; (6) Patanjali Yoga Sutra, Vyasa-Bhashya.

Even as she is busy noting these down, in comes Dr. Virmani, Head of the Department of Neurology, All India Institute of Medical Sciences. She greets Swamiji and is greeted by him. She places before him a few paramedical points to get clarification on their philosophical background. By now both the bank-work and the bag of bills etc. have been disposed of, and Dr. Virmani's questions have Swamiji's sole attention. Her questions relate to the psychic or subtle body, rebirth and *Karma* and the relationship between these two factors.

Dr. Virmani: When adopting psychic therapy by the projection of thought-force, what distance can thought-force cover?

Sw. K.: The distance depends on the intensity of the thought projected; in addition, the object of thought should have been known to and seen by the one who wishes to send the thought-force.

The door opens to receive revered Swami Chidanandaji Maharaj, President of the Divine Life Society, who had come to get the guidelines in the formalities to be observed in the sacred ceremony of the installation and consecration of Lord Vithoba and Rukmani's idols at the temple in Vithal Ashram, the Ashram on the next hill at the back of Sivananda Ashram Visvanatha Mandir. The Vithal Ashram organisers had come to revered Swami Chidanandaji who took them with him to Swami Krishnanandaji for guidance and help in these highly specialised and technical matters, Swami Krishnanandaji has been the Acharya in such Vedic matters even in Gurudev Swami Sivananda's times to guide such religious and Vedic traditions in rituals and the [codes and formalities thereof].

As the Vithal Ashram organisers and Swami Chidanandaji leave, Smt. Swarnalata enters and presents a set of Ras Lila pictures to Swami Krishnanandaji. The beautiful paintings are in Moghul style.

Sw. K.: Why are the features of all these figures Persian? These figures hardly differ from the typically Muslim features in Moghul and Persian art.

Swarnalata: The Rajasthani paintings also greatly follow, it would seem, the Muslim style.

Sw. K.: Historically, the influence of cultures and civilisations spread out far and wide.

Swarnalata: Just behind this Kutir, Swamiji, I have heard that a small vesselful, a *lota*-ful, of ancient coins was found when digging for the foundation of one of the Ashram structures.

Sw. K.: Yes, the markings on the coins were deciphered as Greek characters and the coins were said to be perhaps of the Salukas' period. Somebody must have buried it for his own use, but did not come for it! The *lota* of coins was handed over to the government, for buried treasures belong to the government.

Swarnalataji, in the Ras-Lila which the group from Brindavan had been presenting, they used a peculiar language. Ancient Sanskrit was not what is now Braj-Bhasha of Mathura-Brindavan. But it was the language that Lord Krishna spoke. It is difficult to decide as to what the original language in India was. Of course, Hindi came into vogue only after the Persian influence spread in Northern India. [*Noticing a young man now entering*] "Come in! How are you? Your health? How about your job?"

Thus lovingly greeted and blessed by revered Swamiji, the ashram-educated young man replies duly. He is on his way to elsewhere, so taking Swamiji's blessings he leaves. Another youngster comes in and gets his scholarship for Sanskrit study in the college sanctioned.

Sw. K.: (*to this scholar*): Go and find out exactly the present condition of Swami...who has been admitted in the Ashram hospital. Come back and give me an exact report of his condition. Go and come quickly. (Looking at us) His condition is serious since three days. I dreamt that the Swamiji was dead.

A sadhak disciple: But long life is predicted for the one who in dream appears to be dead.

Sw. K: While in essence the dream is an actuality, it need not be so in the case of a third person dreaming that so-and-so was dead. On the other hand, your own dream that you are dead is said to indicate a long life.

The messenger returns to report that the condition of the ailing Sannyasin was the same as it had been earlier. He *wasn't* dead !

A visitor (*who had joined in some time earlier*): What is the relation between a dream and the body of a dreamer?

Sw. K: The simultaneous consciousness of being in this body and being just here as also the consciousness of being up and above in a much subtler form is experienced by the dreamer. And if an outline of the relatedness can be geometrically given, it would take the form of a triangle.

A young foreigner who has been attending Yoga classes for about three weeks comes in and requests Swamiji to give her a certificate of efficiency, so that she could start a class in her home town. Swamiji replies in the form of a story: A young man went to a sage and requested him to be his Guru. The Guru replied that it is not easy to be a disciple, it would be a hard job for the disciple to be in the service of the Guru all the time and obey him faithfully and undergo great discipline as required of a disciple. "Then make me a Guru," prayed the young man ! [*Laughter led by Swamiji filled the place. Then turning to the young visitor*] "Ask the teacher from whom you have been learning here to ascertain your success in the *asanas*, and we shall ask him to give the certificate if he declares you are proficient in the *asanas*. O.K?

Visitor: Yes, Swamiji, O.K.

Swamiji asked a number of questions on the various details of cooking and recipes, etc. In essence, it turned out that the same ingredients were used in preparing different dishes like dry vegetable, one with gravy, or semi-liquid (dal) *sambhar* or clear soup of *rasam* of the South Indian meal. The main difference in the making of dishes was the proportion of the cooking medium and the ingredients used.

S. D.: ((*laughing*): Is Swamiji going to write a book on cookery?

Sw. K: (*seriously*): No, I had something else in my mind. It was in some way connected with philosophy—*Panchikarana*. The same thoughts with different emphasis and different context "cook" a different pattern of thought. Strange thoughts come to my mind ! What is wrong, I ask myself now, in staying in one's own home ? In those days I used to think it was not right to do so. But now I feel I can stay anywhere—even in a Harijan's house.

Sri Karthikeyan comes in with the day's correspondence. While dealing with it, Swamiji continues to converse with the devotees present.

Sw. K.: Here is a letter of a 'mystic' to me (moments later) —she is only an ordinary person and she has never seen me.

As his revered self was laughing away when reading the letter to himself, several of us pleaded: "Please, Swamiji, read it out to us." Swamiji did so. The letter gave an account of the writer's ecstatic experience of a vision she had had of Swami Krishnanandaji. To us it sounded very much true, but Swamiji only laughed it off. Soon the job of dealing with correspondence was over.

Sri Karthikeyan: Swamiji, why is it that we should go alone for walks? This is particularly emphasised to the *sadhakas*. They do not go out for walks with anyone else usually. Why?

Sw. K.: The egos of those you walk with restrict your ego when you go out together for a walk. Each one's ego is cautious and guards itself. The trees and other objects in nature do not exert their ego upon you. They have no ego. And so you are not affected by their presence. No limitations are brought to bear upon your ego. So there is no tension due to caution which has to be maintained when walking with other persons, and you get relaxed and free. The walk is meant for relaxation of the mind from tensions, as also exercise for the muscles.

A mother with three children comes in and they offer their *pranams*. The conversation with them is carried on in Hindi and the unsophisticated mother replies with great humility and deep respect.

Mother: We have come only for thy *darshan*.

Sw. K.: Achcha! Sing a song, these people will be happy to listen. [*The mother and her children in a group sing a beautiful short kirtan. Everybody is thrilled.*]

S.K.: Very very good! How did you all learn to sing so well?

Mother: We conduct kirtan-satsang every evening in our home.

Sw. K.: Oh wonderful! I never knew they could sing. I just casually asked, and they really sing so nice. *Dhanyavad* Mataji! Are you staying on here?

Mother: No Swamiji, we have to go back now itself.

Sw. K.: Please, all of you now go and have your food. Swarnalataji, take them for lunch with you. They are new to the place. Oh! There is the lunch bell. Go, otherwise you will miss the lunch. Thank you all for your darshan and satsang. God bless you!

18 December 1978

(Today's diary is not from any recorded tape, but has been actually written in the customary style of a diary).

To begin with, there were just three or four visitors only. As the morning proceeded more visitors came, but it was a floating crowd of hardly 10 in all.

This morning's darshan had come after an interval of nearly 10 days, excluding Sundays when in any case Rev. Swamiji does not give morning darshan.

A Sadhak disciple began the conversation by asking about the division of the chapters of *Durga Saptasati*. The question was if all the *slokas* (stanzas) and *mantras* (hymns) of Devi, should as a rule be treated as three separate portions. Rev. Swamiji replied that it was because they were addressed to Durga, Lakshmi and Saraswati. Were the chapters then spoken from different aspects ? No. The three deities were the three stages of consciousness —Tamas, Rajas, and Sattva—reached in an ascending order.

Question: Are the chapters then suitably written to Tamas, Rajas and Sattva?

Answer: No, because they are all one. It is our incapacity to see all three as one that brings in the distinction. It is the same one *guna* that appears as Tamas, Rajas and Sattva.

Q. Then the number of *slokas* in each portion has no meaning as so many *mantras*? The numbers vary, unlike in the *ashtottara* and *sahasra*—Namavalis.

A. There is no significance in the number as such of the *slokas*. It is all one continuous *mantra* of prayer to one deity only.

Sw. K.: There is a figurative description of the *Karmas* of the individual, his *prarabdha* waiting for the *Jiva*, like a king who is awaited by this vassals. But there is also this logic. For instance, under the circumstances of suicide when the sub-conscious is shocked it results in the restlessness of that particular *jiva*: its astral body.

S.D. Why should the latter eventuality occur when the former condition is already a fact?

Sw. K.: That happens because the soul is ignorant of its destiny. Under the circumstances of deaths due to accident or suicide and the like the soul is restless.

Q. But why does not the *prarabdha* come into action?

A. The *prarabdha* will act at the proper time and place. Till then it will await its turn. The *prarabdha* of every individual is written at his birth, even while in the womb. And it awaits the right time and place for it to come into play. The whole tree is in the seed. But you cannot expect it to come forth as soon as you put the seed in the earth. All conditions for its growth must be present. There must be rain for the seed to sprout. It is our ignorance that makes us incapable of seeing the whole picture—from birth to death. Even the moment of death is written up in the womb. If we have the capacity to see into the time we can see the working of the whole cosmos. There is no present and past, we are used to think in such terms. If it were not for your ignorance you will see the whole history of the individual personality even in the new-born child.

[Ramswarup Brahmachari approaches and pleads with Rev. Swamiji to agree to go to Calcutta for the All-India Divine Life Conference in February. Rev. Swamiji firmly and consistently refuses to be persuaded to comply with the request.]

Ramswarup: But Ram Niwasji has taken it for granted that you will attend.

Sw. K.: But I have cut Ram Niwas's ground from under his feet. My condition of health is very pathetic. Only Swami Chidananda has a little idea of my pitiable state of health.

Ramswarup: Swamiji your feet are exposed. Are they not feeling cold? [*Brahmachari again persuades Rev. Swamiji*]

Sw. K.: Now that you have mentioned it I am feeling cold!

All this time I was not feeling cold in the feet. I was thinking of something else. Now you mentioned it and I am feeling the cold. [*Turning to the visitor from South Africa*] Why are you going to Nepal? What do you want to see?

Visitor: I am going with Mataji (Sw. Hridayananda)

Sw. K.: I see! Then you return to South Africa.

Visitor: No, I am going to Europe, not back to South Africa.

Sw. K.: (*addresses another visitor*). Are you going away today?

Ranjit the receptionist: At 2 o'clock, Swamiji.

Visitor: I am going to Yoga Niketan for a couple of days.

Sw. K.: Very good. Be happy!

Q.: Why do we suffer Swamiji? What is the cause of suffering?

Sw. K.: It is the incapacity to adjust oneself to things that is the cause of suffering. It is the lack of union between the intellect and the act. Suffering is the reaction to an action. When feeling merges into intellect it is philosophy. It is the practical philosophy of adaptation. Otherwise it is armchair philosophy. The art of seeing things as God sees is the real spiritual life, nothing else is spiritual life. To God everything is perfect. Everything, at every time and everywhere is perfect. It is very difficult to think like this. If everyday for five hours, you can think like this, you can grind this thought into the mind. Otherwise it vanishes into thin air like mist before the sun. You see the difference between this and that, you and the others, only due to space and time and the projection of your mind. Our trouble is that we are unable to see things as they are. You see everything as outside yourself. It is this separation in space-time that is the root of all our sufferings. If you abolish the feeling of separatedness, suffering also goes. You abolish the cause and the effect also goes.

Brahmachari Ramswarup repeatedly approaches Rev. Swamiji to persuade his revered self to attend the All India Divine Life Conference at Calcutta. Swamiji's indifferent health does not allow it.

Sw. K.: You go and ask Swami Madhavananda ji Maharaj to attend the Conference at Calcutta and Orissa. Tell him that if he is happy to go, I shall look after all his work and he can have a little relaxation. Go. You are good at all these things, you are an intelligent and capable man. Go and ask Swamiji.

[A couple who have been staying for some weeks take leave of Rev. Swamiji. So also does Dr Padmavati].

Sri Tripathi has come from Delhi, bringing news of Sri Ramana Rai (who works devotedly in the Sivananda Publication League and who is currently suspected to be suffering from cancer of the gullet and is under treatment.) Rev Swamiji earnestly acquaints himself with the details and gets the facts known. Why nose-feeding? How do you say he is improving when he has to be red through the nose? How can fresh cells grow so quickly as in a month over the now raw area, under treatment? etc., etc. (Unhappy though his revered self gets reconciled to the explanations.)

[Sri Yogiraj of America, an old disciple of the ashram who runs an ashram of his own in America has joined the gathering along with his four disciples who have been staying here for a week or so and have been giving *kirtans*—vocal as well as on the guitar.]

Sw. K.: (*addressing the leader of the kirtan group*): You are all very good musicians. You have what in Sanskrit is termed Jnana-Swara. It means a particular type of voice, 'a dignified voice' it means.

[His revered self asks each of them what they are, where they are from, and what their profession is. They demurred from saying that they had a profession, a calling, meaning thereby that they were now only sadhakas.]

Sw. K.: Being a sadhak is a temporary condition. The main work you do is called a profession.

Sw. K.: (*Turning to Yogiraj*) What news? you have come after a long time. What are you looking for in the Ashram?

Yogiraj: I am glad to be here Swamiji. I will be glad if I can help you improve your health.

Sw. K.: You can only help by praying. Tell God "This poor man needs His help".

Then Yogiraj invites Swamiji to go to America.

Sw. K.: Oh ! You have seen how I am refusing to go to Calcutta. You are asking me to go to America!

[Brahmachari Krishnamurty and Sri Amarananda arrive separately. Yogiraj and his disciples take leave. An old gentleman requests revered Swamiji to permit his stay further than now permitted. Revered Swamiji happily complies and fixes no time limit from his side. (The receptionist has noted the same.]

Sw. K.: [*to Sri Amarananda*]: What brings you here? Anything special, otherwise you won't come!

Sri Amarananda: Yes, Swamiji, I want a passport to go to America and need your help.

Sw. K.: (*half in joke and half in earnest*): Everybody wants to go away from India. She is your mother. She has fed you from her breast. Why do you want to leave her, poor thing, and go to foreign countries ? I see only foreigners everywhere. A foreigner is a person who is not needed nor wanted in that place. Yogiraj says that he holds a green card for American citizenship. The American is afraid of such green card-holders. He says it is up to that government not to give that. Politically he is American, an Indian in origin!

Ramswarup and librarian Murugananda come and discuss the placement and entry of "The Works of Mahatma Gandhi" purchased by Rev. Swami Chidanandaji Maharaj.

Swami Krishnapriyananda Mataji, the Librarian-incharge explains that Sri Aurobindo's works are also in the library. So the decision to similarly arrange these volumes, under the same heading, is taken and they both take leave.

Sw. K.: (*to Br. Krishnamurty*): What do you want to tell me?

Br. Krishnamurty: It is personal, Swamiji.

Sw. K.: (*to Amaranand*): Why are you leaving your own place and going to a strange land? Don't you know the proverb that the butter milk made at one's own home is better than the curd offered at someone else's.

Ajay: Swamiji allot me some work.

Sw. K.: What work to give to you who will be leaving in a month's time [*To Smt. Radha Krishna Rao*] Give him some work in the hospital. Train him into hospital work. (to the receptionist) You don't want more hands? Once you were complaining that you needed help. Now?

Receptionist Ranjit: There are three for my help. I don't want any more.

Sw. K.: An overflow? [*After a pause*] These three types of people are needed in the ashram. You must know typing or have a good handwriting to do writing work or to work the machines in the Press. Otherwise there is no need of the person for the ashram work.

A Canadian from Valmorine (Quebec), Rev. Swami Vishnudevananda's disciple comes in, greets Swamiji and introduces himself. Swamiji queries about Vishnudevananda, saying that it was in answer to his call that this disciple had gone to live in Kerala

He had now come to have *darshan* of Rev. Swamiji before returning since he was on his way back.

Sw. K.: Swami Vishnudevananda is in India, in Kerala? And he had called you from Valmorine? What is he doing in Kerala?

Visitor: He is there is *mouna* (silence) *tapas*, for one year. That is why he called me to go over to him.

Sw. K.: For a year he is observing *mouna*! Oh! He will get tremendous will power. He can have the whole world under his control. If you observe *mouna* even for six months, you develop such will power. Work does not waste energy, it is talking that wastes energy. And in *mouna* you store up and stagger up the energy. Wonderful experience! Do you know this line from the Bible? "Before Adam was, I am." The grammar is wrong here. But the affirmation has a ringing sound because of that.

21 December 1978

In winter we gathered in the open terrace in front of Swamiji's *kutir* under the open sky and shining sun for warmth and fresh air. During these months foreign visitors also came in groups and in numbers and the open terrace had space for all to sit around informally. To begin with, there were about half a dozen people.

Swami Krishnanandaji greets a visitor who has come from Yogi Niketan, the Ashram's neighbouring institution. She is from Rajasthan, wife of Mr Singhal who has retired from the post of Chief Secretary of Tripura State.

Sw. K.: So Mr. Singhal is an IAS Officer. What have you been doing? How did you spend your time?

Visitor: I have been doing social work when he was in service. Now I am going to work for the Divine Life Society: I am a member.

Sw. K.: Was your husband Chief Secretary at the time of Hardayal Joshi's chief ministership?

Mrs. S.: No, my husband was in Tripura state, not in Rajasthan. It is only after retirement that we have settled down in Rajasthan. Tripura is near Manipur.

Sw. K.: *Are Baba*! you don't belong to Assam? What is your mother tongue? Rajasthani, Gujarati, or U.P. Hindustani?

Mrs. S: We were in Assam because he belongs to Assam cadre.

Sw. K.: [*Greets a new arrival*] Namaskar Tripathi Saheb! Not feeling cold? You have no muffler, only a sweater. How is it no one seems to feel cold?

S. D.: I have four coverings in all!

Sw. K.: [*laughs heartily*]: Krishna Priya Mataji! You are sitting under the shade in this bitter cold. There is no sun there. Come and sit in the sun.

K. P.: No Swamiji, I am O.K. here.

Mrs. S.: Swamiji, I want the pamphlet on meditation which you have written. I want to distribute it to the people in my town. How To Meditate is, I think, the title.

Sw. K.: That is not a leaflet or a pamphlet, it is a small book: "Meditation. Its Theory and Practice".

S. D.: It is an atom bomb, not a pamphlet.

Sw. K.: [*Laughing*]: Yes, it is like an atom bomb. What news Tripathi Maharaj. You are from Gujarat?

Mr Tripathi.: I am a Maharashtrian settled in Gujarat during the British time.

Francisca: Swamtji, I wish to ask you a question. In the cosmic consciousness there is no compassion; there seems to be injustice.

Sw. K.: These don't exist in the cosmos. These are all human feelings.

Francisca: It ts difficult to live with this idea.

Sw. K.: Which idea?

F. Well, see the suffering and...

Sw. K.: No, no. When you see the suffering naturally you cannot escape reacting to it. And when you see it, you are not seeing the cosmic consciousness. It is out of your sight. You can't see the two things at the same time. When you are sleeping, the waking does not exist. You can't say what you shall do with the waking consciousness; in the dreaming also, you cannot put this question because you have not woken up. If you wake up, you do not put questions about dreams. The matter is closed. And you know very well why you should not put such questions. [*Turning to his errand boy*] Do you know Premananda Rao? Not Premananda Swamiji, but plain Premananda Rao? Call him here. You will never ask me questions about your friends in dream. Perhaps one fell and broke his limb in that dream but on waking up you do not ask, "what happened to that man. I have to take him to the hospital." You do not put such question for obvious reasons which are known to you very well.

For the same reason you will not put these questions when you are in cosmic consciousness. But these questions will certainly be there so long as you have not woken up into cosmic consciousness. When you fall from a tree in the dream you certainly feel the pain at that time. But this is only in a dream. When you wake up you will not say anything about the pain.

S. D.: So when I am in a cyclone-hit area, I cannot think that it is a cosmic action.

Sw. K.: You cannot think like that; the mind will not go there to the cosmic consciousness.

S. D.: It does go, God's will, etc. we say.

Sw. K.: No no ! Only theoretically the mind goes there and that is useless. It has no utility for the mind.

S. D.: [*laughing*]: What does it want, and how does the mind in a practical sense go to the cosmic consciousness?

Sw. K.: Practically means you will become that. Just as you become practically waking—you are not theoretically thinking it is the waking state. Are you simply arguing that it is the waking state, or is it really so? Now you are only arguing that God exists. You are not seeing it. It has not become part of your life. But waking is part of your existence and you would not have any question about it. It is very clear that in the waking state the sun is rising and is bright. You will not ask any question about that. But you ask questions about God, cosmos, and all that. This is because it is not a part of your life. When it does become a part of your life, you will not ask questions. You came from England, you didn't ask from people, "Am I coming from England?" That is very clear to you and you'll never ask such questions. Your name is very clear to you, do you ask others, "Am I called by this name?" These are part of your existence and questions can't arise. That which is outside you and not part of your life, raises doubts. Cosmic Being and God are outside your personality and so you have so many questions. So practically means practical experience and the cosmic consciousness absolution into your personality. Anything that has become one with your personality does not bring doubts. You've no doubt about your being a citizen of England, but you have doubts about your being a citizen of Paradise. If you are connected with another

British national such as Michael—you are connected with the citizens of England. This is very clear to you, it is a part of your existence, you will not ask any question. If you see the world at the cosmic level, you will see it in a different light altogether. Answers to questions will be as clear as daylight.

Francisca: Many traditions talk about the Compassionate God.

Sw. K.: That is only man's creation of God. What man himself has created traditionally, it is that God. There are two kinds of God—God created by man and God as He is. [*laughing*] And the God created by man is like this—He thinks as man thinks. But there is another God who does not think like man but has got His own ways of thinking. And you've to participate in that. He is not prepared to participate with you. [*laughing*] There are people who do not believe in God. When, for instance, the child dies—if my child dies I can't believe that God is good. He is a very cruel, hard-hearted person if at all He exists: He has killed my little child. But if you win elections to be the Prime Minister of England, God is very compassionate. He has given me success in the elections. This is your God whom you have created and who is of this type. Whatever you say, He does. So He is like a servant. You can't call Him a God who does whatever you like. In that case He is only your slave. If you want wealth, He must give it; if you want that your enemy should die, He should kill him. A very strange God that would be! Whatever you say He must do, otherwise you have no faith in Him.

This is exactly what I have been rebelling against for years and years. [*Swami K. laughs.*] As a poet beautifully said: "God is the greatest creation of man. Man has created many things like robots and engines and aeroplanes and also God for his utility. And this God is not going to help you. This is your creation. But there is a God who has created you and that is the real God. If you are able to understand Him, well then, you'll be a superhuman being, and you will not think in the human way.

Even mathematics is of three kinds. There is empirical maths and a cosmic maths, 2 × 2 = 4, 3 angles of a triangle make two right angles. These are arithmatic and geometry of the empirical type. But there is an arithmatic of sub-atomic physics and cosmography, of the theories of relativity, for instance. There 2+2 do not make 4 and the 3 angles of a triangle do not make two right angles. How do you say that it is absurd ! No, it is a geometrtcal truth.

But this empirical mathematics is not applicable at that level and has nothing to do with it. Only a person whose mind has risen to that level will understand what it is. Now, length, breadth and height—this is called three-dimensional perception. But it is not true. It is only an erroneous perception. According to the Theory of Relativity, these are made in four dimensional structure—What four dimensional is God alone knows, the mind cannot grasp. You have reduced everything to three dimensions—length, breadth and height. Everything is in space and time. They say there is no such thing as space and time, there is only a complex of space-time continuation. This is one mathematics. And what this gentleman this scientist, said, God can't understand. Only he can understand.

According to the Theory of Relativity, there is no past, present and future. The past can be future and the future can be present. There is no distinction of the past, present and future; time does not exist. And if the past and the future do not exist the world also does not exist. It comes to that. The world is based on this conception of the past, present and future. The human basis does'nt exist. The whole thing collapses. If the theories of modern physics are to be accepted, you can't even believe that the world exists—except in your head. And this is what men like Einstein have demonstrated to the horror of ordinary thinkers. If physics can revolutionize your brain like this, well, God is something different and you will never think in such terms as this. Your daily life will get completely transformed in God-consciousness. It will not be as it is lived ordinarily, because God will direct your course of actions in the light of the cosmic set-up of things, not in the light of empirical perception of values.

Where is the difference between these? You have no connection with the person sitting next to you. That is your ordinary way of thinking. You may think you are connected with that person who is your sister, etc. But in the cosmic set-up of things it is not true that this other person is not connected with you. There is nothing which is not connected with you. Everything is connected with you just as your nose and hands are connected with you. And if that is the case, what will be your attitude to things? I ask you, if everything is connected with your personality organically, what will your attitude be? You can yourself judge. You can yourself answer this question. If everything is organically connected with your personality and is inseparable from your being, what will be your attitude to things? You will have the same attitude to things as you will have to your own self. You can neither like nor dislike anything. You cannot pass judgment on anything. No opinion about anything, just as you have no judgment or opinion about yourself. And then you will see some miracle taking place, and what that miracle will be you will see at that time only.

People will start appearing in a different light altogether and everything will come to you on its own. They are away from you now and you have to go here and there to get them. At that time you need not go to things, they will come to you. And you do not have to run after them because they are away from you. At that stage they run after you; the tables are turned. Now you are dependent on the world. At that stage the world will depend on you, because you are not an individual, you are something else. Not only the world, but also that which is beyond it will look unlike what it was before. You are now a representative of the cosmic substance. Even the world looks like a dot before the might of the cosmos. Naturally, nothing exists before it and everything has simply to bow its head before it. Now everything in the world which looks so big frightens you. But at that stage nothing can frighten you because you have transcended it in your awareness, and you become a superhuman being. Your logic gails, your mathematics fails and even your ethical consciousness fails. It is supermoral; and not immoral but supermoral.

S. D.: Swamiji, you have said that during meditation, a change takes place in every cell of your being. If there is no concentration will this still happen?

Sw. K.: No, there is no change taking place when there is no concentration—nothing will happen. If you throw a grain of sugar into the ocean, there is no change in the ocean. A spoon of sugar is not sufficient to sweeten it. It is true that you are concentrating, but it is not strong enough to bring about that change. When a strong wind blows even a tree can be uprooted. (*Acting the words*) But if you puff and blow before the tree nothing happens. [*Swamiji leads the laughter from all*]. You will say, I am blowing but nothing is happening! See! your blowing can have no effect on a tree just near you. How can poor concentration affect the cosmos which alone brings about the change in your individual self?

S. D.: So any unusual experience when there is no concentration is not valid? It is only one more phenomenon the senses are creating under these conditions.

Sw. K.: [*Busy with the papers*]: Y-e-s.

S. D.: Even if it repeats itself it is only the senses that are projecting the experience and so it has no validity. Is it only the senses affirming their say and trying to convince us that they are not protecting it?

Sw. K.: [*Still with attention on papers in hand*] Yes, if the experience is not projected by the senses by themselves, you will never have a doubt whether they are true or not. You do not doubt that it is daytime now, you don't ask people around whether it is day or not. The minute you ask questions, it means it is not true. If you are free from doubts, the experience is true. The minute you ask questions it means it is not O.K. It is not the real thing: of the real thing you will have no doubt.

[*Swamiji cuts some jokes, greeting visitors who return the jokes bowing before Swamiji.*]

S. D.: Swamiji, you have said that the eight ways in which the Vedas are recited drives them into the mind. Are all the four Vedas recited in all these eight ways?

Sw. K.: Yes, but especially the Rig Veda is sung like that. (to Franka from England.) What books have you read? (this question is replied). There is Ramakrishna Centre in London. They have published a booklet or a phamphlet on spiritual communion or something like that, have you seen that?

Franka: No. I know that centre, it is on the outskirts of London and it is not easy to frequent it.

Sw. K.: There is one centre in Buckingham Palace. Is it in the Palace or it only a name for another place, not the Royal Palace.

[*A visitor who does not seem to follow any English is brought in and Swamiji turns to Yogi Raj.*]

Are they your disciples? How many disciples do you have? Who are they?

Yogi Raj: They are not my "disciples"; I learn from them.

Sw. K.: They are your teachers? Disciple-teachers? Who are they?

Y. R.: I have only two disciples.

Sw. K.: Tell me their names.

Y. R.: Very difficult to pronounce.

Sw. K.: There was one named Uttaptaat Yut Kata Tvita Prakata Kata Kata Dhvaana Sangghadanachari. This young man on the road committed nuisance. The policeman caught him and asked his name. The young man said Uttaptaat Yut Kata Tvita Prakata Kata Kata Dhvaana Sangghadanachari. The policeman who wanted to *challan* him was flabbergasted. He could not pronounce that name. So he said in a grandiose manner: "Get up, don't do it again." And went off!

Sw. K.: (*Swamiji leads a long laughter at this*) So you are in trouble because you cannot pronounce your disciple's name! All troubles that to the Guru are due to the disciple: for otherwise the Guru is "Alakh Niranjan" (free and blissful).

[*Swami K. gives direction to a member working in the "Langar department"*.] Questioning a visitor as to the object of his visit to the Ashram and the extent of interest in 'Yoga'. The term Yoga is used by foreigners in a very general sense with a casual understanding, remarked Swamiji. When a visitor wanted him to explain what should be the aim of one's life, he made the following observations.

Sw. K.: Let me first explain who you are. You are an individual. An individual is a social being, a member of a certain society. We think of each person in the society as separate individuals. You do not think that one soul is connected with another soul. Suppose you sit here without having any connection with one another. In that case you cannot call it a society. It is only like a heap of pebbles on the road which looks connected with it with each other but is not really so. In fact, society dies not mean merely a group of people. Society is the relationship between individuals and not merely a group of people. There is a difference between a group of people and society, though on the surface it appears that society is nothing but a group of people.

There is, therefore, a difference between group psychology and individual psychology. You may think something individually, i.e. as an individual, but when you are in the midst of a hundred people you think differently. Why is this so? What happens to you? You become a part of the group. This is the difference between society and the individual. However, listen to what I am saying, my dear friend, don't turn your eyes somewhere else. Ah! this relationship between one person and another is the primary concern at present. Whatever you do is in the light of society, the social relationship. You are not doing it absolutely from your own individual point of view, though ultimately that is your intention. You cannot impose upon it your own personality inasmuch as you cannot extricate yourself from social relationship.

But social relationship is ultimately to be transcended in one's understanding of the great fact that society is not independent of individuals, notwithstanding the fact that it is the relation between the individuals which is society. If individuals were not there, society will not be there. So individuals are tremendously important. You have an importance in your individuality because you are an individual. And the importance of one individual is the same as that of any other individual. If you know yourself fully you know everybody else because everybody is made of the same substance. So from social psychology, you come to individual psychology. Though the primary intention is to face society ultimately, that will not decide all your questions unless you read the psychology of human nature. And the way in which human mind works decides the manner in which society works. Because society is a relationship of individuals, it is essential that you know what is the structure of the human mind and human nature. It is made up of certain factors. It is constructed of certain forces and works in a certain manner, and you have to take into consideration the structure of the human personality, the human mind, the intellect, the emotions and whatever there is of the psyche.

But this is also not sufficient. Why should the mind work in that way? This is another question. The human mind works in a given way because of its pattern of thinking, understanding and desiring. And one has to conform one's self to the way in which the mind works. There is the question why the mind works in that manner and not in any other manner. [*Someone interrupts but is dealt with and disposed of.*] This question cannot be answered by psychology. Because psychologists study only the pattern in which the human mind works, as also the way of the working of the mind. The why of it—it cannot say. This is the question which leads us to philosophy, for philosophical enquiry which is in the higher realms of spirituality, religion, yoga, etc.

Your relationship with the universe is the reason behind the way the mind works in that particular way. As human society is determined by individuals, the individuals themselves are determined by cosmic relationship. You are constituted of a particular relationship with the universe of the world outside. You are connected with air, water, fire, ether, sky, the moon, the sun, the solar system and what not! So the way in which you are relatec to the cosmos outside is the determining factor of the manner in which your personality would work—the way in which your mind works and incidentally the society works. And your relationship with the universe outside is the subject of philosophy. From sociology, we go to psychology and from psychology to what they call epistemology i.e. the way of thinking and understanding of things outside and the manner of our perception. Then we go to cosmology the creation of the universe.

When we go to the creation of the universe, the question of the creator arises. Who created this universe? So you go to metaphysics and the Absolute. Just imagine! You are related to so many wonderful things which are unthinkable, and it is enough to make one giddy. Your head will start reeling if you have the time to think of the various relationships in which you are involved. Though it seems you are connected with only little things like shopping and standing at a counter to encash a cheque—silly matters for you—but these things are connected with the Absolute. And this will become clear to you only if you have time to think deeply about small situations. Even the littlest thing of the world is connected with the Absolute. Now I come to your point. You asked me how can I decide the aim of life. Do you think you get some inkling as to the answer to this question? Some idea as to the implications of your question?

The Italian youngster who asked the question: Yes.

Sw. K.: What should be the aim of your life? Tell me.

Italian Youth: You should see to your own qualities, your own intelligence and—

Sw. K.: You should not look to your own quality. You have to look to the various stages of life. I mentioned to you the various stages of the development of thought, from lower to the higher you go gradually. You are not looking to any particular thing—neither to yourself nor to society nor the world nor even to God Himself, but you have to look to all things at the same time in different gradations or ascents, and you must know where you stand. You should not jump too high thinking that you are on a higher level when you are actually on the lower. Generally we suffer and come in conflict on account of our theoretical imagining that we are on a higher level while practically we are on a lower one. That is called worry, mental tension, etc. Tension is the problem that is created by a theoretical future and a practical present. [*laughs*] So you should be very wise. You should not try to soar to the sky very quickly. When your feet are planted on earth, you must know that they are on the earth; you should not think you are in heaven.

People say, Oh! I am concerned only with God, spirituality and Yoga. That is not true. This kind of statement will not work and it is not a fact. The fact is that you are in the world. When the wind blows you feel cold, you have hunger, you have thirst, sleep...See? And many other considerations. So you must eschew the idea that you are thinking only of God. One must be realistic. Though the aim should be to transcend these lower limitations, you cannot ignore their presence when they are there.

[*The interruption is dealt with and disposed of.*]

F.: Swami Sivananda says that while he was doing ordinary things, he had his consciousness on the higher level; he does not talk of any level of perfection but says you should be conscious only of the higher values—

Sw. K.: [*still attending to papers*]: Yes, yes, that is so.

F.: There is no link between the ordinary level without real perfection and the higher consciousness within oneself.

Sw. K: Why do you say there is no link? A link between them is actually present. In fact, the very art of perfect living or aim of living life is the maintenance of a higher purpose. It need not necessarily be the highest purpose, it is the purpose immediately higher, just above your present level. That is what you are concerned with, not with the supreme level. That is not your concern. When you say this is right, that is not right; this is good, that is not good; it should be like this, it should not be like that—when you say "this" you have already set a higher standard than the standard you are following. Otherwise you will not say this is good and that is not good. You have something in your mind as the proper standard to which you make a reference to find out what is right and what is wrong. So your idea of it is already there. If it is not there you will not know what is right and what is wrong. The very fact that you are thinking this is right, that is wrong shows you have a link with a higher idea which you are maintaining in your mind and from the point of which you want to judge the lower level. Similarly when you have reached that you will find a still higher level. You go on like that until you reach the highest step. So, as I said, you must concern yourself with the immediate higher level.

The immediate higher level for an ordinary individual is the social norm. You cannot break the social norm, you know that very well. Otherwise you cannot live in human society. Whether the people in society are correct or not is a different matter. For you, it is correct. The Western society has one norm, the Indian society another and the Japanese still another, different from both. It is very strange that every society has its own norm and neither this is nice nor that is nice. But that is a different subject. You belong to a particular society and you have to follow its norms. So at the earliest stages of existence, social norms become the higher level. When you transcend that, there is a racial level. When you transcend the racial level, then you are independent and you do not have to hang on society for your existence, and you have strength and value of your own. Then you start judging things from the point of view of your own conscience. Sometimes your conscience will rebel against social norms. You will think society is stupid. But you cannot live, get on staying in society with this feeling; you have to get out of it, and that is a different matter. When you are in it, you have to follow it. So when your society relationship is transcended, you begin to follow the higher—the higher reason with which you are endowed. What we call conscience is the next step.

There is no need of thinking too far into the higher levels because the mind is not used to it and will not therefore go to that level which it has not reached, though it will go to the cosmic level itself in time. Your reason may not be of the final norm because that is also an empirical thing. It is conditioned by your body and your needs. Your idea of the necessary and unnecessary is dependent on the needs of the body and mind. Whatever is necessary for the body and the mind you regard that as really necessary. And this something is necessary for the body and mental well-being and you have got to give in. That is the temporary and tentative judgment of the values of things. But you will transcend this value afterwards. What is good at this level is not necessarily good for the body and your indivdual psyche from the point of the law that operates in the cosmos. And that is the next step. Then finally the highest good is that which is in consonance with the existence of God Himself, and anything else is not good. But you cannot reach that level immediately. As I told you, slowly and gradually you must go from the lower to the higher purpose, otherwise you cannot make judgments. Every judgment logically is the standard that is set as the next higher level. In any opinion that you express, whenever you pass an opinion on anything, hold an idea or a concept or a judgment about anything, you have connection with a higher purpose which becomes your standard. Otherwise you cannot know what is right and what is wrong, what is perfect and what is not perfect, what is true and what is false. So there is a real link. But the link will develop into higher and higher dimensions. You cannot see the higher dimensions but only the immediately higher.

Italian Visitor: What is Shakti? How does it work?

Sw. K.: What is Shakti? Which Shakti? First of all you tell me what you mean by Shakti?

I. V.: Well, Shakti like creature power, Shakti like the Divine Mother.

Sw. K.: It works everywhere and in everything, and everything is its manifestation. It is cosmic energy. And every thing is constituted of that. Do you know what the latest modern scientific discoveries say? They say that every material object, apparently looking material, is nothing but a formation of cosmic energy. Everything including your own body, is made up of that one energy, Shakti, which means energy, power, force, etc. It is the stuff of everything right from earth to heaven—nothing else except that. And the more you are able to participate in its working, the more strength you derive. Shakti is not merely physical but also psychological and even spiritual. But you must know how to participate in its working. That means you have to transcend your ego and to some extent also your personality and your individuality. Because cosmic substance is all-pervading, it is not affiliated to some particular individual. So to participate in the universal substance means to get over the limitations of personality, that is to transcend it. What else do you want to know. What is your question?

I.V.: Is the Shakti connected with feminine quality?

Sw. K.: No, no! It is not connected with any quality because it has no such distinction as masculine or feminine. It is a universal, impersonal force. It may split itself into various shapes, into not only feminine and masculine but also into matter in the animate and the inanimate, etc., etc. This is a discussion of animate and inanimate. Even that is the creation of the ways of human perception. It has no such distinctions in itself but it looks as if there is distinction when you look at it from your point of view. It is not male or female, it is impersonal. It is endrogenous. You know what is endrogenous?

I.V.: Yes!

Sw. K.: It is that.

I.V.: It works also in the individuality.

Sw. K.: It works also in the individuality; it works everywhere—in every atom of the world it is working. It alone exists through all that appear as substances. But it looks to your empirical perception as if it is divided, whereas it is cosmically integrated.

I.V.: There are such things as positive and negative forces. Can the male and female be regarded as such?

Sw. K.: This would be a very gross and crude form of expressing the two forces, positive and negative. These two forces of electricity, for instance, you don't call them feminine and masculine. That is a very peculiar human way of looking at things. They are two electric couplings—neutral forces: one becoming complete by combination with another and they appear to be different on account of the manifestation of Space-Time causal relationship. There is further distinction of male-female positive-negative, etc. But in what people nowadays call the fourth dimension, there is no such distinction of positivity and negativity. The split of positive and negative, male and female, arises after space and time have been divided. So what you say in this context is correct. But everything is contained in the fourth dimension—the uniformation of the continuum in its essentiality has no division within itself. There's a difference between the head and the legs for instance. You have a head and you've legs. They are not different; you can't say either that one is the same as the other. But you don't feel the difference; you feel it is one whole—you feel one living mass or personality extending from head to foot. You don't see the distinction from one part to another part of the body.

Likewise the energy will not see any difference such as that which the mind sees. It is one mass in which everything is comprehended: pure awareness.

I.V.: Then why are we not endogenic of this?

Sw. K.: We are not endogenic of this. We are cut off from it—Cut off from the source. This is what is called the Fall of Adam and Eve from the Garden of Eden.

I.V.: What is the meaning of Yoga, please?

Sw. K.: The meaning is the realization of the mistaken notion—that of the isolation of the individual from the cosmic, your feeling that you are cut off from the world. You feel that you are outside things, isn't it? There are so many things like the sun, the moon, the stars, etc. They aren't connected with you, but it is not true: you are connected with them. The solar rays and the cosmic rays constitute the substance of your body itself. But you feel that you aren't connected, this is your mistake. Our mind is not so made as to appreciate the connection of your existence with other things. This is the inability of the mind to think correctly. That is our problem. And the practice of Yoga is nothing but a gradual process of self-identification with the different levels of reality, until gradually you identify yourself with that to which you originally belonged. A great art, a tremendous, life-long process—life-long, not a question of a few days and months. And you exist only for this purpose and have no other duty in life. Every other duty is only for this purpose. What can you do in this world is a setp in the achievement of this purpose.

I.V.: So Yoga is connecting the individual reality with the Cosmic Reality?

Sw. K.: Yes, yes; right, right!

I.V.: Have you to use the mind too....

Sw. K.: In the beginning, you've to use nothing else: You've got no other faculty. The only faculty you've got is the mind and the intellect in the beginning. But later on, there is no need for you to use the mind and intellect, soul itself will act. Your soul is your total personality. It is not working always. Generally only a partial part of your total personality works.

I.V.: It is the individuality that works.

Sw. K.: Yes. Personality is the outward expression of your individuality. Your individuality is superior. You feel you exist as a person or individuality does not work for all times. Either the intellect works or the emotions etc. but the soul does not work. The whole intellect works, emotion works, will works. And the soul does not, only very rarely it acts.

I.V.: Is it because the intellect and the mind are conditioned very much?

Sw. K.: They are very much conditioned and they are not going to be of help at all times. But when you have nothing else, you have naturally to take their help for the time being. When you have no apparatus to rely upon, you have only the mind and intellect, hence you have to take their help.

I.V.: What about the feelings? Is it conditionless?

Sw. K.: It is equally conditioned as much as the intellect and mind. It is no less conditioned. Your whole vision of things is conditioned in a particular manner by space and time. As I mentioned to you, you cannot get over this conditioning. But the intellect will help you finally in knowing its own limitations. That is, when you know your own limitations, you have automatically outgrown your limitations. When you know, you can go up higher and further to this level, you have to some extent known what is above you. When you know the limit of a thing, you also have an idea of what is outside that limit. So when your intellect has reached its farther limits of logic and understanding you would get a flash from the higher level. And then the soul acts and the intellect stops.

I.V.: What happens to your own personality afterwards?

Sw. K.: It all just goes afterwards. It will not exist then. You will become something different. You will become a larger personality and not an individual personality. You become inclusive of all other factors in you. That is what is called a superman. You must have heard of superbeings. Superman is nothing but a higher being in whose personality the existence of other personality is subsumed. He is a larger individuality with greater dimensions tending towards still higher realisation, stage by stage.

I.V.: What is the difference between Jnana Shakti and Kundalini Shakti?

Sw. K.: Kundalini Shakti is everything. Jnana Shakti is knowledge. Jnana is a Sanskrit word, the power of knowledge is Jnana Shakti. Kundalini Shakti includes the power of understanding, of feeling, the power of action. It is every kind of Shakti, action, volition, feeling—all these are comprehended within it.

I.V: Is it included in the practice of Yoga. Can we use this term?

Sw. K.: Yes! Kundalini Shakti is included in Yoga. All types of energy are included therein and it is inclusive of everything.

LV.: What is the difference between knowledge and wisdom?

Sw. K.: Knowledge is the lesser of the two—wisdom is deeper—almost bordering on intuition. Many times in practical life, we have knowledge but not wisdom. You know that very well. When you know how to live properly that is wisdom.

(Interruption—Someone has come for help).

Sw. K.: This person helps that person and that person someone else. Who will help me in the end (sniffing the air). What is this smell ?

Someone answers that it is the scent used by (foreign visitors).

Sw. K.: They want to exclaim their presence by smell? You know what smelling a person means? (laughs heartily)

Y. Raj: By helping someone, one helps oneself Swamiji.

Sw. K.: No, my dear friend. This is what the Bhagavata Gita tries to tell you through a whole chapter. Karma Yoga is not meant merely to help somebody but also to participate in the system of the cosmos. Incidentally, it looks like helping other people. That is a different matter. That is a secondary thing. You are participating in the law of evolution of the universe; that is Karma Yoga. And in that, of course, it would look like helping others.

The lunch bell ? Went long ago ? Go, go, and have lunch. If you go late there would be no lunch. God bless you. Thank you for giving me your *darshan*. We have enjoyed good *satsanga*.

23 December 1978

About ten people, mostly foreigners, disciples of Yogi Raj, a couple and their friends who had come to see the Ashram, were present at the start of the morning *darshan*.

Revered Swamiji welcomed them.

Question: What is the cause of our perception of change? Is it purely physical, and, therefore, pertaining to the body, or is it due to the structure of the mind?

Sw. K.: Changes are both perceivable and not perceivable due to the mind and the body.

Question: Are they interdependent?

Sw. K.: Yes.

Q.: How to overcome this interdependence?

Sw. K.: Interdependence of the body and the mind can be overcome by transcending both, and this is what is meant by the word 'Meditation'. What kind of meditation is suited for the individual can be found only with the guidance of a competent person. Find someone in the world—may be in your own place or elsewhere—and ask him which type of meditation is good for you.

Visitor: Can not Swamiji tell me what is suited for me?

Sw. K.: I will study you first, only then I can answer that question. Psychoanalysis, which is essential to understand the structure of the mind, is part of Yoga itself. Yoga is the highest kind of self-analysis.

Visitor: Do you believe in dream-analysis as relevant to Yoga practice?

Sw. K.: Psychoanalysis includes dreams, etc. The function of the mind is studied in this analysis and all the various mental functions have to be studied, and it requires time. It is a long process of analysis undertaken leisurely. You need a guide for this, because you are studying yourself and, therefore, will be prone to justifications of your own way of thinking. You hold an opinion, because you are sure that it is right. But it may not be so in the final analysis which we have undertaken. Therefore, a personal guide is needed, because it is better to have two heads than one. Specially in the advanced stages of meditation, you need the guidance of a competent person.

(A messenger brings papers for Swamiji for his attention and disposal. It is done while Swamiji continues to talk).

To find out the type of Yoga suitable for you, you must first fix up the aim in your taking to Yoga. It is useless to proceed if you cannot fix up your aim. When you undertake a travel, unless you determine the aim and purpose you wish to achieve by travelling, how can you reach anywhere or fix up your travel programme? 'Why are you sitting like that? What are you thinking with your eyes closed?' [*These questions were put by Swamiji to a teen-aged German, a great devotee and follower of Rev. Swami Chidanandaji Maharaj.*]

Revered Swami Krishnananda Maharaj had observed that the lad was always sitting with his eyes closed and in a meditative mood, at all the morning and evening satsangas, even in the presence of Rev. Chidananda Maharaj.

In answer to the question from Swamiji, the lad, whose name was Alexender, said that he wished to study Yoga.

Sw. K.: Why do you want to study Yoga?

Alex: I want to know what I am. I sit with my eyes closed trying to find out what I am.

Sw. K.: How did this question arise in your mind? There must be something in your mind which is prompting you into this question. Why do you want to know yourself?

A.: Because I am not satisfied that I know myself.

Sw. K.: Not satisfied? Why? Are you not happy?

A.: Sometimes I feel unhappy, but generally, quite happy.

Sw. K.: Note down what makes you unhappy.

A.: I am not able to follow my own way of thinking, I am not in my own path.

Sw. K.: Why do you feel so? Are you sure your way is right? If you are not sure, then why do you wish to change? There are different ways of thinking—how to judge which one is correct. If each one is correct in his own world and cannot harmonise his way of thinking with another, find out what the reason is.

That the world of one's own is different from that of the other is what results in war. Is your unhappiness caused by the necessity of following the law? Actually appreciation of the law is happiness. That is the first thing. Secondly, because you don't want to agree to other's opinions, you feel unhappy: this is wrong, this is selfishness. Thirdly, happiness is the result of agreeing to the law and thus avoiding trouble. Philosophical thinking brings about understanding. We must direct the mind to understand the law. Education is the capacity to understand. Philosophy is not for writing for the examinations. It is an education in the art of life itself and not any compartmental knowledge. Philosophy means comprehensive thinking. You need not follow Plato or Kant. You can take their help to the extent you find them helpful. A wider vision and sympathy should be the result of philosophy of thinking. All these need to be studied under a competent guide for a protracted period of time, just like in a university where they have the course chalked out systematically. (A new visitor is introduced to Swamiji by the reception. By now the gathering had swelled to about 20 with people coming and people leaving after the *darshan*).

Sw. K.: Because the subject here is more difficult, there is a great necessity for such a systematic course and a guide. Yoga is not one singled out subject) It is fundamental, your existence itself. Understanding of the subject depends on the level one is at. The different qualities of different people is due to the fact that they are at different levels of understanding. It is not enough to meet one of your own level, but one who is at a higher level, so that you can progress. As human beings, we act alike in general. But we think differently in particularised details. Since Yoga deals with the fundamentals of one's existence, there is need to harmonise by adjusting oneself to all the levels one meets with. That amount of adjustment is necessary which is needed for harmony, specially in such things as in differences of outlook, mind, aim, etc. of the individual.

When a person thinks rationally, there are, side by side, feelings of personality also. A man of understanding is also a man of feeling. It is in consideration of this that the great tradition of guru-disciple system of education had been planned with great wisdom by our ancients. But in modern times, we are trying to overstep this wise and necessary guru-disciple tradition. The modern ideals of independence is the cause behind the impetuousity of severance from guidance. Self-dependence plays the key role in the misplaced idea that a Guru is dispensable. I repeat, you require a guide.

[*A visitor who has just joined the gathering remarks that if one ponders over spiritual problems, one becomes depressed.*]

Sw. K.: Thinking becomes depressing, because you don't understand the subject you are thinking of, and if your reading has not been understood, you feel more so. A medicine it meant to alleviate and not to aggravate the illness. If this happens it means it is a wrong medicine. The disease has not been properly diagnosed and competent prescription has not been given. Three things are necessary for Yoga:

(1) Continuous study under a guide.
(2) Contemplation of what has been studied.
(3) Meditation on what has been understood. Contemplation is lighter in depth than meditation.

In meditation you become the object of your meditation and, therefore, have gone much deeper into your own personality and the relationship to the object of meditation.

Q.: Which is the best religion which gives the right direction?

Sw. K.: What is good, bad, above, below, right, wrong—all this depends upon the position of the observer and, therefore, they are relative and not absolute in themselves. There is no new philosophy. All philosophies are so many different aspects of theology. The old and the new concept of God is what you learn in the Old Testament and the New Testament. So, there is no right or wrong type of philosophy. All depends upon your level of understanding and your type of thinking. I will not say this is higher or that is lower. Do you know Judaism? You know nothing about it. What religion have you studied?

Visitor: I am only a student and my subject is Theology. I have studied only in the university and I like Hinduism.

Sw. K.: What books have you studied?

Th.: Mostly about Hatha Yoga and other Yogas.

Sw. K.: Why do you like Hinduism?

Answer: Because I feel it is more open than the other religions that I studied.

Sw. K.: What is the outlook of Hinduism? In what way is it different from the ways of other religions? How? Or, is there no difference?

Th.: It has more practical value.

Sw. K.: (To another Visitor): Topiwalla! Where are you coming from?

Th.: I had been here, Swamiji, some years ago. You were much more healthy then. I want to become an inmate here in the Ashram and I want to learn Yoga here.

Sw. K: If you say that, I will not allow you to stay here even now! (*laughs*). Yoga can't be learnt in fifteen days. You can stay only as a visitor. You can't stay as an inmate. See Swami Madhavanandaji. How long do you want to stay here? Stay for sometime and you see how things are. Stay for 15 days like all these so many visitors who come and go. Sivananda-Ashram must also be enjoyed by you. [*laughs*] Don't be in a hurry to decide what you plan to do.

Mr. R.N. Chatterjee: Please note my name. I wish to see you some time later. My name is R.N. Chatterjee.

Sw. K.: I will see you some time later. (Seeing Sri Kartakeyan at the side of the gathering), Yes, come. As Swamiji goes through the correspondence the luncheon bell rings. People disperse after taking leave of revered Swamiji who blesses them and says, Thank You!

26 December 1978

The people assembled this morning were newly arrived foreigners as well as an English couple with their child. They had come from Delhi where the husband, an engineer, had been deputed by the British Government to help with the knowhow of some machinery that had been presented by them to India. The wife more particularly was interested in spiritual path and I quote her own little summary which I had requested her to kindly give to me. She had put questions to Swamiji who answered them. I had joined the gathering much later and therefore could not get the continuity of Swamiji's conversation.

"I asked Swamiji whether he could suggest a simple method to start concentration—meditation. He said I could do *japa* (repeating of a *mantra*) or follow any method suitable to me. He asked me (the times of the day I keep and) how much time I could devote to thinking and contemplation which he said was essential. One must have time to oneself. When asked, I told him I wanted to see things in their proper perspective and (correctly) but could not do so because of sudden interference of other thoughts. He talked about the difference between objects and their perception and (separation of objects and the perception which separates them). He asked if I could (see with) follow him. I said I could. Then he asked me if I could see him with any other organ than my eyes. I said I could see him with my mind. After that, he seemed to be saying that I was seeing him as if two points of the same consciousness reflect each other. Hence they reflect also the same thinking. So I must realise this unity of all things and live accordingly, by being aware of the manifold but not obsessed by it to the point of forgetting the underlying unity of the whole structure of the Cosmos. After that, he said once this realisation of unity occurs, the mind does not differentiate between one object and another. He then went on to talk about the subject and object saying that nothing is completely a subject or an object. There is always 50 per cent of both. Hence our minds are the same. But when we encounter in the object something we dislike or like or like the subject and the object are not of the same 50/50 per cent proportion. I could not grasp the meaning behind this bit. So it is difficult for me to remember what he said. May be I will remember later."

Swamiji said in conclusion, there is only one consciousness, only one ocean, but the ocean is not the millions of waves (*from my own notes*). If each wave thinks it is different form the rest, it is not true because every single wave is ocean. To understand this, it is essential to sit by ourselves, and meditate. Activity in terms of multiplicity and consciousness in terms of unity is *Karma Yoga*. Study, *japa* and constant thinking on the line stated above will induce concentration. The goldsmith and the carpenter see only gold or the wood, the material they work upon. Their thoughts are not concentrated on the various articles they produce. A piece of jewellery to a goldsmith is not jewellery but so much gold; similarly the table or chair is not a meaningful item for the carpenter but the log of wood from which these have been produced. 'I don't think I have told you everything that has to be said, but I hope I have said something worthwhile," concluded Revered Swamiji.

One of the visitors put the question: "Is the distinction between one and the other due to what is in between the two? What creates this distinction?"

Sw. K.: Don't believe the senses which say the opposite of the inevitable unity which alone exists. Every cell in the body is interspaced, from each other. Well, you see them as your own and are sure they are unified in your body, despite the space between them. Likewise, if you see the unity, multiplicity will disappear. This is what *Bhagavadgita* tells us. The *Bhagavadgita* is like the Sun which looks fresh and beautiful and young every day, every morning, fresh and full of loving essence."

And thus concluded the answer to my question.

There is a request to the Swami regarding some suggestions for the working of his department.

Sw. K.: More work? I was only greeting you and you are pouncing upon me and giving me work. (*Laughs and the gathering also joins in the joke.*)

Someone: "You are found of solving problems, Swamiji, that is why this request has been made to you.

Sw. K.: Because I have none of my own. I laugh and joke otherwise I will go mad. Two things must be kept in mind. Nothing in this world is meaningless. Everything has a reason or a meaning to it. Therefore, be happy and smile. Everything is divinity charged with the Divine Absolute.

Q.: What happens to us after death?

Sw. K.: If you exist after death, there is no need to worry. If you do not exist, there is no point in worrying. What does it matter even if it is a continuous existence after death. Tomorrow is no botheration because it is yet to come. Therefore death is not a problem. Look at it either way. So why bother ? Because you have a hazy notion both of existence after death and also of non existence, because you have 50/50 per cent of both these notions, the problem has risen before you. There is always a problem when partial views are taken. A partial view gives a double attitude. There is a big philosophy behind this problem. As the *Brihadaranyaka Upanishad* puts it, the subject and object are 50/50 per cent mixed with up each in the other because neither is 100 per cent. Therefore the problem of likes and dislikes arises. If this double attitude goes, the problem goes too. When you project God as an outside object, then you say God has no sense. He sends cyclones, earthquakes, etc. He is very unkind; He is very cruel. The problem before you is because of conflict between the subject and the object; your understanding is in conflict with the understanding of God. Your understanding is in the light of the report of your senses and the mind is ever ready to rely upon the report the senses bring. God's understanding is independent of the senses. And Yoga is withdrawal of the senses, from the objects, because senses act like the prism that splits light into seven colours. Hence to get the pure light of understanding, Yoga, which is the withdrawal of senses from the objects, that is the solution. Then the double attitude of subject versus the object goes.

An old devotee from Meerut comes in. Swamiji enquired of him what he was doing. He said that he had become a civil lawyer, as his parents wished.

Swamiji jokingly said, "Are bhai! You have become greater than a sannyasi. You will advise even the sannyasis." He added: "This gentleman wanted to become a sannyasi, and now see he has become more than a sannyasi." (To Ajay, a young aspirant who wished to go to America to study nuclear engineering while his father wanted him to become a lawyer.) "You also become a lawyer as he has done. You can be greater than any of the sannyasis because they shall have to seek your advice."

A Japanese gentleman had been sitting in the forefront all through this morning. Addressing him, Swamiji asks: Do you follow English. Have you understood anything of what has been said?

Jap.: I have almost understood all of it. I know in general what has been said.

Sw. K.: What do you do?

Jap.: I am teaching ladies the Japanese language.

Sw. K.: You say you understood in general what was said. Is it the thought in general or is it the words in general that you have understood? Thoughts need a background to be understood it. Have you read any books?

Jap.: I read in the library, "Elexir Divine" by Swami Sivananda. The sales department of the Sivananda Publication League does not have this in stock. Can I have a copy from you?

Sw. K.: I don't have a copy of it either you will have to wait for the reprint.

Ajay: What is the difference between feeling and emotion.

Sw. K.: The two are like the wind and the cyclone. Feeling is mild emotion; emotion is strong feeling. A singled-out emotion versus all other views and emotions of even collective nature is passion. A preference for a particular emotion is passion. Passion is a thought that overpowers personality. For example, the politicians are overpowered by passion for a thought so they seek to suppress all other emotions by promulgating such laws as Sec. 144.

Q.: What is the difference between devotion and passion?

Sw. K.: Devotion without understanding is only emotion and later becomes a passion—fanaticism. Mr Bill Isler an American recluse who has been staying in the Ashram for some years and a dedicated devotee of Rev. Chidananda, asked: Swamiji! You had started to give us talks on the Gita. Why not continue it?

Sw. K.: It is not possible for me to undertake this because I have some hardships to overcome in this matter, and I cannot explain what these hardships are. I alone know it.

Q.: If all devotion ultimately reaches the Absolute in whatever form it is offered, why is there such an elaborate arrangement for devotion to lesser deities?

Sw. K.: Shankaracharya in his commentary on *Brihadaranayaka Upanishad* says, "Why quarrel with the lesser gods by objecting to the worship offered to them? Please them. There is no harm in it."

Q.: Why can we not think of God as such.

Sw. K.: You can't think of God as such because the minute you think God, He becomes the object. You think of God as a particular potentiality, power, force, conduct or beauty. History of mankind is the manifestation of God's potentiality in any or all these forms. It is said that before manifestation, it was all dark, unknowable, ununderstandable etc. and this potentiality has no beginning nor end, even as there is no beginning nor end, of Cosmos. Only for man who thinks in terms of the present past and future, there is a beginning, a process and an end and there is history.

Q.: Why is this *Yuga* called *Kali Yuga*?

Sw. K.: The *yugas* come in a cycle. There are four *yugas* which come in rotation. The *Satya Yuga, Treta Yuga, Dwapara Yuga* and *Kali Yuga. Satya Yuga* is the golden age. The golden age is a condition of things where consciousness of externality is minimum and consciousness of universality is maximum. In the golden age, there is the highest consciousness of universality. The question whether creation is a reality or not cannot be answered. Both ways of answering it, yes and no, land us in one or the other kind of problem. So, why creation was of the highest consciousness of universality in the golden age cannot be easily answered. The reason why we feel that now in *Kali Yuga* we are in a non-golden age is because the sense of externality is overpowering the other view, viz., that there co-exists consciousness of universality. Hence the consciousness of universality is reduced to the minimum. There are books written by a Chinese author *Infinite Way* etc. In these books, he gives the same thoughts as those contained in the Indian system of thought explained by Patanjali. Matter is another name for externality, in other words sensory perception, and if there is 100 per cent perception of externality, it is inferno. At one stage, there is a balance between sensory perception of externality and the consciousness of universality. At another stage, there is complete abolition of this balance. Then the catastrophe occurs as in the case of the Yadavas being exterminated by Lord Krishna, an *Avatar.* Thus starts another *yuga.* The golden age, is the harmonious self-existence. It is the harmonious relationship of all forces in the world. *Kali Yuga* will be followed by *Satya Yuga.* The world is not going to dogs. The Supreme is ever Bliss and happiness.

30 December 1978

The following points were made to the group of Austrian visitors, led by Mr. Sobers, who had come by appointment. Some of their points had been put earlier to Rev. Hridayananda Mataji, who was also present that morning and to which Revered Mataji had replied. To the question, "Why do we have to search for our own souls," Revered Swami Krishnanandaji Maharaj replied as follows: "There is logical contradiction in that things are outside us. By logic it can easily be seen that the universe is one whole of which we are parts. For example, the hand in our body. It appears to be outside our body. But it is really not so and if there is no conflict between the hand which is outside the body, why should a conflict arise when we perceive the world as outside us? Yet conflict is raised. The world versus man. The greatest conflict however is the relation between man and God. There are four types of conflicts that assail man:

1. Conflict of man in society;
2. Conflict of man in his own (individual) personality;
3. Conflict of man, between the individual and the Universal, i.e., the cosmos;
4. Conflict of the relation between man and God or the conflict between the spirit and the Supreme.

God created the world and therefore it is outside God. That is the idea we have. This is a wrong notion and it is with this wrong notion that we complains against Him. The world is not created in the sense of apace-time relationship as far as God is concerned. This space-time relationship being foisted upon God is also a wrong notion. Now the dream proves to you that you can exist independent of the physical body. The parallels can be seen in the existence of God in the world and beyond it. What is it that exists continuously in both states of dream and waking consciousness. We had no awareness in sleep and yet we know that we slept. This is the contradiction. It is a recollection which is a fact also. How does contradiction in this recollection come—of the sleep of yesterday and the waking consciousness today ? We say it is memory of the dream which is recollected today. Now what is memory ? Memory is a rememberance of previous experience which is not possible unless there is consciousness of the previous experience. For example, the stone does not have any recollection or memory of the time-space complex, though a degree of consciousness does exist in it. Therefore consciousness is independent of mind and body. Consciousness alone is present in deep sleep. Therefore it is a proof that you can go beyond body and mind, but not beyond consciousness. If there is no consciousness, who will know that you slept, you had dreamt, etc. It can only be if consciousness has been continuously present. You cannot believe that there is anything beyond and outside consciousness, therefore consciousness is everywhere. Thus your essential nature is somehow that existence everywhere. Do you search for your own soul was your question. How can you search your own soul outside this existence which is everywhere, the Absolute? This all-Soul is God within whom rests the whole world. God did not create the world for you as an object and you as the subject opposed and outside you. Yoga aims at reconciling all the conflicts we have now mentioned. (1) Social (2) Individual (3) The individual in the Cosmos (4) Spiritual and the Absolute.

These are the stages mentioned by sage Patanjali and are based on intense scientific investigation. Yoga is meant for every one because every one has these four conflicts which have to be resolved by reconciling the contradictions. Therefore Yoga is for every one. Yoga is the art of the science applicable to anyone, anywhere every time, for Hindu monks or for other types of monks in other religions.

OM is a symbol of the vibration from which is supposed to emanate the manifestations of the world. Science says electricity is vibration. Not only that, Science further says that all materials, the so-called objects of the world, are nothing but vibrations ultimately. A substance is hard, soft, not palpable, etc. according to the vibrations our fingers register. Even so, universal vibration is the energy of the whole Cosmos which is OM.

Hence we may say that the world and we and God are not separate from one another, but constitute a continuum of consciousness. To realise this, the four conflicts mentioned above must be resolved at the very start before we try to go to the next stage. The first conflict must be resolved before trying to resolve the next stage of conflict. We must go stage by stage and not overstep any stage. If you know well the level at which you stand now, the next stage is not difficult to reach. The difficulty will come only if you try to jump levels.

It is but natural that you must have time of your own to ponder over the level you are on. Only then you can resolve the conflict one by one and progress towards your goal, and it is possible to find time for yourself because you are not occupied all the twenty-four hours of the day. Nor do you have to be in the midst of people every hour of the day. This is never the case. So tell people, for one hour—any hour that you decide upon—I will not see anyone. Every problem must have a solution. Problems cannot exist as an eternal fact. You may feel that while devoting time for your own self in this manner, you are not doing your duty by other people. This is not so. If your problem is service of people you can do more service by being alone this one hour and resolving the problem of conflict. That way you have drawn more strength and thereby have fortified yourself for the object you say you have viz. service to people. The scientist when working in the laboratory is alone with his experiment and not in the midst of people. The doctor in the operation theatre is alone with the patient and does not operate in the midst of people in the ward. So the conditions necessary to tackle a problem is clear from these two examples. It is necessary to be alone to resolve your own problems because from the generalities observed, it is not possible tc find the solution to the individual's problems. But like the ocean which remains calm even when the waves are dashing on the shore, you must remain calm and rest in your own individuality when the waves of problems of society dash upon you. From this analogy that relationship which exists between the society and you is clear, and the art of Yoga is this art of keeping calm like the ocean. The art of Yoga is to become a superman, and Yoga will make you that. The only trouble is you are in a hurry and wish to get on quickly with it and be through it. There is no point in hurrying to the goal, as we have seen; every step must be given its due time to resolve itself into the next higher step.

The reason why the psyche or the individual takes on many incarnations is because the psyche is taking a new body for every new experience it desires to undergo. The psyche's desires are many. Why these desires arise is a different subject of philosophy. In a nutshell, you may say that the infiniteness of desires results from the fact that the pryche is seeking the Infinite every time in every experience. This is why the body is cast off when the psyche withdraws from it because the psyche knows that in this body the experience of that particular desire is not possible. When this body is cast off, psyche gravitation pulls the materials needed for the body that can enjoy the desired experience and builds the new body. It is like the magnet that pulls the iron fillings in different patterns under different conditions. The psyche pulls the atoms of the universe in the same manner, giving rise to a suitable incarnation. No-desire is God. Hence once you have reached God, there is no reincarnation, or, in other words, once your desires are nullified, you reach God, which means God realization, which means no more reincarnations. Once you have understood the nature of Truth or realised the Truth, which means God realisation, then there is no desire. Only because this Truth has not been realised, the search for the Infinite continues in the form of desires and therefore there are repeated reincarnations of man. The notion that the world is outside you is what makes you go to the world for the satisfaction of your desires and for obtaining happiness. And for this you engage yourself in a number of activities in the world. The actions you perform in the world and their reactions are the cause of your being caught up in a net of action which the Hindu philosophy calls *karma*. *Karma* means the impressions on the psyche produced by your actions and the reactions to them. These impressions in turn prompt you for more actions on the same lines. Movement of the psyche towards an object is for the fulfilment of its desire. Ignorance of Truth produces desire and in turn produces action. All these three go together, hand in hand. If all these three factors are absent, then your action is God-action, and this God-action is what is explained in the Bhagavadgita as *Karma Yoga*.

What man likes is the ordinary freedom, but freedom in its real sense means ultimately to be in tune with the Absolute. That is real freedom. The psycho-analysts have told us that we are not free in the sense we understand it and our freedom is not what we imagine it to be. Take any action in which you feel you have freedom. Now you have freedom to eat. But do you have the freedom to eat whenever you want? Unless there is compulsion of hunger in your system, you don't eat food. How then have you acted in your own freedom when what has made you act as the hunger factor ? It may now be possible to understand that the urge for the recognition of the soul, that is realisation of the Atman, or God realisation, is possible under special circumstances.

When you are driven to the corner by the external, inevitable and irresistible urge and the purpose of reincarnation is tightened, you can re-organise the phenomena of the empirical world of time-space complex. But unless this urge is there, it is not possible to get into those special circumstances which drive you to the Truth, and so due to this, evolution goes on from the atom to the soul until the soul gets identified with the Absolute. Evolution is because it is a movement towards the Absolute. The Absolute is the only thing that does not evolve because it is the whole of the evolution and therefore with the attainment of the Absolute, evolution ends.

19 March 1979

The weather has warmed up and so the open-air terrace becomes unsuitable for the morning *darshan*. We sit before him in the closed verandah of his *kutir*. This is the first day after a week of severe illness that we get a blessed hour with Swamiji.

A group of Japanese have come to see Rev. Swamiji. And as usual Swami Shankarananda is the interpreter.

A question is put as to why the mind is unable to concentrate on the Buddha. (The questioner is a Buddhist.)

Sw. K.: The reason is simple. There is fear in the mind that the Buddha cannot give everything. So the mind is not going to the Buddha. There is something that the world also can give and which the Buddha may not be able to give. When you are hungry and you pray, your mind will say: 'O man, you are hungry and you are praying to the Buddha. Go to a restaurant.' This is the dual attitude of the mind. This is a very general statement I am making. Mainly the reason is that there are many tensions in the mind, nervous complexes, emotional frustrations, etc. These are the reasons why the mind will not concentrate on what you wish to concentrate upon. Remove all tensions and frustrations. This is the method. Remove what you do not like and have only what you like; there is something the mind longs for and cannot get; or you may hate something whole-heartedly and that is what troubles you. Though these factors may be small or subtle, they are important factors in the psychology of the individual. Buddha is not a personality, a human being. The idea that he is a human being must go. *Buddham saranam gacchami* is only a concept for the Universal Reality. *Dhammam saranam gacchami, sangham saranam gacchami* these are the three great proclamations of Buddhism. These mean 'I take refuge in Buddha which is Reality. I take refuge in Dharma, namely, Love for all creation. I take refuge in sangham which means the organisation.' These three are the three stages of ascent, of which first is Reality. Then it manifests as Law of the Universe. Then it further manifests in concrete organisations in the human society. So from the organisation you go to the Universal Law and from the Universal Law to the Absolute. When such a grand concept is before you, how can you think of anything else and be distracted. Buddha was not some gentleman born at one time and now dead and gone. Dharma Kaya is what He is called. [*The Japanese here makes a statement.*] Yes, there are three stages, no fourth. Tatatha Gata is the third. Dharma Kaya is the second and Bhuto Tatatha is the first. It is something like Sat-Chit-Ananda. Bhuto Tatatha is Sat: it is the whatness, the thatness, the suchness or the whichness of things.

At this stage by vivisecting type of questions Swamiji elicited from the questioner that God exists everywhere and therefore had answered his question, where is God.

Sw. K.: In the heart of the man? Not in the head of man. Not in the animals.

Jap.: "Yes, also in the animals".

Sw. K.: If God is sitting in the same place as yourself, how can another, you, also be sitting there? But these are very high and abstract thoughts. Do not go too high in your concepts. Be humble and simple in whatever way you can think of God without bothering about such high flights into philosophy.

Jap.: Where has man come from? What is his connection with God? Am I and He different from one another?

Sw. K.: Why does such a doubt come to you? God is all-pervasive and you have to surrender your will to Him. You contemplate on God as the creator of the whole cosmos. Whether He is one with you or different from you, this question should not have come into your mind just now. Why do you let unnecessary questions come into your mind? Pray to Him and seek His grace. That will make everything automatically O.K. God will tell you what the Truth is.

Jap.: The Christians believe that God and man are different.

Sw. K.: But you are following Buddhism. Why worry about

Christianity? There are things which the mind cannot grasp and these should not be thought of; the understanding will evolve by itself. Now we talk of three dimensions of a thing! length, breadth and height. But the modern physics says no, there is a fourth dimension. Everything is a four-dimensional reality, not three. What is the use of saying this to the ordinary mind. Such a thing cannot even be thought of by the mind. But the scientist says that it is the only thing that exists. So you can imagine where we are. If that is the only thing that exists and that is what we cannot even think of in the mind what is the kind of paradise you are living in? Tell me.

Two Israelites had been touring India complain that wherever and whenever Indians helped them they asked for money. In their own country the religious leaders concerned themselves with society because they set an example to them. Why does not, asked the Israelite visitors, an ashram like this tackle this problem?

Sw. K.: I am not interested. [*Laughs heartily.*] I am not bothered. Nor do I want to concern myself with what God has created. He created people on different days, and so all are different from one another. I find fault with God who has created this world. So let Him manage it. Why should I bother about it? It is not my world, I have not created it, and so I have no responsibility whatever for it, proper functioning. Why should worry, my head when it is somebody else who has blundered? [*There is visible amusement all round in the gathering.*]

A Visitor: Why,did Swami Sivananda found the ashram here in India?

Sw. K.: There are branches all over the world.

Visitor: My point is why at this place?

Sw. K.: Why is Ganga here and not in America. Similarly, the ashram is here. The geographical and historical circumstances and certain factors produce certain influences on the social life of the people, that is to say, the humanity living there. These influences form the very thought and outlook on life of the people living under such influences. Why was Christ born in Israel, Jerusalem? asked a boy. The missionary's answer was, because it is in the centre of the earth! To the East and the West there are other lands! When I was a small boy I myself put this question to an Evangelist who gave me this answer. The centre is Palestine and so God is born there, for. He is born only in the centre of the Earth! (*A slight plays over the lips of Swamiji.*) Even so, there are theories and theories of the theologians, doctrines and doctrines of the theologians and babblings and babblings of the sectarians. But nobody understands the mystery of these things. There are mysteries and mysteries and they are not what you see with the eyes. It is not visible like the sun to the eyes, nor like the bullockcart on the road, the shop in the market or the bus stop, etc. These are not the Reality. These are the outer phenomena which projected by certain secrets that are working behind nature. Unless you know this mystery, neither can you have peace nor can you give peace to others. So you must go deep into your personal self, and when you go deep into it, you will find that you are entering an ocean which includes everything else. So, this is my message to you this morning. (*laughs heartily*).

(Sw. K. now paid individual attention to those present as was his usual way of communing with everyone. The visitor from Anandamayi Ma said that he would like to stay on till 7 April).

Sw. K.: It is very good that you wish to stay till 7 April, because 7 is a very good number. There are seven days in the week, seven rays of the sun, seven risis, seven layers of human personality and seven human problems. [*Laughs before he has a fit of bad cough due to his recent illness.*]

S.D. It is very kind of Swamiji to restrict man's problems to seven! [*Another hearty laughter from Sw. K.*]

Sw. K. went on making kind enquiries of visitors already in the ashram and also those freshly arrived, discreetly questioning them in detail as to their comfort in their *kutirs*, their health, any special problems they had, as also extension of stay of some of them.

Jap.: Are you happy (because, perhaps, you have had a glimpse of the Truth)?

Sw. K.: I will not answer that question.

O.K. Time for lunch, thank you all. God bless you all!

22 March 1979

A German visitor had been invited by an Anandmargi to learn meditation. Her question was that it was difficult to concentrate on the centre of her eyebrows. It is considered a very suitable point to concentrate upon during meditation. This landed her in physical disturbance. Was it right and was it the ony place to concentrate upon? "I am unable to control the mind in meditation," she ended.

Sw. K.: Has anyone controlled the mind? None except the Realised Souls. As for the centre of the brows, it is NOT necessary to fix on that point for more effective concentration. The control of the mind is a very difficult matter. The mind is not a thing, it is not a person, and it is not an object. It is like air. Therefore, how will you catch it? But there IS a way, a technique. The air is everywhere and you cannot catch it. But it is concentrated in some place. Find out where it is thus concentrated, the source from where it is flowing everywhere. Even so the mind is concentrated at some spot or object that it is aware of, and the location is there. What the object is of little importance. But it should be made to stick there and never move away from it. It may be only a tree the mind is located in; that is, thinking about, PIN it there and do not let it move seven an inch from that place (location-object). Do not move it to another place because the mind then will become very strong. The mind is always thinking about something. But if it is thinking of one thing, let it think of that only, and NOT of any other thing. That is called meditation. You go from shop to shop when you want to purchase something. You do not find it in this shop and so you go to the other shop, and so on until you find what you are looking for. It is for the same thing that you are looking for you go searching one shop after another. It is not that you go from shop to shop for nothing and get fatigued. Is it not ? So mind is searching for something in the various things it is thinking of. What is it searching for? Here rises another question. The first question is that it is moving. Where is it moving? have answered that question that it is searching for something. Now the question is what it is searching for?

Visitor: It is going here and there, thinking of the Divine.

Sw. K.: It is not thinking of the Divine. It has no idea of the Divine. It wants to unite itself with some object, and when there is a union with that object, it gets pleasure. And it looks for pleasure. It is pleasure that the mind is looking for. It does not want objects which are only instruments in creating the psychological circumstance called pleasure. If an object cannot bring pleasure who wants it! There is the tiger and the cobra i.e., Will you search for the tiger or cobra? Will you love it? But you will love a child because you get pleasure by hugging it. Will you want to hug a tiger or a cobra ? Hugging a child gives satisfaction. What you seek is pleasure and not an object. So do not make the mistake of thinking that your mind wants this or that object. You do not want anything, only pleasure. And if you think that a particular object can give pleasure you go near it, but if it does not give satisfaction you will leave it alone and go to another place for another object. In this way, your life is spent looking for pleasure and not for a particular object which it really cannot find. And nowhere you will find this pleasure you are seeking—nowhere. Because it is not a commodity of this world. It belongs to some other realm altogether.

I have given you a simple picture of the state of affairs. You cannot get what you want in this life that you live. Now comes the next question—where else you can get it? One question leads to another endlessly. You can find it only where it is. You cannot get water from the Sahara desert, you can get it only from the Ganga. So you must first know where the Ganga is, then only you can go for water. Mind is looking for what is not in an object. If there had been pleasure in the object itself, there would have been no necessity for it to move from one object to another. That it moves from object to object shows that these do not give satisfaction. So it is not available anywhere in the world, it is available somewhere else. Where is that place? It is not in books, universities. Even Mahatmas and Gurus can not give you that. If you know where it is, you will never open your mouth thereafter to ask for it. Do you understand what I say? These are the answers to your various questions on meditation. Do not concentrate on the *trikuti* (middle of the eye-brows) unnecessarily. It is not going to give you anything at all.

Sri Erhart Vogel, an old American devotee who is running Yoga Centres—"Nataraja Yoga Centre"—in California is now on a visit to the Ashram for a refresher course as it were. His was the next question.

E. V.: Why is it compulsory for us to read the Glory of the Gita which runs into several verses reducing the time available for the verses of the Gita itself? Why? I never read them. Sounds like blackmail to me, this compulsion.

Sw. K.: It is only to give you an incentive to read the text and has no importance by itself. We have a peculiar system of glorifying everything, the greater the glorification the more compelling the incentive to read it. Not worthwhile by itself. When a product is advertised, you have a peculiar weakness to go for it. It is a tradition and you may give it that value. After the death of a person they read the sacred text like the *Garuda Purana* in which there is a vivid description of hell. When people hear that such and such torture is meted out to a miser, or for lack of due respect when called for it, they get frightened and do a lot of charity, and so on. Because they think Oh! Let me be saved from such torture. The *Garuda Purana* picturesquely and vividly describes what happens to the soul of man who has not done charity or fulfilled his duty or lived a bad life etc. etc. It is an incentive for the living to mend their ways! (*laughs*).

S. D.: Does not charity etc. done by those left behind benefit the departed soul?

Sw. K.: No, nothing of the kind. It has no connection with the departed soul: It is meant only for those left behind.

E. C.: The glorification is much longer than the verses which you can complete in a given time!

Sw. K.: (*laughs*) Yes, yes. Reading even one *sloka* of the *Gita* is enough if you can understand the meaning properly. One single verse is sufficient for contemplating upon its glory. A foreign visitor who had been sent by his Guru (Major Ramachandran) to meet Rev. Swami Krishnananda Maharaj asked a few inconsequential questions on Yoga, etc. Almost at the end of the morning after he had been in the gathering for about one full hour, he asked Swami Krishnanandaji.

Foreign Visitor: What is your name?

Sw. K.: (*Without showing any emotion*) I am he whom you have come to see.

Its reaction on the gathering was one of shocked amusement. This instance has a place in chronicling of the diary because it is a typical example of some Western visitors who come to the morning *darshan* without any interest or knowledge of why and for what purpose they join in. There was another instance—that of another Westerner—asking Swamiji how long he had been a Sannyasi? To which his Revered self replied after a moment of silence in an even tone: "About 35 years", adding as if thinking aloud, "all my life." At the end of the session later when all but a couple of old disciples remained, S.D. remarked that these people reminded one of urchines throwing stones into a pool, just something to do, at which Swamiji smiled indulgently.

E. V.: What is karma yoga?

Sw. K.: Activity in terms of multiplicity and consciousness in terms of unity is karma yoga". can you, do you understand that sentence? Ponder over it.

E. V.: I shall, thank you Swamiji.

Sw. K: The luncheon bell—Namaskar—Go and eat hot food!

* * *

Q. Kant, Descartes, Heggel, Hobbes Edward Kail, W.T. Sates, Bergson, Bradley, Debunke—all these are great philosophers, but not alike in their views, quite often diametrically opposite, the one even decrying the other logically and philosophically. Sankara's works on the other hand constitute an omnibus, as it were. Whom should we read Swamiji?

Sw. K.: They are all great masters of thought who will chisel your thoughts and make them very sharp. You may agree with them wholly or partially or not at all, that is a different matter, but they can help make your intellect sharp. That is a great help. I am very glad to hear all this from you. Very good. After that, you read Acharya Sankara. Acharya Sankara should be read to give flesh and blood to their thoughts.

G. Yes, Swamiji; And *Yoga Vashishta* contains Berkley's thoughts.

Sw. K.: Berkley?

Q. And I read his work and *Yoga Vashistha* also.

Sw. K.: They have great similarities.

G. Not merely that, it looks as if Berkley plagiarised it!

Sw. K.: (*Laughs heartily*) He might not have plagiarised, but it looks as if it is done! Oh! all this is good. Have you read Paul Dawson? You must read his exposition of Sankara, because Sankara's original commentaries are very long; Paul Dawson has given an exposition of Sankara. It is a beautiful volume, system of Vedanta. Yes, very exciting to talk of all this. You practise meditation on these thoughts, on the maker of all things and you will get all the answers—isn't it? Answers will come from everywhere, from every nook and corner and even from the very bricks, not merely from masters and teachers, kings and sannyasis. The very bricks will give answers to your questions when you are able to commune yourself with all Reality, because when you become friendly with anyone, that friend will tell all his secrets to you. Isn't it? He will not tell all his secrets to you unless he is a real friend. So the brick will not tell you what it is unless you become friendly with it and become one with it. See? Likewise, the secret of the whole universe is known when you become tuned up to its essentiality.

Q. Why are dogs far more faithful than men? Is it a silly question?

Sw. K.: Animals act on instincts, and instinct is supposed to be nearer to reality than intellect. At least, according to Bergson, this is so. There is some point in it. Man is very untrustworthy, unreliable, and he suddenly changes his attitudes, but dogs are not like that. Even if you give it a kick, it will follow behind you.

Q. But why can't it be argued that they act so because they have not got reason?

Sw. K.: That reason is a "bondage" which has made you fall into the hell of this social life, whereas they are happy without that. What is the use of reason which tells you wrong things—that you must punish somebody—wreak vengeance on somebody? Is this reason for your good? The dog doesn't remember all that. Even the monkey doesn't remember that you threw a stone at it yesterday.

Q. But I will at least know that I should not sit near the person who will kick me. But the dog doesn't.

Sw. K.: Reason is like a double-edged sword. It can tell you that it is doing a wrong thing and yet also remember some evil done to you. You will remember it for ever! "The evil that they do lives after them, the good that they do is interred with them." You can never remember the good done to you. But always you will remember one wrong done to you out of the hundred good things I have done for you. This one wrong will wash off all the hundred good things. But dogs are not like that. Everyday you give it a little bread and it will always go wagging its tail behind you.

Q. Why? Why is that so? [*The question came from someone in the gathering.*]

Sw. K.: Because the intellect takes you away from reality to some extent, though it has a virtue also, because it can tell you what is truth.

Same Voice: Is the intellect all the time taking you away from the reality?

Sw. K.: Not always, sometimes. When it gets mixed up with emotions, it takes you in the wrong direction. When it stands independently it will say to itself that it is also committing a mistake. Reason has this other aspect also; it can find its own limitations. Sometimes it asserts its absoluteness when it goes with sentiment and feeling, etc. By reason you know you must love all children in the same way you love your own. But emotion dictates that your own children are better! Emotion speaks and says mine are dearer to me than others' children. But reason tells you. No, it is not the proper attitude, all children are equally good. So in certain attitudes there is a mix-up of emotion and reason.

Same Voice: Are reason and intellect the same thing?

Sw. K.: Yes! Reason is a higher power of the intellect like the electricity that is working through the bulb. Electricity ist he intelligence—that is the reason. The bulb is the intellect; it is the vehicle.

Q. What is the meaning of Satsang, Swamiji?

Sw. K.: Satsang means holy company. Spiritual company is satsang. Well there is the luncheon bell—go for lunch. Thank you all for your *darshan*. God Bless You! Namaskar.

* * *

Sw. K.: Yogi Raj, how is your mother?

Y. R.: I am coming from her. She is well and will come after about a week. I first went to see her, it was my first duty to see her, on my return to India from America.

Sw. K.: She knows that you are staying here for some weeks. You wrote to her? O! I see, you visited her on landing, as your first duty. An ideal son, yes, mother comes first, usually people don't bother about the mother.

(A couple of Brahmacaris belonging to the Andhra Ashram Temples, both Siva and Venkateshwar temples, visited Swamiji and recited the Vedas in various orthodox styles, Ghana, Jata and so on. They were the same pieces recited in these varied rhythms.)

S. D.: Why is the same piece in the Veda recited in three different and very difficult styles? Were all the Vedas learnt to be recited in this manner only?

Sw. K.: Yes, the Vedas were memorised so that you should not forget them. And they have created such a complicated method that you can never afford to forget it. If, for example, you go on troubling me every day, I cannot forget your existence. That is one way of making me keep remembering you. Everyday you harass me and I remember you without effort. Like that it is a harassment to the brain to such an extent that you cannot forget it.

S. D.: Ingrained in the brain!

Sw. K.: Yes, like the repeated visits of your creditor! Now, will you forget a creditor? Everyday he comes and gives *darshan*. His visit gets imprinted in your mind, does it not?

* * *

Q. Why did Krishna play that leela with Rukmani who, he said, had made a terrible mistake in choosing Lord Krishna as her husband when there were so many other suitors who were much worthier than himself. Lord Krishna goes on telling her that he is a poor man, that he has been called a thief, that he has got many enemies, like Sisupala, who hate him and so on. Poor Rukmini swoons and Lord Krishna revives her. With eyes filled tears, Rukmini explains how she is unworthy of his greatness. Why did Lord Krishna frighten Rukmini like this?

Sw. K.: Lord Krishna wanted to present an unpleasent picture of himself to test whether it was the essence, the real qualities in him that she liked. He tried to put off Rukmini. Lord Shiva is represented as a tapasvin full of ashes, as a meditator in the burning ghat, as a beggar with not even a good begging bowl except a skull. Further, he does not even have clothes to wear and goes about wearing tiger skin or elephant skin. And he lives on Mount Kailas. All this description is to deter people going to him for the nonce. Even Parvati complained that he had no house, no roof over his head and he had no respect for the guests who, when they came to see him, sat on the snow. She wanted him to build a nice place for her. Lord Shiva tried to dissuade her, reasoning that it was useless wanting a house and such other things. Parvati would not listen and she insisted on building a nice place worthy of Lord Shiva and his consort. Brihaspati the divine *purohit* was called and told of the plan to build a palace at once. He said that the period was such that if Sani (Saturn) had one glance at the house, it would burn up. Sani was bound to come to know of the building of the house and he was bound to see it and the house would burn away. If Sani could be stopped from coming at the *Grihapravesa* (House warming) time then everything would be all right. Parvati agreed to keep Sani away and she requested Lord Shiva to go to Sani's house and keep him in his house until the *grihapravesa* was over. If Sani insisted on coming to see the house Lord Shiva should play the Damaru at which she herself would burn the house. Lord Shiva agreed happily and went to Sani's house and innocently explained everything so that Sani understood that Lord Shiva had come to keep Sani bound to his house and if Damaru was played Parvati herself would burn the house! Cunning as he was, Sani started praising the Lord, "O Lord, this is Sandhyakal (the meeting of Day and Night) and it is wonderful to do kirtan with you. At 'pradoshkal' (the sacred hour of twilight) you dance wonderfully. Let me see that glorious sight. Let us sing and dance". The Lord was happy and he started dancing to the beat of the Damaru! Parvati who heard the Damaru, thought that Sani was insisting on coming to see the house, so she herself burned the house! The point of the story is that Lord Krishna or Shiva is quickly pleased, because they are simple in their nature. That is why Lord Shiva is called a simpleton, Bhola Nath. This aspect, namely, the simpleton's attitude can easily please the Lord. And like a mother who plays with the child, covering herself with a cloth to frighten it, the Lord plays such Lilas.

Another Visitor: When you are in doubt, another doubt and yet another doubt comes, how to clear the doubt?

Sw. K.: When in the first doubt, best remove it first before the other doubt crops up. How will you remove it?

Visitor: By study?

Sw. K.: Yes, And by frankly placing yourself under your Guru. A Guru need not be a spiritual Guru only. Any one who helps you to understand things better is your Guru.

Q.: What is grace? Is there any particular type of yoga which can bring this?

Sw. K.: Effort from outside, you may say, is grace. Effort from within the individual is effort, but the one cannot exist without the other. That is, they follow one another. Do not speak of the yogas as either effort or grace. It is their transcendental finality. Einstein or the Upanisads or the Bhagavad Gita will say the same thing in the ultimate view of all the different types of yoga which these state. One is supposed to often enter into the other. This is something which the mind with its capacity to think only in three-dimensional pattern cannot transcend this stage. To enter into the fourth dimensional consciousness, the mind even if forced is not fully prepared for it and will even go berserk—mad. This fourth dimension, this transcendental state is like the fourth state of sleep known as *turia* which is difficult to comprehend, though a sense of understanding of it may exist. It is said that a shadow is a second dimensional concept of the third dimensional physical body. In the same sense, in a continued sense, the body is the third dimensional concept of the fourth dimensional Brahman. The point is not what happens as each philosopher like Aurobindo or Radhakrishnan discusses it in his books. It is the reaching to it that is the point and this is the finally transcended consciousness or the fourth dimension mentioned at the start.

Q.: (*From a visiting Sannyasi*) While Adi Sankara's philosophy expresses most clearly the concept of the illusion of Maya, both Aurobindo and Radhakrishnan are critical of this attitude and comment that we should give the world its due and not overemphasise this maya aspect.

Sw. K.: Before we go to this state of critical thinking, we must first obtain enlightenment of the absolute by a clear concept of the steps in yoga and progressively fix upon the higher steps by which you get enlightenment one by one. How can you know how you will act and be, unless you reach the fourth stage of consciousness; in other words, in that state when we have changed the content of our consciousness. And when the mind sees separation in space and time and the mind gets gross then the mind can see only the gross things, you cannot get into the higher state of consciousness. 'Vrittibheda' is the cause of the mind feeling that, I, the drop (of the ocean) is different from the ocean. The Cosmic Being is the split-personality so to say: it is all the three: the Drashta (the seer) Drishya (or the act of seeing), Dhric (or the object seen).

Q.: Swamiji said the other day that when God comes, he swallows you like the ocean. And God comes like an Atlantic Ocean. The World or God comes to swallow you, that is, swallow my ego, my dearest personality?

Sw. K.: God will swallow you. The World and God are the same thing. You have seen people committing suicide when they are defamed. What is suicide? It is throwing off the physical body; one throws off the physical body merely because one does not want to throw off the ego. Getting a bad name means having the ego defamed, the ego which is shaken. He does not want that. Even if the body goes, the ego should not go. It shows the intensity of the ego of the person and his attachment to his personality: the psychical, not the physical. It is not possible to exist without personality, because it is the dearest of possessions. Similarly what is the use of going to God losing my existence itself by merging in Him is the question the ego asks.

Q.: Is meditation a means to conquer the body, the soul and the ego?

Sw. K.: The meditational stages are explained in the Bhagavad Gita in the arrangement of the Chapters. First, second and so on —in which Chapter are you? You find that out. You can find out where you are. Each successive chapter is a description of a higher ascent, and when the last stage is reached, you become like Lord Krishna. And what is it to become Lord Krishna. Nobody can understand that except Lord Krishna himself. You become a Cosmic person. You get adjusted to everything, tuned up in one second to every cell of the cosmic body. When you wake up from dream, you get tuned up to your waking consciousness. Every cell of the body is your cell only. There is no cell outside you. Likewise when you wake up into this universal consciousness, you get tuned up in every cell, in every atom of this cosmos and just even as you say every cell is "I", the whole universe, you will say, is "I". That is the God experience that the Bhagavad Gita tells you.

Q.: Swamiji!, why is the Last Chapter not the Eleventh Chapter? You have the Viswarupa in the Eleventh and thereafter, seven more Chapters?

Sw. K.: The Eleventh Chapter is not the end of the story, the end of the experience. The cosmic vision is not the end; it is only a terrifying vision which Arjuna sees. He has not entered into it. The entering takes place afterwards. Merely seeing is no good.

Q.: Yes, In Chapter XVIII, Arjuna says 'Now all my doubts are gone?" So, seven more Chapters after the Eleventh.

Sw. K.: Yes, I suddenly bring you face to face with all the wealth of Rockfeller. You only see it, you cannot get it. If you get it then it is a different thing (*laughing*) and is the end of the matter. I just show it to you; but you cannot get it. In Chapter Eleven He has shown all the tremendous magnificence but as yet that vision is not yours. You don't even touch it. But if it becomes yours, then you can have it, then you really get it—this great achievement cannot be by just seeing the Vision. It must go on till then, so the Eleventh is followed by more chapters.

Q.: Is there any significance in the Twelfth Chapter describing Bhakti following (cosmic vision) in the Eleventh Chapter, that is, if you are a dedicated Bhakta even this terrifying vision becomes a beautiful form to you.

Sw. K.: Before you reach Zen—that is an old saying in Zen—before you reach Zen (and by the word Zen they mean the ultimate experience) the mountain is a mountain, the tree is a tree, and a river is a river. But in the process of reaching Zen, when you try to gain Zen you do not see a tree as a tree, a mountain as a mountain. This is the answer to your question. The cosmic experience is not a stunning resolution of the existing law. This is the middle stage only where a tree is not a tree, a mountain is not a mountain, a friend is not a friend, an enemy is not an enemy. Everything changes when you are in the middle stage. In the third stage, the tree is a tree and so on. You don't have to abolish the existence of things in God-realisation or Zen. And, this is the experience when you transcend the middle stage to the final—the ultimate realisation of God when a tree is a tree and a mountain is a mountain, because it is no more a renunciation. First you get attached. Then you withdraw. Then you go back to it with a new vision. These are the three stages. First stage is attachment. But afterwards there is no attachment but efforts towards the detachment business. In the first experience you want the world only. You don't want God. That is usual and that is the first experience. A normal man's experience is I am concerned with the World. And not concerned with God. The second experience is, I am concerned with God, not with the world. I don't want the World. That is renunciation, Vairagya—Tyaga—giving up. Then the third stage when everything is O.K. There is no withdrawal because there is no attachment. There is no attachment and therefore no renunciation is called for, for everything is perfectly O.K. Suppose a person has schizophrenic experience. You know what is schizophrania? There was a very learned philosopher. He was master of all philosophy, Western and Eastern. But he was in the mental hospital where Pandit Jawaharlal Nehru visited him in the course of his visit to the hospital. The man very learnedly discussed all schools of philosophy with Pandit Nehru. He spoke beautifully. At the end of their interesting hour, Panditji met the doctor-in-charge (the Superintendent of the Hospital) and asked him why such a learned man discussing philosophy in such an excellently cogent manner was kept an inmate of the mental hospital. There must be some mistake. The doctor listened to Panditji and said, "You want to know why that man is in the mental hospital. Come with me, I will show you." Together they went back to the Philosopher. The doctor put out his finger to touch the patient. Immediately the philosopher screamed, cringing away from the doctor's finger, "Don't touch me! I am made of glass. I will break ! Don't touch me." (Swamiji acted all this bit of narration). The doctor turned to Pandit Nehru and said, "You see why he is here." He may be master of all philosophy and many such things. But he thinks he is made of glass. This is the mental problem that he has.

Now, I have given you an example. When a person thinks he is made of glass, the purpose is to treat him with a medicine, so that he may realise he is not a glass, i.e. the consciousness is withdrawn from the so-called imaginary object which is glass. That is called renunciation. You are saying this is a tree, this is a mountain, this is my father, this is my mother, this is my property, this is my land, this is my building. This is exactly the kind of identification that man did. In imagination he was a thing which was not. There is no tree, father, etc. They are all imaginations in the mind just as there is nobody made of glass. So you are treated by an antidote that is called Vairagya. The withdrawal is what you call renunciation and you go to a chapel, or a monastery, or a desert, renouncing everything. That is an antidote you are giving to this wrong feeling that something is yours. When you come to the consciousness that you are not the body made of glass or that you are not the building, tree, etc. you are in the second stage. You realise that you are a human being made of flesh and blood. But afterwards that medicine of renunciation is not necessary. You need not repeat the injection. So once you come back to the realisation that things are what they are the attitude of renunciation becomes irrelevant and is not applicable any more. What are you renouncing? You have already renounced the wrong idea and the right idea has come. And so further renunciation of the things is not called for. Thereafter you live under normal conditions. The first stage is wrong thinking, the second stage that of *medication*—not meditation but medication. The third stage is the normal realisation. Now, in which condition are we? That each one should understand for himself. We are mostly in the first stage (pause) with a little of the second stage mixed in. Some 75 per cent first stage and 25 per cent second stage. The third stage has not come. It may not come in this birth. God knows in which birth it comes. We are wrongly thinking and are in need of an antidote. That antidote is this medication, spiritual study and going to satsang and good company and renunciation, etc.—all that you usually call the religious life. We always make a distinction between religious life and secular life just as you say there is a difference between medication and illness. But that difference exists only as long as there is illness, and when the illness goes, the medicine does not come into the question at all. So we have a tremendous hope of transcending the first stage, where we believe that this is a building only. We cannot say it is but a building. You may read any scripture, you cannot get out of the idea that this is a building of bricks and that it is my house, my garden, my plantation. Who can renounce this idea? However religious you may be, however spiritual you may be, however God-fearing you may be, you will still say, this is my garden, etc. This idea will not go. So for most people in the world, real religion has not started yet. It is still in the preliminary stage of spirituality. But when we come to the decision that this is not correct and we require a rectification of this idea, you decide to undergo the tremendous discipline of the practice of Yoga. Now you are in the second stage. Even the practice of Yoga is not a healthy condition just as the necessity to take medicine is not a healthy state. Medicine must be continued for you are still sick. But you cannot say it is a natural condition and go on eating indiscriminately. Likewise, this meditation and yoga are not natural conditions. They are necessary as an antidote, as a counteracting element for your earlier mistake. These clash at each other and cancel each other. Then neither illness is there nor the medicine. So is the case with the practice of Yoga and meditation for instance. You don't go on meditating. I am the daughter of so and so. You know that, so there is no need to meditate on it. Why were you meditating? To make this clear. If a thing is clear, then you don't need to meditate on it. Why you meditate on is it day time ? It is very clear that it is day time. Are you going on meditating Oh! it is day time, it is day time, it is day time! Why will you do that? It is foolishness. Only if a thing is not clear, then you need to think it out, If a new vision comes in no renunciation is needed for there is no attachment and when the third stage comes and everything becomes so clear and no practice of yoga is necessary. No meditation. No God-realisation. No Bhakti. No devotion. Nothing. They are all only methods like medicines and drugs. So this is what the Zen master said. In the beginning it is a tree—mistaken notion. The second stage it is not a tree withdraw yourself from the idea. You are now in the third stage and so a tree is a tree, due to the new vision that has come. You are seeing the same person with the idea "I am not a glass, but a human body." The mistaken idea has been rectified so the answer to your question has come. The Viswarupa is only the second stage. Where it is a counteracting force for Arjuna's wrong notion. Things are not different from one another. They are all integrated in a Cosmic whole. That is what he shows in the Viswarupa. But afterwards what happens? You have to continue to live in the world only: while that Cosmic consciousness tells you that nothing is different from another and that there is no need to have to abolish that duality, because that duality does not exist, then that idea of duality has gone completely from you, and you are free—after this realisation. Suppose you have a microscope for your eyes instead of what God has now given you physically normal eyes. Then you won't see bricks and trucks, you will see only atoms! Now if nature had made your eyes microscopes then you will not struggle to get out of ideas of bricks and wall and this and that but the atoms alone. So at that time you have eyes with which you see things as they are. And no question of the practice of Yoga arises to get that vision at that time, because you are perfectly in normal condition and this is what has been said in the last six Chapters of the Bhagavad Gita which state that we are on a dangerous path for we are asked to see the spirit, the soul, through every thing and be spiritual. Spirituality is a dangerous path, in view of what I have told you, the desperations you have to pass through in traversing it. And if you think of it, you will not go near it. It is such a terrible thing. Namaskar, I go my way! You will say.

Suppose you have to suffer like Christ. Will you like to pass through that stage? You will say, "I don't want to go. Next time, not now. Now I cannot undergo all this amount of suffering." But that is absolutely necessary. You cannot escape it if you want God. He comes like fire, like the Ocean, like the wind, and you cannot stand the wind or the ocean or the fire, —not possible with your ordinary strength as man. You like a very delicious cup of coffee and apple juice. But He does not come like that. In the beginning, that is, in the first stage everything is satisfactory to the body. The body and the ego are our enemy. We have no other enemy in the world. These two will not want to give themselves up in favour of spirituality and God.

Q. But the body only exists because of the ego.

Sw. K.: Yes, the body is the outer expression of the ego. The one a gross form and the other its subtle form. Two troubles you have. Hunger, thirst and sleep, they are all problems of the gross form or the physical body. Who can bear them? If these three attack you, you cannot resist them nor exist, without them. And that is the body ego problem. You know what the ego is. Everybody calls you an idiot. You don't like to be called such names. You think it is better to go away somewhere, instead of continuing to live here. But at the time of going the going is with such force that it looks as if the disease is made worse like in the Homaeopathic treatment. This is the same case when the need comes to surrender to God in every instance, like Jesus did. This ordeal you cannot understand by reading any book on philosophy, because philosophers are not saints. They are only expounders of the logical implications of your problems. If you read the life of saints, you will come to know how to meet such problems. You read of Buddha or Christ, and of the Desert Fathers—you must have heard of Desert Fathers who lived in the deserts of Egypt ? The worst that can confront us is not to be wanted by anybody, it is the worst experience you can imagine. Even hunger and thirst will not be so bad as the feeling that nobody wants you. This is so very strange a thing that you cannot live with it a day longer. You cannot understand what such a wretched feeling means, unless you go through that stage. If you are hungry, you know what is hunger. By reading a book you won't know what hunger means, what poverty means. Only a poor man knows what poverty means. A rich man cannot read a book on poverty and understand it. You will like to go to hell rather than live a life where no one wants you. You will pray to God to throw you into hell which you would say would be better. Do you now understand why? Why doesn't God come though we pray so much? Because we are not wanting that kind of God who gives such wretched problems. We want a nice God who speaks nicely, smiles and is motherly. Our illness is so intense that the medicine must be equally intense. It has become chronic, and it is such an illness that no medicine on earth can cure. It requires surgical operation of a divine type as makes you pray God to give hell rather than this and that would be a help! And God is prepared to help you if you consent to be treated thus and surrender yourself to Him and if you accept His ways. Otherwise even through the ordinary routine meditation nothing will be achieved. Because we have got a subtle lurking feeling that we belong to this world still and you don't belong entirely to God even when you meditate; you say God! I will meditate on you, but still don't take me away from the World! And that is the ego speaking! that is the desire of the ego to exist without an end—never to die!

Dr. P.K. Rao: Are World and God not different?

Sw. K.: (*Emphatically*) Yes, they are! You always make a distinction. We cannot say they are identical. If they were identical, it would be still worse for you. You cannot believe that people are God to you. It would be good to divide them as separate from God. And keep the meditation for the temple and the world for shops and shopping etc. If you believe they are identical, you have to behave with the shopkeeper as God Himself will! It is a very difficult thing to imagine what that would be. So we are not prepared to undergo that ordeal which is a great experience. What you say is worse than what the other alternative is. To behave like judge in the Court and a father in the house is better than to be like a judge everywhere. You cannot exist like that. It will be a very difficult thing to do. Even to your wife, you are a judge! and to your son also! To the shopkeeper also a judge! They will say, he is a horrible man (*laughs*) To a shopkeeper, he is an ordinary customer though in the supreme Court he is a judge. Of course, if you can become like that and you can bear the consequences of behaving like the divine being the same everywhere and with everything, wonderful in that case you are immediately in the soup—in one second! Your identity is in God! You don't want to slip into the soup all that quick. But slowly slowly perhaps? There is another thing, sometimes you would like to do something, you want to get out of all this confusing problems and in trying to do that something, you don't know whether you are doing it out of your volition or God is impelling you to do it. This is another problem for you. You cannot immediately make a distinction between God's impulsion and your ego. You will say, "Well, I am going to the mountain-top for meditation. I am not going to live in this terrible city of noise and foolish, stupid things." Now, who is telling this? If God is ordering you to do it, very good; he will help you at the top of the mountain, but you may be doing it for some other reason. It may be that you are unable to bear the pain of living in the midst of anti-social persons. It is a pain. Isn't it? And you are trying to avoid the pain. That will be a subtle psychological reason behind your getting out of a city and wish to reach the mountain top. But worse things are possible at the top of the mountain. So now are you going to the mountain top because you want God or because you don't want pain? Which is that reason? These are all very subtle matters not easily to be left out on the basis of simple assumptions.

Q.: But Swamiji, God is supposed to be wanting to receive us with open arms. He is pulling us to Him all the time.

Sw. K.: He wants to receive you the Y capital. He does not want the lower y. He wants you with the capital Y alone. He wants you, the Real you. Not the legal you or a social you or the gender you—masculine and feminine you, He does not want these. That is not you, the real 'you' and so then it is the unreal. You will ask for the unreal God only. It comes to that when your prayer is conditioned by the foot-note "provided that. . . ."! The proviso of the law usually takes the edge off the law! Yes! Now it is clear why God does not come when you pray, 'I am thine' etc, is it not?

Q.: Yes, Now it is clear why God does not come.

Sw. K.: You want God. Who are you? Tell me. Let me know, if Bhagyalakshmi is wanting God, then a corresponding thing will come. He will send an Amin not Himself (*laughs heartily*). When you do 'Japa' by rolling the beads and God will say, mind your business. Do not trouble me unnecessarily!

Q.: And has he also told you what your business is?

Sw. K.: (*laughs*): When you tell a man "mind your business" you do not intend anything in particular. Your intention is to get rid of the man. Whatever it is, mind your business is a way of talking idiomatically. He does not tell you what the business is. I don't want you to talk to me. Don't interfere with me unnecessarily. This is what He now seems to be telling me also! I am very unhappy about it. What to do? There is no mystic greater than God. He is the highest mystic. That is why Lord Krishna is depicted as a tremendous naughty boy. Otherwise why do you depict the incarnation of God as mischievous and naughty. That is how Vyasa depicts Lord Krishna. He could have depicted him as a wonderful, beautiful, sympathetic person instead of as a very mischievous and troublesome element ! It is a spiritual interpretation of God's attitude towards you that the author has given you. He marries a thousand wives ! He is a householder. Yet He is described as a Brahmachari. Every social law is broken in His life. He has His own law and his law is a super law with which social laws have to be consonant.

(*As if thinking aloud*) In one moment I can solve all the problems which I am called upon to solve by leaving the Ashram. I can just leave and no problem can touch me. The problems of the Ashram are most tiring. (*snapping his fingers*), In a moment all troubles will end if I leave and go away. But who is telling this to me to leave and go away? Who says, "You can be free of trouble"? I must know that, I must be sure of that, only then I can act! See, now have I solved all your questions? Thank you for the *Satsanga**, *Namaskar*.

*More such conversations *satsangas* are published under the title, "Swami Krishnananda in Conversation" by Vikas Publishers, Ansari Road, Darya Ganj, Delhi. Price : Rs. 125.

PART II

SWAMI KRISHNANANDA —THE MENTOR

Vis.: How can yoga practice get us strength?

Sw. K.: Your affiliation to God is your strength. It will save you in this life, in your future life also. What I am telling you is yoga without giving it a label.—Yet it includes all the yogas—you do not want yogees. You want a living yoga which is helpful in our practical existence—not yoga only for demonstration or an institution. This is a thing with which you can exist and keep yourself balanced and happy and without complaint against anything. The yogi sees everything in its proper place—when you see a thing misplaced, then it is not yoga and then you complain.

And yoga is nothing but a comprehensive outlook on things. Yoga is not just the Bhagavad Gita, it is not just the Upanishad. You may call it by any name you like. But you cannot be a comprehensive person, because of the weakness of the mind, and the incapacity of the understanding to grasp all aspects. You always miss some points. And then you say something is wrong—if you see that point you will say every thing is okay. You have perfect peace. Your peace will spread the aura of peace around you. You become a magnet of completeness—radiating strength, energy and peace. But if you are a partial being, you become wretched yourself and make others around you also wretched.

S.D.: All right, accepted. But how do I take my pains? Saying that cosmic balance is being set up! That does not help.

Sw. K.: Your suffering is due to lack of understanding! Ah yes! It is the philosophy of Madhusudan Saraswati—have you heard of this man?

Madhusudan Saraswati was a great scholar and saint who lived about a hundred or two hundred years ago. He is a master in philosophy. He is also a great devotee of Lord Krishna. He is a Jnana Yogi—Jnana Yogi and a Bhakti Yogi—he believed in Krishna only and in nothing else.

(*Turning to Dr P.K. Rao*) You are reading Benjamin's Naturopathy? What is the matter with you?

P.K.: Got to read something or the other, Swamiji. (*Showing a few books.*] I got these books yesterday morning only. Has Swamiji read this book? (*Hands over a book*)

Sw. K.: No. I want to read this book; I have never read it. I will have a glance at it. May I have it? Thank you very much.

Dr P.K.: That is why I brought it here to show it to you and ask you if you have read it. I have received a parcel of 23 books which I had ordered, mostly from Motilal Banarsidass of Delhi.

Sw. K: Thank you. Mataji! he was a philosopher. And yet, nobody was equal to Madhusudan Saraswati in the philosophy of the Absolute. He is the top-most philosopher of Advaita Philosophy—and how he combines it with Krishna's devotion is a wonder. That is the knack of the man, the greatest man is capable of reconciliation of anything with anything.

Someone: The intellect and heart joined together.

Sw. K.: Everything; that is the sign of greatness. He can be reconciled with anything. He is not an irreconcilable personality. That is the sign of greatness. He never refuses anything. He never rejects anything. He does not disbelieve anything. He does not say anything is wrong—that is the sign of greatness. Everything is okay and in its proper place, at the proper time, in the given circumstances. So this is again Yoga.

S.D.: But, Swamiji, it is said that Lord Krishna's ways, his lilas in his Avatar were all a breaking of social norms—so to speak. And that was said to be a spiritual interpretation, an explanation of God's attitude to man. How can it be a spiritual interpretation?

Sw. K.: Because, to say that the Ganga water is very cold is just a human attitude. But God does not say it is very cold, because it is not cold. It is cold only to your skin. To the fish in the Ganga it is not cold. So is Ganga water really cold? Tell me. Now you can very well see that your statement is not correct; for any statement society makes is partial. How can God take it as perfect? You may be right from your skin's point of view in saying that the Ganga water is cold.

But the fish in the Ganga does not say it is cold; it does not want a blanket or a quilt because it has adjusted itself to the atmosphere. You cannot adjust yourself to it in the same manner. And if your temperature of the body is the same as the temperature outside, you will not say it is winter. So all social laws, personal predilections are judgements made on the basis of the experiences from the point of view of your present state of personality. And it need not be correct. [*Emphatically*] It cannot be correct. It is partial.

And you will not see things as before. If you have got a microscopic eye, you will not see the wall in front of you—you will not see the building, you will see only vibrations, you will see electrons, or protons and if I tell you it is a building, you will say where is a building? I cannot see any building. But God has given you a very gross eye and you see a large structure. So, who is correct? Is the microscope correct or you? The circumstances are different and you speak from different levels of being. God speaks from all comprehensiveness.

S.D.: What is the ear or the eye with which we should see for hear His lilas so that we understand His purpose?

Sw. K.: You understand your level of existence first. You speak from your level only. Do not overestimate yourself and try to see as God sees at the comprehensive level.

S.D.: You mean to say, what I cannot understand I should leave alone?

Sw. K.: You should not try to disturb your present feelings. The disturbance arises on account of the fact that you try to overcome the limits of your feelings. Whether they are right or not is a different matter. They may be right. They are right only as long as they are incapable of transcendence. When they are capable of transcendence, they become wrong. When you are dreaming, the objects that you see in the dream are real but now they are not real—you have transcended them. So when I say it is real or unreal, it depends upon the point of view, the level of being from which I speak. You cannot get over the idea that you are a human being. But it is not true that you are a human being ultimately. You are something else. You are a unit in the Cosmic Force—but you cannot understand it. It is no use talking about it. So what is your present state? I am a human being. You cannot forget that you are an Indian. You cannot forget that you are a woman. All these are false notions ultimately. But when you realise that you are not a woman then your law changes and you speak in a different language and you experience different things.

So long as your feelings and your conditions are inseparable from your present level of understanding, you have to follow only that law. That is what Bhagwan Krishna says in the Gita: do not disturb the present state of affairs nor speak to others from your point of view of God. Their point of view may be quite different; do not disturb that. You have to go stage by stage, from one level to another. All Yoga is transcendence and not negation. You do not negate anything, you transcend it. You should understand the difference between negation and transcendence. You do not negate the nature of a child, but you transcend it when you become an adult. When a child behaves in a particular manner, you do not call it a stupid behaviour. It is a valid behaviour on that level. But if *you* now behave like a baby, it is invalid. You have transcended it. Work on that level till you transcend it. And when you fulfil the law of that level, you will automatically be liberated from that bondage, which would mean that you have taken to another level. And then you work on that level. Like that, you go higher and higher until you reach the Absolute. You should be a happy person at every level. You must always be friendly and happy and balanced and coordinated with every type of atmosphere—that is your wisdom, the wisdom of life. Never reject, never disagree, never become irreconcilable and never be intolerant.

S.D.: It is very difficult to decide at what point one should act. I increase my sufferings which could have been forestalled if I could have had—

Sw. K.: That is due to ignorance—ignorance of law is no excuse. Every law is a kind of system which has a reaction.

S.D.: Swamiji spoke of intolerance—now that is exactly the point I want to know. Up to what point should you tolerate?

Sw. K.: No limit to tolerance. Christ also suffered due to his goodness. But you cannot say he did a wrong thing. And you will be taken care of by other forces which will not let you feel at ease. Because, you follow a system of perfection and due to that you suffer, well, really you will not suffer—it is a mistaken notion. If you follow the law from the level on which you are, then you will not suffer.

[The following pages contain revered Swami Krishnanandaji's replies and advice given to a young American Scholar, Jim

McMichael, then engaged in research in the Banaras Hindu University. He visited the Ashram during May-June to discuss his thesis on the concept of Isvara and get guidance. I was away from the Ashram at this time, hence this contribution from him.]

Emphasising that there is no easy short-cut to God-Realisation, Swamiji told Jim not to think that God-Realisation could be had from books and described the agonies of Christ before the Ecstasy. "Like Christ all must be crucified. Like Buddha all must suffer before Enlightenment. We must endure patiently these sufferings if we really want to realise God. If we don't want God, then we will be free of these tortures; but if we truly seek God, we will have to weep from our soul for God, not merely with tears from the eyes. When this happens and the ground is cut away from underneath you, as it were, when you cry in desperation, intensely longing for release, then the Grace of God or whatever you want to call it, comes and you are free."

Question: Revered Swamiji has said that a true disciple never asks God for anything. What if you ask for liberation?

Sw. K.: In that case you are asking for God Himself and God only; you are not asking for another entity. You must not use God as a means to achieve some end—God is an end in Himself.

J.M.: How are disciples classified?

Sw. K.: (*Laughingly*) There are three kinds of disciples, according to their ability to get ignited with the fire of wisdom: One type is like a banana stem or wet wood. No matter what you do, it won't burn. Yet if it stays in the fire long enough, some effect will eventually be seen. The second type is like firewood. One must blow on it, tend it carefully and it will catch fire. The third category is like gunpower: it catches fire immediately.

Referring to the warm weather (it was the middle of a very hot summer), Swami Krishnanandaji compared our attitude to the weather to the attitude of ordinary people who think they are Bhaktas of God: When these Bhaktas get a lot of material things which they wish for, they praise God as if giving Him a Certificate. When the Oxford University wanted to confer an honorary degree of Doctorate of Literature on George Bernard Shaw, the latter said: 'It is an insult for you to offer that to me'. God does not care for your praise. It is all purely subjective—it gives you pleasure when you praise Him. This is like the way you admire the sun in winter. But when these Bhaktas suffer materially or physically, they condemn God, in the same way you curse the sun in summer!

J.M.: What is the meaning of *darshan* ?

Sw. K.: It is seeing a holy thing. The influence it has on you can be great, depending on the strength of the source. For example, you sit for an hour out in the sun today at noon and you may get sun-stroke (or at least a good tan), but a candle light will not affect you in such a way.

J.M.: What is prasad?

Sw. K.: It is a consecrated thing. Taking it may affect you immediately or much later.

J.M: Is pilgrimage of any use? So many pilgrims are daily passing through the Ashram on their way to or back from Badrinath, Kedar etc.

Sw. K.: It depends on your motive. What is your motive? Is it for going to heaven? Any action may produce good reaction, bad reaction or a mixed type of reaction, according to the attitude of the doer. Pilgrimage is an action, a Karma. To get Moksha you have to go beyond all Karma, good Karma as well as bad Karma, that is, in other words all types of motivated action. A Jivanmukta also engages in action, but he has no selfish motive and the action does not affect him in any way. A Jivanmukta without Karma would vanish: so he must have some Prarabdha Karma yet to be worked out, which makes him engage in good actions; otherwise he would not act at all.

J.M.: Is there really such a thing as Grace? Karma seems so relentlessly binding.

Sw. K.: (*light-humouredly*): You want God to be partial? Why should he be partial to you? God is *just*. He has established the law and fixed it permanently. God's nature is His law. But this law, the law of Karma, is not like the laws of Physics for example, mechanical. The cause-effect relation of Karmas has always been there, but not a fixed mechanical law for everyone. When Ramana Maharshi attained Realisation at such a young age, it is not that he got there quickly as it may appear. He must have passed through all the preceding stages in his previous life or lives. In a few minutes at the convocation ceremony you may get the Ph.D. Degree; but you know, you have laboured for it for, may be, six long years.

J.M.: What is the difference between Mantra Japa and Meditation?

Sw. K.: Japa is the verbal or mental repetition of words, whereas in meditation we are dealing with concepts. Usually you cannot separate the two, that is, words and concepts. When you think of a tree, for example, you also think of the word "tree". Practically the two are inseparable, but theoratically they can be distinguished. A Mantra is that which protects you and elevates you. All Mantras are equally good. Different Mantras are selected because of different temperaments; but they are all equally good.

J.M.: What is the definition of Brahmacharya?

Sw. K.: Brahmacharya is living as a Brahman lives. It is not merely a vow externally imposed. If it is only that, then the mind will rebel against it. It should be spontaneous. It must come from within. If there are lapses now and then in the beginning, don't worry about them, but carry on. After a while it will become a habit.

J.M.: What is your definition of morality, Swamiji?

Sw. K.: Morality is the attunement of oneself to the atmosphere one finds oneself in at any time. It is always changing with the evolutionary process to which the individual is subject. Morality is relative from place to place, time to time, but the necessity for morality is absolute. You cannot sever yourself from the environment, because you are virtually related to it. To find out if an action is moral or not, apply it to everybody and imagine what the result would be. Suppose everyone tells lies, for example, then lying will not work! Suppose everyone is a thief, then stealing will not work! If it works when universalised, then it is good, it is moral. Morality is realising that everyone is an end in oneself, not a means to some end. Others are also subjects, not objects to be exploited. Anything that conduces to the higher integration of personality is moral. Anything that leads to disintegration of personality is immoral. The intention behind the action is what is most important. A man may be making a hole in this wall—it is quite all right if he is a construction worker fixing a door there. But the same action is not all right if it is done by a thief intending to steal.

J.M.: They say that the path to hell is paved with good intentions?

Sw. K.: Only if the intention is bereft of understanding, then it is merely emotional, and you may get a bad result. All factors must be taken into consideration. A king had the good intention of giving away one thousand cows to poor people, but by chance a cow belonging to another, a Brahmin got into the herd and the king unknowingly gifted away the entire lot. Later, when the mistake was found out, the king offered to compensate the Brahmin with ten, twenty, fifty or even a hundred other cows, but the Brahmin would not agree to accept any other cow but his own and he cursed the generous king, who had to be reborn as a lizard. Suppose a man takes Sannyas, you would say it is a very gcod thing. But suppose his wife dies the next day, because of her sorrow at separation from her husband, she suffers a heart-attack, does he incur sin?

J.M.: But is the really spiritual man beyond the laws of morality?

Sw. K.: Firstly, at that time you cannot call him a man. Rather, he is a Universal Being. Though he is beyond the law, he cannot break the law. The law works only for individuals, not for akasa, for example, which is universal. According to circumstances one may modify one's rules of behaviour. When you travel on the train, you modify your programme somewhat—you cannot take a proper bath and the like. You have to change even more if you are a General on a campaign there you cannot act as in peace time. One might even have to steal, rather than die of starvation! The spiritual man knows the exigency of the prevailing circumstances and hence it is imperative for his disciple to obey him. Swamiji told the following story: A disciple and his Guru journeyed to a land where they found any quantity of food cost only half an anna. The Guru said: "We must leave here immediately, this is a place of fools". The disciple, however, stays and becomes very fat. After two years, a wall collapses and a man is injured. The king of that place wants to hang the man responsible. They find the mason who built the wall, then the cement mixer, then the water-carrier, and each claims he is not responsible for the bad construction now 20 years old. The water carrier says he was late in bringing water because he was singing. They bring this woman who is very thin and are ready to hang her, but they discover the loop of the rope is too big for her neck. The king says: "Bring a stout man and hang him". That disciple, who stayed back unheeding his Guru's warning has now become quite stout and so he is brought. He prays: "Oh, Gurudev, please save me." The Guru was an Omniscient Jeevanmukta and he immediately appears in that place and says: "Don't hang that man. I want to die. This is a very auspicious time. Whoever dies now will be a king in the next birth." They report this to the king and the king goes to the gallows saying Oh! in that case let *me* die! Thus the disciple is saved and the Guru tells him: 'You should have listened to me. I told you this is a place of fools'.

Question: Which is good to wish for a short life or a long life?

Sw. K.: If you *want* to live a hundred years, it could be an error. If you *want* to die, it is also a mistake. You should not condemn life outright; make the best of your life here (100 years is only symbolic). A negative, pessimistic attitude of utter condemnation of the world is wrong. But excessive love, being captivated by the beauty of the world, is equally wrong. The truth is somewhere in the middle.

Question: Is it a sin if a Mantra is mispronounced due to ignorance or physical defect?

Sw. K.: Some people become fanatics and think only their mantra works and only if pronounced correctly. A devotee in Tamil Nadu used to recite 'Namah Chivaya' (instead of 'Namah Sivaya') with such faith that he was able to walk on water reciting 'Nama Chivaya'. One day a grammarian taught the devotee to pronounce the mantra correctly as 'Namah Sivaya'. But with the correct pronunciation the devotee could no longer walk on water—he fell into the water. Because he was concentrating on the pronunciation of the Mantra and had also lost faith in his Guru who gave the mantra.

S.D.: Swamiji this story is like the "Tapla Curry" Story.

J.: Please tell me that story also.

Sw. K.: There was a sweeper women who approached her employer, a pround Namboodiri Brahmin of Kerala for a mantra she could recite. He was angry that she should ask for a mantra, as she was of a low caste. But she persisted. The Namboodiri got angry and yelled at her contemptuously "Go and recite 'Tapala Curry', meaning frog curry. The woman took it in good faith and went on repeating the phrase with such devotion that she became enlightened. People asked her who her Guru was and when she told them they went and praised his disciple's saintliness and how good a Guru he must be. But the Namboodiri had forgotten all about the low caste woman. Now he remembered the incident and felt sorry for himself; for he was still in Samsara while she had become enlightened with the 'frog curry' mantra! All these parables emphasise the importance of the attitude or Bhava in mantra-japa, the attitude is much more important than the mere sound of the word.

J.: Some sages had families. Is not celibacy compulsory?

Sw. K.: I may live in a garden, but I don't think of it as my garden. So I am not affected. The Rishis had no psychological attachment to house, wife, children, etc. The mere physical presence among wife and children, did not, in their case, mean anything. So they have to be regarded as celibates.

J.: Iswara is associated with sleep, Hiranyagarbha with the dream state and Virat with the waking state. Does this mean that all our individual experiences come out of sleep, as the world comes out of Isvara?

Sw. K.: The consciousness in the waking state, the dream state and the deep sleep state is more and more dull in the Jiva, in that order—but the reverse is the case of the Cosmic, where Isvara is greater and antecedent to Hiranyagarbha, and Hiranyagarbha is greater than and comes before the Virat. It is like seeing a reflection of yourself in the water while standing on the bank of a river; the reflection is upside down. Everything is upside down here in the individual, (*laughing*) as in sirsasana when everything is upside down for us.

You must see the object as the subject. When you think of someone or something as an object, it is an insult to that person or thing. When the object becomes the subject, it is Yoga: You are not able to see that the object depends on the subject and that the subject is in the object. When you do, see it so, you are a Yogi.

J.: How do Vedas provide knowledge of Nirguna Brahman, if they were revealed by Saguna Brahman?

Sw. K.: If the Vedas are eternal, they cannot be said to come from anyone else. If they come from someone else, they cannot be eternal. So to say Isvara created (or revealed) the Vedas is only a way of speaking. The Vedas are a thorn to remove the thorn of ignorance. They negate the *Vyavaharika* plane, but do not give any knowledge of Brahman. A tiger in the dream experience can remove the dream experience by waking you up with fear!

J.: In the Bhasyam on the Brahmasutras, Sankara says gods have knowledge of Vedas. Are gods omniscient and on the level of Isvara?

Sw. K.: Only Isvara can really be omniscient. The "knowledge of the Gods" is only a concession—it cannot be equated to Isvara. No one can be equal to Him.

J.: In Mundaka Upanishad 3.1.1, Sankara says, God is pure, wise, free and Omniscient. Then how can He be limited by Cosmic Ignorance—Maya? Maya is often called the Upadhi of Isvara—is it not a mistake to call it an imperfection?

Sw. K.: You can see the sun. But suppose you have a cataract in your eye, then you cannot see the sun properly. But that is your fault—not the sun's. It is an imperfection of *your* vision to say that Brahman has limitations or adjuncts.

J.: Some advaitins say *Sarva-Mukti* means we attain Iswara when all (everyone) finally attain Brahman; but Isvara is not different from Brahman, so how can we attain this entity?

Sw. K.: This is only a theory that may appeal to your sentiments. It is not real. When you say 'all attain' you have an idea of a finite number of souls. But really the souls are infinite in number. There can be no end and no question of all attaining anything. So this is a democratic theory that can be misunderstood. There is no ontological entity called Isvara to be attained. Isvara is like the 'X' in a mathematical equation. It has no ultimate value but it helps you to solve the problem (of Reality) just like 'X' created by you for the purpose of solving the problem. You think that Isvara is Infinite and the World is finite. You think that the finite has come from the Infinite. But it really is not so.

All these theories of cause and effect (*i.e.*, creation) appeal to you. But if the *Sruti* tells the Ultimate Truth that the Infinite has come from the Infinite (which means nothing is really produced), you won't be able to accept it. But the *Sruti* teach us metaphysically, not literally. They mean to teach non-difference, not really creation as different from the creator.

The Infinite is also in the finite, the whole is in the part. The soul pervades the body, that it how the Infinite can be in the Finite as it is said in the Gita. The Ocean is in the drop, but really the Ocean which it so vast cannot be in the tiny drop. So the Lord says in the Gita: "I am in all creatures, yet I am not in them.. " [*laughing*] No one can be as difficult as God. He is a

Master of Confusion. For, really the drops are in the ocean and the ocean is in the drops in a way which we don't understand. The essence of the ocean and the essence of the drops are the same—it is water—they are not two, they are one.

S.D.: Swamiji, someone with a definite purpose of his own, in order to provoke me into an argument, remarked in the presence of a religious Muslim who had married a Hindu, "Hinduism is nothing but one god fighting with another!" I knew his mind and so refused to say anything and get excited. But what is the meaning of these so-called wars between Visnu and Brahma, for instance, when Lord Siva vanquishes them both and quells their pride? Lord Siva establishes at the same time that He is the Most Supreme! Is it because in such contexts the Manifested God gets accretions of their level which is lower than that of the Supreme Being? The Puranas and the Epics are full of such incidents of war among the Gods.

Sw. K.: The subject-object opposition in time and space, the affirmation of the ego as superior to and supreme over everything, causes the clash, no matter at what level. This clash of the positive and the negative, both of which are inherent in everything finite, produces a spark as a Higher Synthesis and is absorbed in the Higher Synthesis. But this level of the present Higher Synthesis is, again, not the highest, it is still only in the process of evolution into the next Higher Synthesis. So this clash and this spark are repeated, so is the absorption of the spark into the next Higher Synthesis, from level to level. This clash or "war" between the gods—deities of the different levels—goes on until the last Higher Synthesis is absorbed into the Absolute. This process of the sparks getting absorbed thus is explained in the Puranas and the Epics as one god warring with another and a third god conquering (absorbing) both within Itself.

J.: What is the benefit of Sirsasana? Swami Sivanandaji says it is good for memory and brain power; Rajneesh says it makes you stupid. Who is right?

Sw. K: Sirsasana is the best asana. But it should be done only for a maximum of five minutes. You will get good memory immediately. Something can be good and bad also. Someone says, 'Eat this, it is good for you, you will be strong.' Another says, 'Don't eat it, it is bad for you, you will get diarrhoea.' Actually, your memory improves as your body consciousness decreases. The more the body consciousness, the less the memory and the ability to concentrate.

J.: Swamiji, what is the locus of *avidya*? It is in the *Jiva* as the Bhamati school asserts; or is it in Brahman as the Vaisvanara school asserts?

Sw. K.: *Avidya* can have no locus, no place to be in, for it is not real. Each thinks it belongs to the other. A guest showed up at a wedding party. The father of the bride thought that the man had been invited by the groom's family and the family of the groom thought he was a guest invited by the bride's family. He stayed there many days enjoying their hospitality. Finally, one day the bride's father and the groom's father were talking about him. When they were about to ask him where he really belonged, he vanished. [*Revered Swamiji laughed heartily when he gave this illustration.*] *Avidya* is like that—it is not real, so it vanishes the moment you enquire about it.

Isvara is like the Government. It is not perceptible, but it is everywhere. You cannot say where it is, but if you do something wrong you will feel its effects. You say the Government is in Delhi, but if you break the law (or if you want an extension of your visa, etc.), you will feel the Government's presence here! Isvara is a logical thing—not an ontological or metaphysical entity, not the Reality. The Government is like our body. When you are aware of your body, it means something is wrong with it; my head aches, you say. When a king rules righteously, no one is aware of his rule. Even so, when you realise Brahman even the Mahavakyas will not matter much to you. 'Aham Brahmasmi' will then be only words—and you will be beyond words. You will attain that *silence* which is beyond all theories. Would you want your books even then? If one could attain God by books, you could spend a few days in the National Library in Calcutta and have realisation. But getting God is not so easy. Even if you memoried the entire Encyclopaedia Britannica, you would not have knowledge of God.

There are different names of God: Isvara, Hiranyagarbha, Virat, but they are the names of one Single Being. Just as Michael is one person but he can be analysed medically. physically, psychologically, etc. If you exist as an individual, He (Isvara) also exists. But once you lose your individuality, even Isvara goes on realisation of the Absolute. Actually, Isvara is not different from Brahman. The same Ultimate Reality is there in both. The name Isvara is given only for relational purposes (Brahman is Isvara in relation to us)—just as the same man may be a father, brother, son, etc. You call It Isvara because of your isolation from It. You pray to your own higher nature which is so vast that it looks to you like another person altogether. Because Isvara is a Cosmic Individual, you pray to Him—like you bow to an individual who is a leader of the nation, whom you yourself have elected, whom you yourself have put it that supreme position!

To think universally, as God thinks, is our goal. The only problem is we think as man thinks. When the milk becomes curd, it ceases to exist; it is totally in the other form—the curd. But when God 'becomes' the world, He continues to exist in Himself. Really nothing ceases to exist, for there is no difference between cause and effect.

J.: Is logic the same as metaphysics? Is the law of the mind the same as the law of the Universe?

Logic is the manifestation in the mental realm of the Ultimate Metaphysical Principle. Vedanta Metaphysics asserts that Reality is non-dual. So the psychology, and the epistemology or logic of Vedanta must be based on this non-difference of the knower and the known?

Sw. K.: This is based on the problem of whether there is a metaphysical thing in itself (noumenon), on which the logic of phenomenon is based. This is a great mystery, but it is unsolvable. Even Kant died before he got the answer. Isvara is thought to be logically the highest, whereas Brahman is metaphysically or intuitionally the highest. But these are not two. The law of ultimate existence manifests itself in various ways: law of cohesion, integration, love, sanity—so the universal cosmic law regulates our individual and social and mental life.

A Visitor: Is self-luminosity the same as self-consciousness?

Sw. K.: 'Self-luminous' (*svayam-prakasa*) means consciousness itself. You are not aware that you are aware. It is awareness, pure and simple. The question of self-consciousness, as you think of it, is that of an individual subject as opposed to an object. The Absolute does not have self-consciousness, rather, it is Consciousness itself. Isvara is the highest self-conscious being. It is the universal Being aware of itself as existing. You cannot imagine what this kind of self-consciousness is. Isvara is aware of the object as identical with Himself. He regards the objects of the world as you would regard your hands and feet. Hands and feet are objects in one sense, for they can be seen by you. But they are vitally related to you, just so is the whole world related to God. Brahman is consciousness itself. Isvara is self-consciousness. *Jivanmukta*, you may say, is a little lower. He has not merged completely into Brahman (until the final death of body, and so still needs some external objects to maintain life.)

J.: If life is a movement from Ananda to Ananda, why is it that we shouod be detached from it?

Sw. K.: If you know life is Ananda, then everything is fine! What do you want detachment from? You want detachment from wife, children and property, because you think these are the causes of sorrow—you want to renounce liabilities. Really you should think about being attached (to life). God is not such a fool that he cannot understand these tricks of the human mind [*Emphatically.*] 'Stone walls do not a prison make', nor do the stone walls make an Ashram or church. So you leave the stone walls of your home for other stone walls. What is the difference? Religion is a continued idea of the world and in this sense it is the opium of the people. Religiosity—conservatism—will enable you to get on in ordinary life, but it won't cut ice with God! Religious groupism (sectarianism) has the same purpose as political groupism (parties or nationalities). Whether the left leg is broken or the right leg is broken—it is a broken leg. You cannot be a religious person until and unless you renounce religiosity. Don't call yourself a Hindu, Christian, Advaitin, etc. There was a man at Stanford University who wrote "The Religion of No Religion"; again there was William Cantwell Smith who wrote the "End of Religions". When you know that you know nothing, still you have knowledge. Cut it all away and something remains [*With great emphasis.*] At Dakshineswar when Ramakrishna was alive, a poor, dirty man came and recited something in a temple. No one could understand the language but all present felt a spiritual presence in the temple when he was there. They went to Ramakrishna and told him. He said, you fools, that was a God-realised man, you should have prostrated before him. Go find him out! The people went looking for him and found him in a gutter in Varanasi. The filthy sewage water was flowing down (to the Ganga). The people asked him, 'What is truth?' He replied, when you see this filthy water and the holy Ganga are one (not different) you know the Truth!

One Mouni Swami of South India used to keep a pot of spit, urine, rots etc. People thought he was a great saint, so they went for initiation. He insisted that they drink the contents of the pot and the people ran away. One half-crazy man went there and when ordered he drank the scum in the pot. His senses had been conquered and he tasted no 'scum'. He went into Samadhi. They asked him later what it tasted like. "He said, it was sweet nectar!" These are real men of religion—but you want someone who tells you to read Gita, do Japa; you want comfortable answers.

J.: So ultimately we have to give up everything?

Sw. K.: What do you mean by everything? Wife, Children, etc.?

J.M.: No, I mean theories, beliefs, sects, etc. Are these to be given up to attain God-Realisation?

Sw. K.: No, it is something quite different from that. You must discriminate as to which thoughts to retain and which to dismiss at any moment. When a man comes to a doctor with 105 degrees temperature and eczema, certainly the doctor treats the fever first. Commonsense is the most uncommon thing in the world (*laughs.*) When you have been starving, eating is more important than meditation, but when you are drowning, being saved from the water is more important than eating. When is the best time for eating? It is when you are hungry. Same with meditation. Samsara is timeless. Time began with creation, so in that sense, it is said to be beginningless or eternal. But remember it is not real. Jivas in bondage exist to a realised being just as the people you saw in a dream last night exist for you in the dream. Where are they today ? They have been absorbed into your waking consciousness. Your recurring question is based on the assumption that there has been creation. Why do you assume this? No one has seen God creating.

Vis.: But the Srutis teach us there has been creation. Why should they mislead us?

Sw. K.: When you think the Srutis mislead you, they cease to be scriptures. A friend ceases to be a friend when he robs you. The tiger in the dream can wake you, though it is unreal.

Q.: Is not social work an ultrimistic ideal?

Sw. K: If you investigate all social organisations from the UNO down to the family, you will find that they are all based on selfishness [*Laughing*.] Love everyone but trust a few, they say.

Question: Why does my throat go dry during meditation? It makes me cough.

Sw. K.: It is due to the stopping of saliva; emotion dries up the saliva which is connected with emotions, and in meditation your emotion on the object of concentration may cause this. Hunger, thirst, grief, sorrow, joy are all emotions which affect salivary secretion. When you are very angry the mouth dries up; you cannot speak at that time; the mouth closes, the liver is disturbed and immediately your mouth dries up, the lips tremble.

Q.: There is also palpitation during meditation?

Sw. K.: It is all due to concentration at the time of meditation. Sometimes you feel the locking up of the teeth also. It is nothing unusual. It it natural—all due to concentration only.

Question: When in the course of doing Japa, there is a time when you are unable to go on with it, as if you were in the grip of something other than the distraction of the mind; the mind does not seem to be coming into play here; there is joy for the time you are in this grip of something which you are convinced is not a false experience but are convinced of the reality of the experience. It is not slipping into sleep or dream. Simultaneously you are aware that your concentration on your Japa is not all that deep. Can this be taken to mean a flash in meditation if such an interpretation is permissible here?

Sw. K.: It is due to deep concentration only, although you may not be aware of it. Concentration can be even unconscious. Concentration need not be consciously set up. There can be effortless concentration and that is more natural than the concentration with effort. When doing Japa it is tremendous concentration; but concentration is done unconsciously and is more effective than the concentration with which you are speaking to me now. You are naturally feeling that you are Bhagyalakshmi and that is a tremendous concentration that has been predecided for years and so intensely practised that it has become a part of your being. And therefore, there is no effort in thinking you are Bhagyalakshmi, while it requires a little effort to listen to what I am saying and so on. In Japa, you have concentration at its sub-conscious level. Your name has become a part of you, you are that: Even so the experience and the Japa.

The conviction that there is a world outside us does not require great concentration of mind. We are born with the feeling that the world exists though it really is a false notion. And yet that false notion has got into our blood so powerfully that you do not require to go on looking at things to feel that there is a world outside. So that even wrong things can become a result of concentration.

Question: If no one is helping, how can one achieve anything for the common weal?

Sw. K.: You can do anything alone. Mahatma Gandhi led alone the whole of the Indian nation. Churchill singly defeated Hitler. Swami Sivananda was alone when he started the Ashram. If he had waited for help or cooperation from another person or persons, this Ashram would never have come into existence. Lord Krishna all by Himself delivered the Gita and won the battle of the Mahabharata. You also can do it all on your own any by yourself.

Bill Isler: So Swamiji, you mean to say that it requires concentration when you wish to concentrate on, *i.e.*, think of God? How to concentrate when you want to think of God?

Sw. K.: Be conscious that God exists—the only thing that exists. This requires concentration. But we do not require any concentration to believe that the world exists which really does not exist. You can imagine the trick of the mind. A thing which really is requires tremendous concentration to get it into our mind. But for a thing that is not there, it requires no concentration at all. It simply sits in your mind like a devil and takes possession of the entire area [*laughs*!] You can imagine the catastrophy that has taken place and it is not going to be so easy a matter to rack one's head hard and struggle even to be aware that something exists while in fact that is the only thing that exists. And to get free from the clutches of a thing which is not there see what an effort or attempt it is. You are struggling throughout your life to free yourself from the clutches of a thing that is not there; and cannot think even for a single minute a thing which is really there. It is a case of complete hypnotisation and brain-washing to the very core by the mind. Brain-washing is really a poor word for it, much worse has happened. Brain-washing is only a psychological function.

B.I.: The brain-washed mind does not wish to believe that it is as swerious as it really is.

Sw. K: Yes, yes, yes.

B.I.: In fact, that is the real brain-washing we do! We do not realise that it is as complete as it is.

Sw. K.: Yes, yes, yes. A tremendous catastrophe has taken place and yet you are brain-washed in another way, to make you feel that nothing has happened to us. Though are you a prisoner in fetters, you are made to believe that you are free. And that is a very interesting way of brain-washing! When you are in prison and you are aware that you are in prison, that is a blessing. But you are brain-washed again to believe that you are a free man.

B.I.: If there is confirmation that you are in prison there is no more struggle necessary to believe it is so. But you are brain-washed into thinking that you are practically free.

Sw. K.: Yes, yes. Many great men think that they have realised God and are self-realised—Buddhas-Bodhisattvas, there is nothing else to attain, it only remains to give salvation to the world. Even many thinkers think like that. This is a topsy-turvy sincerity.

Sarju: When did this change from reality to brain-washing begin? How?

Sw. K.: It has no beginning. When you say 'begin', you are thinking of a particular point of time. You are imagining a beginning of time [*laughs*].

Sarju: Okay. How did it change then? Why did it come about? What caused it?

Sw. K.: If you know that you are no more Sarju, you will cease to be that. That secret means God speaking in the end. He does not want to tell you! Because if it lets the cat out of the bag then everybody will be happy! He has a small cat in the bag. He will not let it out; this secret He keeps to Himself. He has done something without letting you know what He has actually done.

S.D.: Is it because man's own efforts will get rusted?

Sw. K.: He wants you to put forth effort and know it. And He will not answer the question like that. He has worked the miracle. It is a miracle, well, merely because it is beyond the intellectual capacity to reach the cause. You are putting the question why: Why is a question connected with logic. And logic means intellectual activity connecting cause and effect. And these are all after-effects of this phenomena. And the effect cannot know the cause. So the question why is connected with effect and effect cannot know the cause, because logic cannot know the cause. Therefore, the question why has no answer. The question itself is a misplaced question.

S.D.: Swamiji, the other day you said that the contradiction that arises between the waking consciousness and dream consciousness creates all the restlessness and problems of the waking consciousness that there are many more layers of the personality before the Atman is reached.

Sw. K.: Yes, many, many more layers.

S.D.: [*Continuing*] And Swamiji you further said that God in His mercy has hidden these layers from us. How is it mercy?

Sw. K.: Have you read my small book "Struggle for Perfection"?

S.D.: No. Swamiji. It is only now, after hearing you for a period of seven years, that I have the courage to read your books. Earlier I always kept them for special attention to the subject and for concentrated understanding. This opportunity did not come before I came to live in the Ashram, and only now the ground is familiar and I can read and follow what you write. Because of this background of only the earlier days that I had all those problems when I translated your book "Meditation—Its theory and practice."

Sw. K.: You read my book "Struggle for Perfection." I have mentioned all these layers there.

S.D.: You have mentioned the layers in other contexts also.

Sw. K.: I have also explained the layers there and not merely mentioned them. The explanations cannot be exhaustive for a small book like that, but that is enough in that context.

S.D.: I see. So I will get my answers by reading that book?

Sw. K.: Yes, specially in the first part of it. That book is condensed and provides the essence of the whole matter. Lieutenant-General Chhibber says he has kept this book in his pocket always—like a Bible. He says, this is sufficient for me, I do not want to read anything else.

A visitor from Switzerland: Why does God create women?

Sw. K.: Why? Do you think He can create only man? [*laughs.*] Because God is a man, He wants a woman! So He creates woman! If God is a woman He will create man! Yes, He is a very mischievous person. He creates woman. He does not like one like Himself—He wants variety. Unfortunately, He is a man, so

He creates a woman. Mischievous He is. Understand? Now, how to clear this doubt? God created man that He may be worshipped. Nobody worships Him. If He were alone there, who, would worship Him? Is this the solution to His creating man? This is very interesting. God has no work ! Fancy His creating someone just became He may be worshipped. This is another doubt. You go to God. Okay. But after that what happens? What work? And what do you get by going to God? Any nice eatables? Or a cosy bed to sleep well? Or some such good thing? What is it that God gives or can give you? These are the doubts. If these doubts go, then your mind will concentrate. Immediately in one brief second concentration is achieved. But they are there and will not allow you to think. Though just now they are not there in the mind when you are thinking something else, on occasions they will come. They remain subconsciously buried, and do not leave you happy. And after all, how do you know God exists. Who told you He is there? This is another doubt. May be, may not be. I am fooled. This is another doubt, Eh! And you can have doubts like this all connected with the same matter. Who has seen God? Let me see that man who has seen God to tell me "I have seen Him."

So you must clear up your mind before anything starts to pull you down. You must clear your mind of all these cobwebs before you start anything [*laughs.*] You require a very scientific approach to the problem. And this is a problem. This is a variety presented by a single problem. All these questions which I put to you are the various forms taken by a single problem of the relationship between you and the universe. That is the simple matter. And this relationship is not easy to understand. Even if you try to understand, it will elude you. That is why you have to dedicate yourself completely to the spiritual life like the scientist who dedicates himself to the telescope or microscope till he hits what he is looking for, and you must be sure that you have no doubt in your mind. Of course, you need not go on clearing the doubt of somebody else. You are not bothered. At least you must be sure that 'I have no doubt', 'I know why God created the world and I also know why God created this kind of world and I know everything you should not have" "Why?"—"Why?" "Why like this?" All these should not be there. "Why should I pray to God, what is it that God will give me after going there and what will happen to me after seeing Him?" "All this I know very well". This is how you should clear yourself. When these doubts disappear, then see how you will meditate! Like an arrow, your mind will go straight to the target. Otherwise you will be stunned and tremble. These are questions which cannot be answered by the Bhagavad Gita, the Upanishad, or the New Testament. These cannot be answered by any book. Though they may openly give indications, they will not answer any such questions, because, they are concerned with something else. They are under the impression that all these doubts have gone frcm your mind. So they tell something else. But they do not know that persons with these doubts want to go there!

Question: Where else to get the answer, then, Swamiji?

Sw. K.: Where then to get the answer? Tell me?

Vis.: The answer is not to ask for an answer to such problems.

Sw. K.: When you know the reason behind the problem, there is no problem. The problem ceases. When the sun is hot, you understand why it is hot. To trouble you is not his intention. It is a phenomenon natural to him. And why do you feel that the heat is a different thing? That is another scientific point. That point is science, connected with physics, physiology, biology, etc. And if you understand science, why they are arranged thus, you understand why things happen as they are and you also know how to adjust yourself afterwards. Water is not created by God to drown you. That is not His intention. But it is possible you may get drowned but the intention is not to do that. Why one gets drowned is another point. The fact is that there is no proper adjustment of your personality with the atmosphere outside. These are all scientific points. And you must get out of these problems by adjusting yourself to these different levels of experience. And how to get the answer? It is not in the book. Ycu will get it only from a spiritual guide, because, he has seen all these things. Only a person who has fallen into the pit will know there is one and he will tell you, here is a pit, do not go there. A person who has not seen it will not know that the other man has passed through it.

Dr Aruna holds a screw driver before Swamiji.

Dr. A.: Yesterday you said you could not find one. Here is one.

Sw. K.: The whole world has been moving to get a screw driver—the whole world active for a little thing ! In every event the whole universe is in travail. This is what a great writer wrote in his own language. At the birth of every event the whole universe is in travail. Everything is active, the whole universe is active just as the whole body is awake at the little pricks of a thorn. It may be a little prick, but the whole body reacts as one stroke. Everything is active for a little thing. So your rescue comes not from one man or one person. The whole universe is helping you at one stroke. But it ejects the help through some channel or some object. Your heart should be intensely craving for it when it is supplied with it through some miraculous method. Nobody knows how it comes. You will see this in the lives of saints. 'Hundies' and bundles of money are released by unknown persons. You know 'hundies'? Hundies mean a V.P.P. coming from the bank.

There was a person called Narsi Mehta—Narsi Bhakat. He had to get a hundie released, and somebody released it, no one knew who. And in the case of Badrachalam Ramadas, a bag of gold coins was thrown before the Nawab because he was imprisoned by the Nawab whose money Ramadas had spent in building a temple. That is how miracles work. No one knows how!

An Ashramite: What is "Paryanka Vratam", Swamiji?

Sw. K.: It is in the Upanishads. In fact, all this is there. Rama tells of it. Brahma is sitting on it. "Paryanka" in Sanskrit means a cot.

[A Japanese visitor, a journalist, has come to the ashram to collect information about Yoga in all its aspects.]

Sw. K.: Tell me about your gods... You want to have the meaning of the Hindu gods explained?

[Sankarananda, who speaks Japanese fluently, acts as the interpreter.]

Sw. Sankarananda: [*translating*] The gods in Japan are represented like the ancient Rishis, in the ordinary clothes of men. But Hindu gods have very complicated dresses—snakes and all kinds of weapons—so difficult to worship.

Sw. K.: Hindu gods are not Brahmins! They are Kshatriyas! They have got weapons! And the Brahmins are asked to worship them! And the gods are all house-holders. The Hindu gods are not Brahmacharis or Sannyasis. This is also an interesting thing. Every god has a wife, even two. All this is something more than sociology.

Sw. Sankarananda: He wants to know which is the correct way of worshipping God? Which is the right method? Should food be offered to God?

Sw. K.: Anything that is offered is called food. What is it that sustains the soul? Tell me.

Sw. S.: Body is sustained by food.

Sw. K.: Body is sustained by food and what is it that sustains the soul ?

Sw. S.: The soul is sustained by the body. The body is a disease of the soul.

Sw. K.: Swami Sivananda used to joke [*pointing to clothes—the dhoti and the upper wrap.*] This is a bondage put upon the sore, a carbuncle that has grown on the soul ! Every day you clean this carbuncle, put medicine and bandage it [*laughter.*] The soul is sustained by God, by the Supreme Being, by God Himself. The body can be sustained by a cup of tea and food, but the food of the soul is God Himself; it cannot be satisfied with anything less. It wants only that. And so it goes on crying, and until that is got it won't become quiet. And though body can be satisfied with little things, the soul cannot be satisfied with anything but God. Only when it comes in contact with God, it loses itself. And when it has contacted Him and has realised it, it feels happy then and, only then.

Question: We offer food—*pindam* etc. during those ten days of mourning to the departed soul. How does that affect the departed soul ?

Sw. K.: Yes, it will affect the soul. Just as you send an M.O. to someone and the money reaches him. Although it is not actually the cash that is sent from your place to the other place, it is the intention that is conveyed to the other end. And even the kind of currency sent need not be the same; you may send it in rupees and it can be paid to the receiver in German Franks or American Dollars or British Pounds.

Vis.: But the soul does not require any food, etc.?

Sw. K.: No, no! The soul has not reached God yet. It is in a helpless condition as it cannot act. So it requires some external help. If that soul has reached God, then your *pindam* has no meaning. It does not want anything. But you cannot take it like that. It is implied that he is hanging in some realms and so, may be, his meritorious Karmas are perhaps not sufficient to sustain him. So you add on your prayers, charities, your *danam*, etc. If

I get some good from somebody, it might be because of the prayer someone has offered on my behalf. Goodwill and sympathy, or rather a telepathic communication that you establish in whatever place, in whichever realm the soul exists, it will reach it by a vibration which is set up in the Cosmos by your mantras, by your feelings etc. It does not mean that your *pindam* i.e., the same food will go there. Like the M.O., the intimation is given there and whatever amount is necessary is paid in its own currency to the addressee there.

Vis.: So then, the *pindam* and the like helps it to go to God?

Sw. K.: That is a more difficult thing. It cannot reach God like that. Your *pindam* and all that cannot reach God. But it is a lesser help that you are rendering. It has got sufferings of various kinds because of demerites that have accrued to itself. So, it may take a rebirth or it may have other kinds of agencies and all these are natural things. Who is there so perfect ? So you render help so that you may also be helped by others. Whatever help you give to other will be given back to you as a kind of mutual return help, as sympathy and love.

S.D.: We can pray for their rebirth also?

Sw. K.: You need not say any prayers for that. They will take rebirth anyhow without your saying that too.

S.D.: "Please grant that a good rebirth"—Cannot you pray like that ?

Sw. K.: That is again a kind of help you are giving it by offering your prayers to God. You are appealing to the Supreme Master, don't put Him in prison and all that.

S.D.: Yes, that is how it is.

Sw. K.: You are appealing. You are advocating. You are a counsel on the part of the soul and you are pleading before the Judge, the Supreme Being—don't punith him unnecessarily and commit him to prison.

S.D.: Is that a foolish act or is it a part of the prayer we may offer ?

Sw. K.: No, no. Why do you say it is a foolish act? It is a great charitable feeling.

Vis.: You are pleading for that soul?

Sw. K.: Yes, yes. Perhaps you will also be pleaded for by somebody because you have done some good deeds. Somebody will help you. Law work like that. It is natural. When offering *Pin-*

dam generally the "Heads" (of the family) only are counted [*laughs*] in the prayer for the departed ones; because every year after a few years, some new persons will be added to it and then you omit the last of the earliest ones.

Vis.: If that soul has already left the world as time passes, is it still in Pitriloka or in other lokas?

Sw. K.: You cannot say that. How can you know? It depends upon his karmas. He may be in Pitraloka or Swargaloka—anywhere. But it does not matter where he is. As far as your charitable deeds are concerned, it will reach him wherever he is.

S.D.: Swamiji, if the soul has already taken birth—is it not the wrong address?

Sw. K.: No, no! It will reach him. Your mind will tell you where he is. The vibrations you set up—you have got a picture of that person in your mind and before the inner eyes, so wherever the soul is, that force will go and touch it—in any world even if he is reborn. He may be sitting near you here! And it will have some benefit. You may not know it works. But it will work.

S.D.: And I wouldn't know that it has worked on this person next to me.

Sw. K.: Nor will he know that you have helped.

Vis.: Some Risi curses—like the one which cursed Ahalya to become a stone—have had great potency. How does a curse work? Ahalya is also released from the curse conditionally. How?

Sw. K.: It is a force that is working. It is his mind that is working there. His mind goes and impinges upon the person with such a force that whatever the thought, it immediately materialises in that personality. It is a force of his mind's thought.

Vis.: I thought that perhaps it is prediction that is going to come.

Sw. K.: Prediction by whom?

Vis.: By the person who curses.

Sw. K.: That way, everything is predicted by God. It is said that when the universe is created, everything is determined by Him. That is too far-fetched and cosmic a view of things that you are taking. But normally, relatively thinking, it is this man's thought that is working. But why is he made to think like that? That is but a different thing. Why has he the impulse to curse others? Who is prompting him? Then you are going behind the causes which lie behind causes. That is too much. But we are thinking of the immediate cause. The immediate cause is his intention to do something and affect that particular experience in that person and that is a blessing or a curse. It is the materialisation of the thought of the person who expresses it.

S.D.: Blessings do not seem to have their effects as quickly as curses have.

Sw. K.: It only shows that your power to hate is greater than your power to love. That is all (*laughs.*) That is why that quick effect. Otherwise, if your love is as intense, it will work—why not ? After all, it is your thought that works. But our love is niggardly and our hate very powerful. The love of Savitri for Satyavan her husband was such that she defeated the Lord of Death himself! And it is not any inferior to the curse. It is much more powerful. Such a terrific force of thought she had that she would not budge until she attained her goal. The story is not an ordinary one. It is love that wins the blessing at once.

Vis.: Dasaratha was very happy when he was cursed with *putrasoka* (grief caused by separation from his son because the curse implied that he would get a son, and that was his greatest desire. The curse did not impress itself as forcibly on his mind.

Sw. K.: Yes, yes! Dasaratha was happy because without a putra (son), he could not have experienced *putrasoka*. So he knew he would get a putra. That is why he was very happy. "After all I will have children," he said to himself. Otherwise, how could this curse work? [*Laughs*] Very interesting!

Dr. R.: A blessing in disguise!

Sw. K.: A blessed curse! My grandmother used to tell a story.

A householder was eating his luncheon served by his wife. The vegetable she had prepared was very tasty and it was his favourite. So he said to his wife: "Keep some for the night. I like it." Just then laughter was heard from the outer verandah where visitors, until invited in, waited. The husband said: "Go and see. Some visitors are waiting". So the wife went and greeted the guests by doing them obeisance. This is the Indian tradition. Greeting her in return, as is traditional, they blessed the lady "Dirgha sumangali bhava" (May your husband live eternally)! The husband had his meals and came outside to greet the guests. Greatings over, he asked them, "I heard you laughing. What was the matter?" And they replied, "We are Yama Dutas--messengers of the Lord of Death." In those days, long, long ago, my grandmother used to say the Yama Dutas came visibly in person to take people to the world of Death and before Lord Yama. So these two guests that had been sitting in the outer varandah while the husband was eating, were Yama Dutas. "We have come to take you with us to Lord Yama just now and you were telling your wife to keep some food for the night. You won't be here in the evening. We are taking you just now to Yama Loka. So we laughed, amused as we were at your saying that." The husband was taken aback. And he called out to his wife and reported the matter to her. The wife was an intelligent and quick-witted woman and she said to the Yama Dutas: "How can you take my husband away now ? Just now when I greeted you, you blessed me, saying, Dirgha sumangali bhava.' How can you go back on your word now?" This was a sort of bombshell to the messengers. They woke up to the situation. They had made a mistake. They had pronounced that blessing in a traditional way, mechanically so to say. When they reported the story to Lord Yama, he said, "You foolish fellows, you should not have spoken to them. All this blunder has been caused only because you were visible to the mortals. From now on do not be visible to the moral world. Go in an invisible form and do your work." Thus it is, my grandmother would conclude the story, that now-a-days the Yama Dutas. are invisible to the mortal world. [*laughs.*] These are all interesting stories. But some creatures like dogs sense it. When death comes, they say that dogs howl and whine because they become aware of the approach of death. And vultures, days before the corpse actually is to come, sit waiting perched upon a tree. That is why they say, "Oh, it is a bad omen, the vultures are seen sitting !" They seem to sense the vibrations set up in the vicinity.

Vis.: The dog accompanied Dharmaputra and he would not enter heaven without the dog if it was not allowed in.

Sw. K.: Hey! Yes, yes! It was Lord Yama Dharmaraja himself that was following Dharmaputra to test him if his generosity would prevail unto the very last. There were three tests for Dharmaputra (Yudhishthira). Once at the lake of poison where the Yaksha, pleased with Yudhisthira's answers to his queries, asked the latter to ask for the life of anyone of the brothers who had died as a result of their failure to answer his queries. Yudhishthira asked for Nakula to be restored to life. The Yaksha said: "Why do you ask for that brother's life? Bhima and Arjuna are better people. You should ask one of their lives back. To this Yudhishthira replied: "We three are the sons of Kunti, while Nakula is the son of our other mother, Madri. Now that I am alive my mother will be happy. And if Nakula too were to return alive to his mother, she would also be happy". When Yudhishthira passed the test the Yaksha revived all the brothers. The third test was in hell. Nothing but suffering everywhere. His brothers were there too. And Yudhishthira, after he had seen his brothers there, was asked to go to heaven. But he refused to go. "If my brothers are suffering in hell, how can I go to heaven alone? I too will stay here until they also go with me to heaven." And any amount of pleading that while his own *karma* would allow him only a glimpse of hell, those of his brothers were such that they had to stay there long, would not change Yudhishthira's mind. Thus he passed the third test also. And all the five of the Pandavas went to heaven.

* * *

8 October 1976

Of the devotees gathered around Rev. Swami Krishnanandaji for the "morning *darshan*", Jim McMichael was the main interviewer. Although his questions had a bearing mainly upon the thesis he was engaged in writing under Prof. Atreya of the Banaras Hindu University, the discussion was a general one with anyone present also taking part in it.

Q.: What is the *lila* of God? What does it mean that the creation is His *lila*?

Sw. K.: This is the same as creation. If the electrons of the stone have really become a stone, then you cannot see the electrons but you can certainly see the stone. If it does not become the stone, how do you see it? So the electrons become the stone, but why? No answer can be given. So, creation does not exist; it means it is only a misconception in the mind—it does not really exist. The more you think of it, the less you like to speak about it! *Lila* is an indescribable sport. You don't know why it happens.

Q.: Is Ishvara a personal God?

Sw. K.: There is a person as long as you exist. When you expand your personality, the personality of God gets diminished correspondingly, because two persons—you as well as He—cannot be there at the same time; and when you become cosmic, He ceases to be completely. He gives place to you. So there cannot be two Gods; only one God can be there.

Q.: You seem to emphasize the creative side?

Sw. K.: If He is the Creator, then He has to be the Sustainer and the Destroyer. But is there any Creator? You must decide that first—then other things would also follow. Has He created the world? If He has not created, He cannot sustain and destroy. I think He has not created the world.

Q.: Some people say God created the world mechanically due to *karmas*; if so, can there be any grace of God to us?

Sw. K.: There can be *karma*, there can be grace, there can be birth and death, there can be every pleasant thing—even if there is no creation! These are no contradictions. God's creation is not necessary for all these purposes. It is a process of consciousness—whatever you call it—*karma*, birth and death—they are not objective events, they are processes of consciousness. They are not outside us—what you see with your eyes.

Q.: You mean belief in the world is a misconception like the belief in the body?

Sw. K.: Even the body is a state of consciousness only; it is not an object which exists ultimately. It appears to be there, but it is really not there. This '*you*' and '*I*' and all that are again phantoms.

You have made a gulf of difference between You and I, which is not really there. It is a mistake that the mind makes. Just as in dreams persons are there, but are really not there, they are only split parts of the same mind, one appearing as the I, the other appearing as you and both are integrated in the single mind in a certain condition.

Q.: Likewise here....

Sw. K.: There is nothing like you and I. What are you seeing? You are seeing a part of the mind only. You are not seeing a person. Just as you see a wall in dream, you see another wall here. It stands in the same relation to the cosmic mind as the dream wall in relation to the waking mind.

Q.: You mean the world is like a dream?

Sw. K.: This world is a cosmic dream. When you wake up you will not see the world. Just as you do not see the dream-world now.

Q.: Any difference between the *jivanmukta* and Ishvara or are both beyond space and time?

Sw. K.: Even *mukti* is a part of the dream only. When you wake up there is no *mukti*. You are on the borderland—one leg here and another there—but really when you go there, there is no *jivanmukti* or anything.

Q.: Then *jivanmukti* is the death of the empirical self?

Sw. K.: It is not really death in the ordinary sense. It is a realisation by consciousness of its presence in everything. That is what you call death.

Q.: It is not aware that it is present in everything. It always thinks it is present only in the body?

Sw. K: This is not the Truth. It is present in everything and the moment you realise this cosmic presence, there is no question of birth and death, the question itself does not arise.

Q.: Shankara and Ramanuja disagree on saguna being ultimate?

Sw. K: There is no disagreement between Shankara and Ramanuja, but it is empirical reality for Shankara while Ramanuja takes it as an absolute Reality. It is something to be transcended.

We may be sitting here—you may not see the person really. You are seeing a part of the Cosmic mind of which you are also a part. One part of the Cosmic mind is in another part of it. It is not one man seeing another man, it is a very crude way of thinking and expressing the fact. There is no man or woman or anything in this world—it is one part of the Cosmic existence envisaging another part of it.

Each part is containing the whole in a hidden form. That is why you are able to catch the whole. The whole is implanted in every part entirely—every cell of the body contains the totality of the personality biologically. If you take one cell of the body you can study the whole of the person, it contains the reflection of the total personality. Likewise the whole Cosmic is reflected in every man—nay, in every atom.

Distinction of Vyavaharika and Paramarthika Levels of Reality.

The distinction appears only to the empirical, it does not exist for the absolute.

You cannot have two things as reals. Two reals cannot exist. The real is only one, either this or that. One of them must be less, they cannot be in the same intensity of delight. Take again the electrons in a stone or as stone.

Can you say the stone is nowhere after it becomes the electrons? It is even now the electron only! So why should it 'become' a stone? So there is no question of jiva 'going' to Brahman. They are already there. They have only become aware of that fact by non-objective awareness.

Your consciousness of objects is your obstacle—i.e. consciousness identifying itself with all things, immediately after you wake up from dream.

As long as the object is seen, you are inside the dream. When the object becomes the subject, the dream vanishes, the bubble bursts. That is called meditation.

Ishvara is an object as a tree is an object. Your point of view in respect of the Absolute is called Ishvara. It is a point of view only, it does not really exist. If you cease to exist, it also goes. You will not see Ishvara when you reach the Absolute.

It is like an X in Mathematics. It is a great help in finding a solution but it is not in itself existing there. Without it you cannot have the solution and it in itself has no meaning. Ishvara cannot be avoided as long as the world is seen with your eyes.

The Ishvara concept is an automatic outcome of your belief in the reality of the world and when the world exists, Ishvara has to exist as the cause thereof, but if the world does not exist, Ishvara need not exist because if the effect is not there, what is the use of the cause?

Q.: I think Ishvara is useful as an object of worship. Does it then matter what object we concentrate on?

Sw. K: There is no hard and fast rule in worshipping anything, provided you regard that as the Absolute. You should not regard that as one among many. That is the mistake which prevents you from going to the Absolute. You can take any particular object as the symbol of the Supreme. There is no question of this object of concentration as mine. The other things do not exist at all for you. The moment other things' concepts exist for you, your own concept of God ceases to be the Absolute for you. A person who regards a deity as the Absolute cannot argue like this. But if I think my deity is Absolute i.e. Visnu, I will argue with Saivites.

The moment you are aware of another person, you have become relative immediately and you cannot regard that object as the Absolute. You must become the Absolute, pervading the whole Cosmos. That sort of concentration you must develop —so, in that way any meditation is correct meditation.

You can take that fountain pen as the Absolute and go to the Supreme by meditating on that because even here the Absolute is present in some form. Through any river in the world you can reach the ocean! These objects are only vehicles to conduct consciousness to the Supreme Absolute. So one object is as good as any other object, if you regard it as the Supreme.

There is no inferior or superior deity, all deities are of equal status.

* * *

The Canadian devotee who had been staying in the Ashram earlier had returned now to the Ashram after his visit to other Ashrams. Pointing to his chest he queried, "There is Atman in me and there is Atman in you and there is (Atman) God outside." What is the relationship of Atman and God?

Sw. K.: What is in between?

Visitor: Atman only!

Sw. K.: You have answered your own question. The words 'inside' and 'outside' are but two terms used because of our physical body, like the inside and outside of a room. There is no relationship as such because they are the same thing. The Atman and God are but two different words standing for the same thing. You have asked the highest question. Nothing else remains.

A Visitor from New York.: Truth is one, although the paths are very many. Often I come across people who dogmatise and say, "This is the truth." I wish to argue it out with them. Am I wasting my time?

Sw. K.: Why do you think so?

Visitor: Because they do not seem to change.

Sw. K.: There are two aspects; one is the time factor. Everyone's grasp is not of the same quickness. Everyone cannot grasp what is said in the same period of time. Some grasp it immediately, while others take a much longer time to comprehend it.

Secondly, there is your own capacity to teach. How quickly the other person grasps what you say will depend upon how you teach that particular person or a group of people.

Visitor: Truth is one and all spiritual friends believe this.

Sw. K.: Teaching is a science in itself, and the psychological understanding of its method and the technique of teaching only a real teacher knows. Thirdly, you cannot teach when you yourself are not hundred per cent sure that your faith is correct. The missionaries feel convinced in this way: all religions are means of approach to God but Christianity is the apporach to God for man. How would you impart your view to him?

Visitor: I shall ask what is the object of Christianity?

Sw. K.: Love of God.

Visitor: Other religions also believe in the same view.

Sw. K.: There are certain tenets of Christianity which cannot reconcile with other tenets. That is the difficulty. And the Bhagavad Gita says; never disturb the faith of anyone.

Visitor: I only want to open their eyes.

Sw. K: Opening their eyes does not mean disturbing their faith. If your heart is sincere, this itself is its own reward and will speak. Christianity, however, asserts that there is none other than Jesus, who is the only incarnation of God the Father. The only teacher of the Gospel of God is Jesus. Judaism is the religion which he taught. As a matter of fact Jesus who is the "WAY" is only one of the several Avatars. To see wrong is itself wrong. And this is the great quarrel. It is the negative way to argue.

Visitor: I want to unify the religions of the different sects of Christianity. They quarrel among themselves as though they were speaking of different truths.

Sw. K: Religion is a unifying factor only. Religions today have, besides love of God, other accretions. Many other activities are included in religion. So you have a difficulty in saying 'God is love' to the customer to whom you speak. You speak in a way different from the one in which you talk to God in the Church. You must see God in the customer. But it is difficult and not quite practical. That is why religions fail, because of this difficulty in achieving the balance between the love of God and the love for man. Religious practice is a hard job.

Visitor: Am I taking too big a job in this task I have set for myself? Do I need training, etc.?

Sw. K.: Why do you have that fear?

Visitor: Because I do not want to aim at the Moon with a pea-shooter.

Sw. K.: By understanding the technique of teaching better, namely, the technique of teaching, you can improve your efforts to teach. And by yourself getting closer to God you can succeed in the job. For, at the point where you get close to God you do not have to speak; your existence itself will speak. If you are truly a religious man, you i.e., your life will belong to the great God! For, living a life as great as God's is to live a Godly life. There is no other or greater service to mankind. To all the friends you wish to talk to, this is the magnificent service you can render. And God will speak through you. You will be told what to do and what to say. You become the instrument of God and it must succeed. This is the greatest duty and the greatest service you can render. His Being will spread an aura around you. Christ was greater than His words. For, "words are partial emanations of His", is a saying; and 'being' is the first thing and doing comes afterwards.

To do a magnificent work you must "be" yourself magnificent first.

The usual audience of various nationalities were gathered under the open sky. Visitors kept trickling in and out. Conversation follows:

Q.: What is the worth of a man?

Sw. K.: You may define it in an aphorism. The worth of a man is his nearness to reality. Now what is nearness to reality? Not physical contact. The agent of the Reserve Bank is sitting over all the moneys in the Reserve Bank. But he cannot take for himself even a single rupee. So nearness does not mean physical distance. It is the nearness to your own reality to yourself. The Bhagwad Gita says, 'Your own self is your friend and your own self is also your enemy'. Now this raises the question again, 'What is reality, the self?' You can see and put your hand out and touch the wall. The wall is a reality. What appears as wall is not the reality of the wall. You will see packs of atom through the microscope! Even so, there are many layers of the 'self'. In dream you are far away from your 'self'. In waking condition you are nearer to your 'self'. Besides the waking and dream consciousness there are many other layers of consciousness and it is God's kindness that of the other layers we are blessed in their ignorance. Restlessness, unhappiness, insecurity, etc. are due to the various layers being at variance with the waking consciousness. The waking consciousness summons you in dream. And so also dream consciousness summons the waking consciousness and causes the world of dreams. When your personality, that is, the 'self' is described as having seven or fourteen layers, it only means that you are still on the path to the destination, 'the self'. And if all these layers were our experiences like the dream and waking consciousness, then we would be in a far worse position than the merely waking consciousness being at variance with the dream-consciousness. God in His kindness keeps us in ignorance of the other layers. Once the destination—the self—is reached there is rest and peace. Nearness to reality is therefore nearness to your own self. What greater thing can be given to you than that of the use of your own self ? Jesus says, what if you gain the whole world and have lost your soul? So we have to say that the worth of a man is not his wealth but his nearness to his self or the nearness to reality.

Q.: I experience pain during Pranayama. Why?

Sw. K.: You are holding the breath for too long and hence the pain. Hold it for 1/4 of a minute only. If you hold it for a longer time you will get headache. Also, this holding the breath is not necessary. Deep breathing in and out is quite enough.

Visitor: What was *karmaphaltyagam*. I cannot understand it.

Sw. K.: Imagine you are a farmer. You plough the field, manure it, sow the seed, and fence it around. This is the maximum you can do. You cannot push up the sprout. Your thinking on it is of no use and your wanting and concern that it must come out is of no use. From now on it is not your concern—not in your hands. There are many factors which have to come into action for the seed to sprout. Lack of rain, onset of pests, hails, etc. are out of your control, but the sprout is dependent on these factors also. The Bhagavad Gita says that the fruit of your action is not determined by your action and intention alone. The Third Chapter of the Bhagavad Gita answers this question. There are various factors that are co-related to your action and motive which also are responsible for the fruit of your action. First, you as the agent, secondly, your intention in doing that action (and this intention may be different from your action) third, the capacity of your sense organ through which you have acted; fourth, the various motives connected with your present motive (when, for instance, you send the boy to the school because everybody does so, sending him to the school is not your ultimate motive; you send him to school to enable him later to earn his livelihood and from his learning you want him to be able to earn that much as is necessary for maintaining your standard of living which is dependent on this and that and a hundred related factors.) Finally, the fruit of your action is dependent on the ultimate factor of the action being in harmony with the will of the Absolute. If your action is in harmony with that will, you get the fruit of your action. If it is in disharmony, you can't get the fruit. Hence it is not wise to think that the fruit should follow from your action as a matter of course. It is wisdom to be content to do what you can do and leave the rest to God. Action is the result of an impulsion to achieve something—you never act just for the sake of doing something. In the ultimate analysis, you are made to take action as per the purpose of the universe itself. It is for this reason that if you don't harmonise your actions with the will of this Absolute, you cannot succeed. And you cannot understand the Supreme Will. Your conscience is a great judge in this matter of whether your action is in harmony or disharmony with the universal will. Even a thief knows that he is not doing a good action in thieving; it is other factors that are brought to justify it. Harming others in the process of your action cannot be in harmony with the Supreme Will. Secondly, what you do in harmony with the will of God cannot harm anyone—for God does not harm A to bless B. So answer to yourself whether in an act, you have harmed anyone else. This is Buddhi Yoga or Yoga of correct understanding. This lack of understanding is what Chapter II of the Bhagavad Gita deals with. It is because Arjuna does not understand what is right and what is wrong, what the will of the supreme is, that he is depressed and confused and bereft of correct understanding. Chapter III of the Bhagavad Gita answers this question of what is harmful, what is correct action, etc. The point is that you as an individual are not a separate entity. You are the universe—one with it. The five elements, *viz.*, earth, air, water, fire, and space, are in your body, in you as well as in the world. It is the same five elements present in all these and hence your harmony with these is a law with which you cannot take privileges. Your own individual personality acts. But your action loses its meaning as an isolated fact in the understanding that you and the universe are one.

And yet you must act because you are a part of and within the universe itself. Your hand is like the world. It is outside your body but is yourself when the hand does something.

It is you who are acting, not the hand as such. That the world is external to your personality is the wrong understanding as in this example—when the hand holds on to something to prevent your falling; it is a spontaneous action of the hand without harming anyone else in the process of its action. And this spontaneous action arising out of the whole universe acting simultaneously is as much a part of you as you are part of the whole universe; this becomes Karma Yoga. It is like the whole body of yours co-operating in the lifting of your hand. Hence there is no question of there being a fruit of an action. Because the 'agent' of the action does not exist, it is not an action outside you. It is like the waves out of the ocean; the waves are the action of the ocean, you may say. But they rise on the ocean itself, not outside it. The wave has no individuality; it is the ocean in action, and when it subsides it becomes indistinguishably one with the ocean. Until you reach this universal consciousness, by your acts, you share your pleasure with others. This sharing is a cosmic tendency, a universal urge, to share pleasure or joy. This is Jesus's meaning when he says, "What you do secretly is rewarded publicly."

Namaskar. Thank you for a nice satsang—

S.D.: Swamiji is to be thanked! not us!

Sw. K.: No, it is you all also that go to make the satsang.

S.D.: Thank you for your faith in us Swamiji in that we have been Arjun:

Sw. K.: (Laughs and repeats) 'Namaskar'.

* * *

Visitor: Is there a place for the police and the military in the scheme of life?

Sw. K.: Shri Aurobindo was asked for a message on his death-bed, and his reply was: 'Mankind is not fit (ready) to receive the message', and he did not give any message. Man needs the police and the military, because he is afraid of the man next to him. There is no confidence in the intentions of a neighbour who appears friendly but may have a knife under his arm. So we have the United Nations. We say we want peace but pile up arms. Even a brother dees not trust a brother. How, then, can man reach God? It is all an empty cover posted without contents!

Q.: What is the 'Direct Path'?

Sw. K.: It is Tantra based on Buddhism in Nepal. It is also known as the 'Sword's Path'. They leave the lower stages and go direct to meditation. This is dangerous. But even now it exists all over India—this Tantric practice.

(*A youngster, a medical student from Gwalior, greets Swamiji. He wishes to give up his studies and take to spiritual life*).

Sw. K.: You should first stand on your feet as far as your studies and the world are concerned. You should also seek your father's advice. What you do should be superior to what you reject.

Student: I have been sincerely practising the spiritual path all along; hence I can now fully devote myself to spiritual life.

Sw. K.: You can be a spiritual seeker through your medical profession.

Q.: Why does the mind wander so much when we try to meditate or repeat the hymns and mantras?

Sw. K.: Because, there is no will to think or take in more than what it is choosing to at a given moment. So the words remain mere words. You must keep insisting on, and hammering in, the thought you wish to understand—insist that you wish to get into the words. The understanding of a thought comes by repeated, continued and exclusive practice of the mind in one single thought which is a very different type of thought from the worldly one of social relationship. But in your efforts you wish to turn it to other worldly pattern of thinking. This is not easy. There should be consistency in thinking. Thinking that the world is real will not stop you from getting to the Ultimate Reality. The shadow must have, and it does have some substance behind it to form the shadow. What is misleading is to separate it from the shadow. What is misleading and can be erroneous is thinking simultaneously that there is Reality and un-reality, of the world. Hammering on a thought will ultimately reveal the Truth. Staying in the Gurukul Ashrama of the ancient days had its great significance. Staying for years with and in the service of the Guru helped in training the mind to eliminate irrelevant thoughts. And then entering into the world into Grihasthasrama did not become an obstacle in the thinking process in the right and helpful manner for the understanding of great truths. Unfortunately, modern education fails to develop this in the students. The atmosphere in which one thinks and its suitability influence one's thinking. The Upanishads present the greatest truths. Other scriptures only repeat their statements, but do not impart any higher truths—no more transcendent.

Ajai: How should we contemplate God?

Sw. K.: Those who are harassed by bondage contemplate God as Infinity. People who are grief-stricken contemplate God as Bliss; they think that He is Bliss, He is Happiness. See? Swami Vivekananda said, "In the garden of Eden of Allah there are rivers flowing everywhere and trees and brooks surround you everywhere. This is Arabian Paradise, full of water flowing around and cooked hen running around! But my country (Bengal) is so full of water, with Ganga and all her tributaries that it is all full of marshes. And, my paradise will be without water! Not the Arabian Paradise!" [*Laughs and all join in with their laughter.*] If Bengal was described as paradise to the Eskimos, it will be hell to them! [*Laughter all around and Swamiji still in the grip of laughter.*] Arabia has no water and its paradise is full of water, and Vivekananda whose home was in the wet lands of Calcutta, says: My paradise will be dry land without water! [*more seriously*] —Whatever we lack is found in God. God is the Bank, a treasure-house where you can find whatever you lack. God is like a statue you can find in a block of stone. Whatever form you want, you can get out of the block of stone; you can carve the stone as you want to. But God is not a statue or any such thing. He is just PURE BEING. Every statue is inside the stone, implicit in it. Even so, you can get anything from this Pure Being: grief, joy, power, infinitude, spacelessness, timelessness—whatever you want. God is an Omnibus, a 'hold-all'.

[*Turning to a Tamilian Swamiji speaks in Tamil*] Yes! Tell me what Seva Vidura meant while telling Dharmaputra about the danger of living in that lac-house and all the bare facts of it. But he could not tell him so openly. So he spoke in a strange language which, according to the Mahabharata, was known as *Mlecha-Bhasha.* I am talking to you in a language only you and I understand. See!

S.D.: *Mlecha*? That word means something —well, like "untouchable"?

Sw. K.: It is not an English word; it is a Sanskrit word. It is a pecular jargon the book records—you can't understand what it is.

Sw. Krishnapriya: Was it Pali?

Sw. K.: No, No. Nobody can understand what it is, some "Ka Ke Ku Ku Kech picha puch Ka...." It reads like that. The meaning is given as a footnote in the book, the original Mahabharata in Sanskrit. Then you understand the *Mlecha Bhasha* Vidura spoke, and only Yudhisthira understood it. "Oh, yes, yes I understand what you said", says Yudhisthira, "Gurudev too uses to speak like that". He would say (in Tamil) "Give 5 Ravanas—5 Ravanas". No one will understand what this Ravana means—or he will say (in Tamil) O! give a Pandava to him! [*Laughs.*] In the presence of all he did not openly say what amount of gift in cash was given to the individual. No one knows what "Ravana" is or 5 Ravanas? [*Laughs.*] Sometime he said 'Kauravas'. [*Laughs louder and louder.*] It means one hundred rupees ! Well *Kartaviryarjuna* would mean one thousand rupees, because he had thousand hands ! But Gurudev did not use such words ! Only 'Ravana' [*bubbles with laughter*] and Pandavas. Only those who had the bag (of cash) accompanying Gurudev will understand it. It was a code-word. Pandavas were five in number, so one Pandava was Rs. 5. See? And Ravana had ten heads, so one Ravana = Rs. 10.

S. D.: So the codeword is *Mlecha* in Sanskrit?

Sw. K.: An unintelligible language is called *Mlecha.*

S.D.: So it is a code?

Sw. K.: But here *Mlecha* means anything non-Sanskrit. Any language which is non-Sanskrit is *Mlecha.*

S.D.: Yes. So, they later distorted meaning is 'foreign' (word).

Sw. K.: Yes, Yes. You can say that.

Q.: Is instinct greater than reason?

Sw. K.: Yes, there is a point in it. The dog follows you even if you kick it, because its instinct tells it that it will get food by following you. (*Laughs*).

S.D.: Why can't it be argued that it is the lack of the capacity for reasoning that the dog does not understand the meaning of a kick?

Sw. K.: Reason is a very dangerous weapon. Reason is a bondage which has made you fall into the hell of social life. The dogs are happy without this trouble. What is the use of that reason which tells you wrong things ? That you must punish somebody, wreak vengeance on somebody. You call this really good? Whereas the dog does not think like that! Even the monkey does not remember that you threw a stone at it yesterday.

S.D.: At least I will know by reason that I should keep away from the person who will kick me but the dog does not.

Sw. K.: Reason is like double edge sword. It will tell you it is doing a wrong thing, and yet also remember some evil done to you once long before. Forever you will remember this evil only. The evil is interred with your bones. You can never remember the good that is done to you. If I do a hundred good things and one wrong thing which you do not like you will remember only the wrong or the bad thing and the hundred good things are washed down the drain. Whereas, the dogs do not behave like that. One day you give it a little bread and it will come behind you wagging its tail (imitates the wagging of the tail and the tongue out) and follow you even if you kick it.

Someone: Why does reason react as you say?

Sw. K.: Because to some extent the intellect takes you away from reality. It is a virtue also because it can tell you what the truth is.

Q.: Does the intellect act like that all the time?

Sw. K.: No! Not all the time. Sometimes. When reason gets mixed up with emotion, it takes you in the wrong direction. But it stands independently—when it will tell you that it is also doing a mistake. The reason has other aspects also, that it can find out its own limitations. But sometimes it asserts its Absoluteness—when it goes with sentiment, feelings etc. By reason, you know that you must love all children in the same way you love your own children. But emotion says my children are better. The emotions speak and says, 'my children are dearer to me than the other children', while reason tells you, no, it is not a proper attitude, all children are equally good. So there is a mixture of reason and emotion in certain attitudes.

Q.: Are reason and intellect the same thing?

Sw. K.: Well, yes. Yet reason is the higher, it is the power of the intellect like the electricity that is working through the bulb. The electricity is the power force and that is what reason is. The bulb is the intellect which is the vehicle.

Q.: Is self-affirmation wrong?

Sw. K.: When you make a statement by way of judgement, it is not that you speak a merely grammatical sentence with just a subject, predicate, and an object without any connotation behind it. So we should never make an affirmation beyond our capacity of comprehension at the present level of our experience. While affirmations are, therefore, good as far as they go, the only thing you must see is whether they are fit for us to make them in the given context.

19 December

[The morning *satsang* begins with just 4-5 persons, later this number grows to about 10. Among today's visitors is a couple—a handicapped blind—professor Surendra Kumar Tripathi and his sighted wife who is also a professor.]

A Visitor: May I be permitted to work in the Sivananda Library, especially be permitted to use the volumes of Encyclopaedia Britannica? I plan to write a comparative study of the deities in the various religions and discover the parallels and, thus, the universality of religions.

Sw. K.: No, there are no parallels. For, there is no such thing as Hanuman, for instance, in other religions. You must meet the best authorities on Christianity, Zoroastrianism, Islam, Buddhism and so on. From books you can't get a correct idea of these matters. What is Britannica ? How can the British give you all you seek ? It is a short indication, that is all. You may now work with those volumes. I will tell you the people you should meet and gather knowledge from various religious authorities. I am not sure of who it could be in Islam. However, we shall see.

Sw. K.: [*turning to the semi-blind visitor, Surendra Kumar Tripathi*]. Are you a musician ? Do you teach music?

S.K.T.: No, Swamiji, I teach philosophy, history of philosophy. The books I base my lectures on—the texts—are:

(1) *Indian Philosophy*, Two Vols: by Dr. Radhakrishnan.

(2) *Introduction to Indian Philosophy* by Datta and Chatterjee.

(3) *Outlines of Indian Philosophy* by M. Hiriyanna.

Sw. K.: I have read all these books. There is also Indian Philosophy by J.N. Sinha of which two volumes have already appeared and a few more are in preparation. They are large volumes. These authors are prolific. I envy them. What did you say your name is?

S.K.T.: Surendra Kumar Tripathi.

Sw. K.: Oh ! Tripathi—you are the learner of the three Vedas! That is what your name means.

S.K.T.: No, Swamiji, I don't know any of the Vedas. How can I become true to my name? I would like to.

Sw. K.: By quality and actions, by the study of the three Vedas, by imbibing the qualities of a true learner of the Vedas. There was a great scholar named Damodar Satavalekar. He was learned in all the Vedas. He lived for one hundred and one years. He has translated all the Vedas most admirably in Hindi. Bhagyalakshmi Mataji, these books are in our library. When Damodar Satavalekar reached the centenary year Swami Chidanandaji sent him his greetings and a purse of rupees one hundred.

S.D.: He lived as recently as that?

Sw. K.: Yes, it is hardly fifteen, or may be about ten years since he passed away. A tremendously learned man. What profound learning ! [*Turning to Srimati Chhaya, wife of Surendra Kumar Tripathi.*] What are you doing mataji?

Chhayaji: Teaching Sanskrit.

Sw. K.: What is the text you follow?

Ch: The method of learning? "Laghu Siddhanta Koumudi".

Sw. K.: That is an old method—very difficult to learn—you can't understand anything and you have to go on learning by heart what you can't understand! But there is a modern method. It is better to teach by that method. Damodar Satavalekar has written 24 volumes. They are small volumes. And it is easy to follow them. He is a great scholar in Sanskrit also and has written on all the eight forms of the Vedas. He has written on everyone of these: (1) Jata (2) Maalaa (3) Sikha (4) Rekha (5) Dhwaja (6) Danda (7) Rathaa and (8) Ghana. Ghana is the most difficult. He has also translated all the volumes of the Valmiki Ramayana in Hindi.

S.K.T.: Swamiji, what are these eight types of the Vedas? Are they to be graded from the lower to the higher?

Sw. K.: No. These are only the eight ways of chanting the Vedas [*repeats the names.*]

Ghana is the most difficult to recite. These eight ways just bore into your brains and won't leave. You can't forget the Vedas if you learn them this way. It is the old method of teaching the Vedas orally. Even if your mind wants to you can't forget them. They just go on rumbling and rattling in your head and it becomes impossible to forget them ever ! [*turning to an American Christian, also a visitor to the Ashram.*] In how many ways do you recite the Bible? Do you know how to recite the Bible? Have you read the Bible?

American Vis.: I used to sing some songs when I was young.

S.K.T.: Swamiji, I want some time with you in private; only ten minutes or so.

Sw. K.: I don't have any private time. Tell me now what you want to say. Yes?

S.K.T.: Please initiate me in meditation.

Sw. K.: Have you been meditating?

S.K.T.: No.

Sw. K.: Then why do you want to do so now ? Curiosity?

S.K.T.: No. I am coming here for the third time and at first I was not interested in these matters. Now I want to learn to meditate. Please initiate me with some mantras.

Sw. K.: Mantras can't be given just like that. Tell me first of all what benefit you wish to get out of such meditation. What is your desire ? Which God form are you fond of?

S.K.T.: I have no desire, Swamiji. I do not believe in Saguna forms of God. I believe only in the Absolute.

Sw. K.: What objection do you have to Saguna forms of God? Why don't you want them ? What harm have they done to you?

S.K.T.: The Saguna froms are all man-made. So I believe only in the Absolute.

Sw. K.: Describe the Absolute to me,—let's have your own idea.

S.K.T.: The Absolute has no qualities.

Sw. K.: You have already given an attribute to the Absolute. Unless you have some qualities in mind, how can you say the Absolute has no qualities? Where is the Absolute then?

S.K.T.: In my heart and all over.

Sw. K.: So again you are giving a definition of the Absolute. The Absolute is not a negation of all qualities. The Absolute is inclusive of all qualities and that is why It is without any special qualities. Tell me, of all things in the world what is it that you like most?

S.K.T.: I have no particular predilections. I have no desire.

Sw. K.: Then why do you want to do something? To learn how to meditate? There is something that is making you want to do this. What is that?

S.K.T.: There is no desire, Swamiji: I want to--

Sw. K.: Unless there is desire, there cannot be any urge to take action. You don't know what your desire is. And Saguna forms of God are as effective as the Absolute in leading you to your goal of life. Now you are a musician, a professor, and you find joy in these and the like. What is that thing of which you are extremely fond?

S.K.T.: *Ragas*—more than other types of music.

Sw. K.: Many saints have reached *moksha* by singing the *Ragas* to their Saguna God forms. It is a very effective way of being in communion with God of the Saguna form. Tell me—don't think I am putting you off. I hope you understand me.

S.K.T.: Yes, Swamiji.

Sw. K.: Tell me, whom among the members of your family do you love most ? Your wife ? Your......?

S.K.T.: My mother.

Sw. K.: [*turning to his very worthy wife Chhaya*]: See! He is creating a quarrel between the mother-in-law and the daughter-in-law ! In the presence of your wife you have said you love your mother most ! Well, you say the Absolute is in your heart. Meditate on whatever seems to you to be the Absolute, even as you perceive it in your heart, and when you come again, we shall have more chat about this.

* * *

[Another professor from Iran is on a year's leave and plans to spend three months in Yoga Niketan for learning asanas, meditation and other Yogas. He wants to be away from his country because of political unrest there. There are no signs as to when and how this position will clear up. Meanwhile he wants quiet and peaceful relaxation.]

Sw. K.: How does the political unrest affect you in a personal way ? You are a Muslim, you follow Islam don't you ? Is it fanaticism that disturbs you ? What upsets you there ? Why do you seek peace away from your country?

Ir. Prof.: I shall give a small example of how the political situation affects me personally like evrybody else in modern times. I had long hair, but they forced me to cut it short like this.

Sw. K.: What does it matter ? Why should long or short hair be a matter of such concern to you?

Ir. Prof.: It is not the hair, but the fact of being forced to do something which is not what I wish to do. This compulsion is disturbing.

Sw. K.: In your country there was a king who had written on the ring he was wearing thus, "This too shall pass away." Do you know that poet ? The king?

Ir. Prof.: What was the name of the king Swamiji?

Sw. K.: It is your ancient king. You do not know your own ancient history ? Do you come from Persia ? Why do you now call it Iran?

Ir. Prof.: Persia is only a part of Iran, and like the word Aryan in your country it means the same—a derivative. So the whole of the land is now called Iran, and not just Persia.

Sw. K.: Well, as your king said, "This too will pass away," all this unrest and its disturbing effects on your personality will also be over. So be happy.

Ir. Prof.: Thank you, Swamiji. I am happy.

Sw. K.: Are you writing something ? You are a great man, very learned. Why don't you write something ?

Ir. Prof.: The mind is not calm enough for such work. I need first peace of mind. Only then I shall be able to do something.

Sw. K.: Yes. God bless you. Be there where you can be happy.

An American explained to Swamiji that he felt confused because he saw visibly with his eyes lots of suffering in the world. At the same time, he also felt that one should turn inwards and contemplate on the spiritual aspect of human existence. What should one do ? Turn inward or turn outward and relieve suffering ?

Sw. K.: You are seeing neither side fully—50% that side and 50% this side; both together are making the confusion in your mind worse confounded. The conflict is between what you see and what you have not seen. Why see only one side ? What is meditation ? In meditation you are thinking something not seen with your eyes. When you are doing work you see the world. There is, therefore, a double devotion to both the world and the abstract object of meditation. Hence, there is confusion and doubt arises as to which one should follow. What you see with your eyes is what is real to your mind, and what you have heard from others also seems real to you, and you keep thinking of what you have heard. Your sentiment makes you see the world, and your faith in the person who tells you that there is something unseen which is real, is the other factor which makes you think of it, because it is different from your sentiment. It requires profound study and learning and a protracted period of training in the correct way of thinking if the confusion is to be got over. What you see with your eyes is not real and cannot therefore affect you. But you erroneously think that it is real. In other words, you behave according to what the eyes tell you. But the eye that has cataract gives wrong visions. One needs special glasses to see things correctly. You have to find the proper guide who will help you to see things and think about them correctly in due course. Even this idea that you have confusion has come to you only now, after you started to think on these lines. So, everything will come in its own time. You say you are twenty years old and all these twenty years these doubts did not come to your mind. But now, because you are in the proper atmosphere, the idea has surfaced in your thinking. Similarly, the proper guide will appear in time and guide you as to how you should think and act.

Mr. Chakravarthy, a visitor to the Ashram, has been staying for some time here. He had the strange experience of escaping unhurt when the bus to Badrinath in which he was travelling rolled down the khud eighteen times, and yet none in the bus was hurt. This experience had made him conclude that God wanted him to dedicate himself to spiritual life and not to go back to the mundane world. Swamiji had been reasoning with him saying that such decisions should not be taken in a hurry. But Mr. Chakravarthy has been adamant and is now a member of the Ashram. He had a doubt about the right way of meditation.

Vis.: First, the small light appears and stays for some time. Then the second light appears on the other side. Why is this ? I do not know. Which is the light I should concentrate upon.

Sw. K.: Who asked you to meditate on light? Your problem is that there is no proper philosophical background for your practice. Your mind should be satisfied with the technique you perform. Otherwise, you cannot answer the questions that come up in your mind. Doubts will come from the very start of your practice. It will even put the question, why do you want God ? Every question of the mind must be answered satisfactorily. The horse must know where you are driving it.

Ch.: I want God. So I am asking my mind to meditate.

Sw. K.: You are not wanting God for the sake of happiness and the mind craves for something which it likes and which will make it happy. So it must be explained to the mind that wanting God means wanting happiness. This is the philosophical point. Your whole idea of meditation is a hotch-potch. Therefore, you are having troubles of all sorts. Wanting God, happiness, knowing what is meditation, and how to achieve success in it—all these require a scientific approach. You cannot simply sit and cry aloud, I want a house. Mere sentiment or emotional spurts will not take you anywhere. You are a very important man ! God is a poor man ! And God is unimportant (*laughs*). God is Ashutosh which means a simpleton, that is, He is quickly pleased by those who approach Him in utter simplicity of heart.

[Two visitors, tourists from Germany, a couple—wife a sociologist, husband, a scientist—want to learn Yoga. They have been to Ladakh.]

Sw. K.: Yoga begins where Philosophy ends. From the social, geographical, geological and astronomical level, you go to the biological level and from there to the psychological level and again thence to the rational level. You cannot go further, because your capacity is only rational. It is only intellectual and hence you cannot go further. So all philosophies generally stop at the intellectual analysis and rational conclusions. But we are not merely reasoning individuals. We have a status of our own—we have an individuality and an existence of our own. You are not merely a function, but an existence as well. Intellectuality is a function; rationality is an activity of a status or faculty. What is in you ? Can you say that you are merely a function or a process ? or a faculty ? (looking at a visitor) You are Mr. Chatterjee. Can you say Chatterjee is only a name for a function. It will be a very poor definition of yourself and something below your dignity. You are not a function, you are a status of your own. People always assert their status. When you assert this status, it is a unique indivisible existence of the barest minimum of the totality of your personality. And this barest minimum is part of the universe. The universe is not merely a function—physical, astronomical, psychological, intellectual, etc. It is a pure existence by itself. These are levels of understanding of the universe. So, on the basis of this understanding of the structure of the universe, you may have to prepare the syllabus of your study of Yoga. And you are to study the lower level first and the higher level afterwards. When you go to school, they teach you only what is visible to your eyes; they own't tell you what is invisible. In the KG class or in the First Standard they tell you a little bit of the nature of your neighbourhood and the people around you to arouse your civic consciousness, and then a little bit of the administration of the country, then a little bit of the geography of the land, and so on. It takes a lot of time to take you further up beyond the earth to the solar system, etc. which will not be taught in the elementary schools; the mathematical or the astronomical geography is never taught in the earliest stages; they are taught much later because, if you suddenly start pouring into the young students' ears facts about the solar system, physics and such things as the atomic structure, these will be horrible things for their shallow minds. And these matters won't enter their minds at all. But the mind can and does grasp things by stages. Gradually, in due course everything is taken up and finally you envelop the entire physical cosmos with your mind. This is the conclusion of physical study. Then as I said you go to the biological, psychological, rational study, finally you go to the pure existence. That you must consider is the spiritual study. That is reached in a very advanced condition, but they are all layers of personality in the cosmic structure. So in the beginning you have to be acquainted with your political relationship, your social relationship and then with your personal relationship to the family, the community and the nation. Then comes your physical structure, then the nature of the relationship of this structure to the physical universe, then the higher studies of life, of the mind and reason; and finally of the spirit. I am giving an idea as to how the study has to be conducted, stage by stage, without hurrying or jumping suddenly to the highest reaches like Samadhi and all such which some people talk of as if it was the second or third lesson of life. Nonsense—nothing will enter the head. You talk of Samadhi, but you don't know what it is. It is only a word—a mere word, and in reality it has no sense for you. How can sense come when you are still at the lower level, when you have not reached the stage when the mind cannot understand the implications of all this? So finally a fear catches hold of you in the end with all your studies. If I enter Samadhi or God's body, what will happen to me afterwards ? What is my future afterwards ? You don't know anything, only there is a terrible fear. This doubt will persist till the end even if you see God face to face.—O.K. Let us say you are seeing Him, a terrible thing in front of you. Afterwards ? What will happen to you ? How long can you keep looking at Him ? You don't know anything, you will be tired of seeing him (*laughs*)—Many people have told me, suppose I see God, how long can I go on seeing him ? I will be tired, I will get up and go away [*laughs*], I will be fed up, I want some work ! [*Laughs loud and long.*] After seeing him you want some work (*chuckles*).

They don't understand that God means a stage of awareness. After reaching that stage, what will happen to me ? That is the fear. And this 'what-will-happen-to-me' will not leave you till the end. Such doubts will never leave you. Sometimes these fears are childish. A disciple was once told by a great Rishi that when you go to heaven you will not have hunger. "Then, I don't want to go there ! It is very bad not to have hunger and thirst !" No appetite ! No sleep! these are all tedious conditions. [*Chuckles heard from the gathering.*] Would you like that condition ? It is a state of sickness [*chuckles and laughs*] ! these doubts arise because you are still very immature. We are but children in our thinking. Physically grown up, yes, but mentally very immature. We cannot understand the cosmic reality. Even doubts which you may not have imagined in your mind come in at the end. What stage have I reached ? You cannot understand. Where am I ? I have practised Sadhana, studies and meditation and still I cannot make out where I am ! Let us say, you find this. This is still a stage of a state of doubt only, and in the end you cannot see any relationship between the world and God. Even learned people have this doubt. What happens to the world when I see God ? Your family and all these things are here. When I suddenly soar up into the empire of God all my children are seen crying ! You wonder what happens. There is another unfortunate thing. You seem to be in a state of anaesthesia. Would you like anaesthesia? What will happen?

Dr. R.: They seem to be quite happy!

Sw. K.: You are happy because you know nothing about happiness. But if you are aware of it, you are frightened of it!

R. Sivdasani.: But why has he made it all so difficult?

Sw. K.: Since you have woken up from sleep you are frightened. They, the world-ridden, are still sleeping. A sleeping man has no doubts; when a man is awakened he is frightened about everything. So the best thing is to sleep, is it not? No loss, no worry, no fright!

S.D.: That also He does not allow to sleep and sleep.

Sw. K.: Because eternal sleep is not allowed. It has to be intermittent. Even the atom does not sleep eternally—it wakes up because of the urge to evolve.

The more the knowledge the more the suffering. So it is better to have no knowledge. Is it not?

S.D.: A devil in the knowing..

Sw. K.: A bird in hand is worth two in the bush, eh? They say knowledge is bliss. But here knowledge is sorrow [*laughs.*] Suppose you have no knowledge that you have lost something—you are happy. When you know of your loss, the knowledge leads to sorrow. Thus knowledge can also be sorrow. Is it not? [*laughs.*]

R.S.D.: Why has He gems on Him? Decorations?

Sw. K.: No, He has not put on anything—you are unnecessarily blaming someone who does not exist.

R.S.D.: Why have I put on something?

Sw. K.: You have put it on because you want it. One does not do anything that one does not want.

R.S.D.: It was silly of anyone to want it.

Sw. K.: Now you mean it is silly? At that time you wanted it and you were very wise ! Afterwards you felt that you were foolish ! Many people, even great people, have this doubt—What is better ? To have God or the World?

R.S.D.: Both.

Sw. K.: No, you cannot say both—you see a man sitting there and you see only the man, not God; man works for man only. He is not aware of the ant or the frog.

S.D.: Yes, I am aware, Swamiji. I see everything, I see the frog and the ant, the world and the monkeys before me.

Sw. K.: Yes, as a nuisance. The monkey is looking at you as a nuisance. It is looking only for the monkeys; frogs work for frogs only, ants for ants. You are thinking of human beings as much more worthy. When a man says, I work for the world, he does not obviously think of the frog or the ant—he is working for man only.

S.D.: Working for the World also includes working for ants?

Sw. K.: No, you aren't concerned about ants—destroy them and you would not bother; what's the use ? Your sentiment will tell you that there is a great use for man's values only. My brother is greater than my father. This is the only way man can think. Man can think only as man, he cannot think like a tree—what can he do?

Dr. R.: How then to work for God, Swamiji?

Sw. K.: [*laughs*]. You cannot work for God. You have a fear that He will leave you in the lurch in the end. He is unseen and we do not know what kind of a person He is, so it would be better to leave Him alone. Don't go near Him---He is an unrealistic person ! Humanity is near: you know what it is. It is better to work for human beings. God is an unknown thing ! To work for an unknown thing is dangerous ! A reliable man (humanity) is better than the unreliable man i.e., God (*laughs*.)

S.D.: Yanjyavalkya says: All love is self-love. Which self? The *atman*?

Sw. K.: That is also a part of that. There are so many selves—political, sociological, social, psychological, rational, physical, vital and mental.

S.D.: It is all myself only—the *jiva's* self?

Sw. K.: They are not the *jiva's*. They are higher than the *jivas*; you cannot call the inner self a *jiva*—but it is self nevertheless. They are all real selves. There are many layers of the self. And he refers to every layer of the self. A universal statement is what he is making. Even the utmost selfishness you have is the urge of that universal self. It passes through, pressed through the body, and so becomes selfish—selfish, because limited to the body. But the force comes from the universal only, ultimately. Other than the Self nothing exists in the universe. But there are degrees of the self.

S.D.: But are you speaking of that highest self only?

Sw. K.: All self. Any self. Anything—

S.D.: It is not love of the self, it is love for the self?

Sw. K.: They mean the same thing. When the self is the only reality for you, then what also can you love ? You can say 'of' or 'for' or 'by' or anything. You love anything because it is in consonance with the structure of your self. So ultimately it means you are loving yourself only. It follows that if something is not in consonance with you, you don't love it.

S.D.: But suddenly it falls into the pit of selfishness?

Sw. K.: That is it. It is selfish—your love is only selfish—ultimately you are loving yourself only. Even the highest love is selfish, until it is merged into the Absolute. Then the 'self' goes. There is no question of selfishness—because love for an object outside it is selfishness. And since the Absolute is not an object, there the self ceases to exist. Every objective level is selfish, unless and until that thing is in consonance with the nature of your self. If an objective is disharmonious, you cannot love it. So you are loving yourself only; it is your self only that you are loving. It follows by logic that you cannot love anything except yourself. Otherwise you will love even an enemy and there would be no such thing as enemy at all. Only that which threatens your very existence cannot be loved because it is disharmonious with yourself.

S.D.: And it is not easy to distinguish it and understand it, as different from selfish love.

Sw. K.: It is difficult to understand it, because it is a deep psychological subject. We are like hypnotised persons. A person who is hypnotised cannot know that he is working under the pressure of some other will. The moment he knows that, he ceases to be hypnotised. But as long as he is under the spell of that influence, he thinks he is acting of his own will. When you hypnotise a patient and ask him, 'Why are you walking this way?' he will give some reason. But the reason is only a concocted reason: he is pressurised from within by some urge of which he has no knowledge—do you know that you are walking on earth because of the pull of the gravitation? But you say, who is pulling me, I walk of my own will. It is not due to your will. If the gravitational force were not there, you will fly in the air. Like this [*imitates flying.*] So it is not true that you have even the freedom to walk—where is your freedom? See! You don't know even this little pressure somebody puts on you. They say that if the sun didn't exert its upward pull, you will be stuck to the ground so much that you cannot even move! And if the earth did not pull you down you would be flying in the air ! So the two forces are pulling in such a proportionate way that you are walking smoothly on the earth. And nobody is aware that such is the fact. You think you are free and go walking, swinging your arms as though you were the master of it all. But it is these two other masters who are controlling you!

"There are more things in heaven and earth than your philosophy dreams of," says Shakespeare. All our philosophy is a husk compared to these mysteries. And if we think of it, it will crack our heads. They say that there are rays called cosmic rays which will melt even the earth if it penetrates deep enough—and that the whole universe is made up of the condensed form of this ray!

It is light rays themselves that have condensed into matter we call the universe, and it is also your bcdy. You are part of the nuclear dust ! You see ? All these are tremendous and frightening truths which will simply take us out of our wits. You cannot exist at all without the operation of these forces because they hold your personality like the thread constituting the cloth. You pull out the threads, the cloth also goes. So is this. So all these forces constitute the universe. And if they are withdrawn, the whole universe will vanish into thin air and disappear.

S.D.: Is this the final dissolution?

Sw. K.: Yes. But they won't withdraw because of the assertion of your personal ego, your individuality. One day they will withdraw and that is when liberation takes place. At that time all the forces are withdrawn into their sources. They say that the power of seeing goes to the Sun, the power of hearing to the 'Dikh Devatas', the power of ego to Rudra, the power of Chitta to Vishnu, the power of the body to the earth and the power of water principle to water. Everything goes to its original source. And you cease to be any more and become the cosmos. That is called freedom, liberation. But that cannot take place as long as you are in the physical body. Since there is great pleasure in this body, we don't want to get out of it! And that dismantling of this body, the warp and woof of the body will not take place in hundreds of births unless you will it and wish it here and now. It is like a house you have built and the entire structure has to be thrown down and the effect has to go to the cause. It is not so simple (*laughs.*) You cannot do a few asanas and reach God. Asanas are good but they are not sufficient for the purpose on hand (*laughs.*) God is not satisfied easily like that (*laughs.*) I cannot satisfy you unless I understand what you are made of. Even so, unless you understand Him, you cannot please Him. If I know your psychology, only then you are in my pocket. So is the case with God. Unless you know what He is made of, you cannot approach Him and satisfy Him. You may offer Him a banana, a little sugar candy in the form of asanas, austerities, etc. You cannot please Him so easily like that. He does not want bananas, because he is not made of bananas (*all laugh. So does Swamiji*). It is like a baby trying to satisfy you, eh ? It puts a toy on your head for your headache. You laugh and say let it go! [*Laughs loudly.*] After all, it is a child, and even if it has no meaning, it shows love.

Sometimes the sun is worshipped by waving the camphor light to it—as if he is going to be illuminated. But your feeling in the act is appreciated.

S.D.: It is not to illuminate it, Swamiji. It is to pray that he burns up......

Sw. K.: No, no. you are not thinking of all that, you are showing some affec'ion or fear through that act—not that you think of illuminating the sun. Sometimes when a guest comes you offer him a cup of tea—it does not mean that he wants it. You show your concern for him—your gesture is appreciated. God also knows that it is out of your simplicity that you do so. That is why Lord Krishna says, even a leaf is enough. He does not mean leaf, but your sentiment is understood. His meaning is you have got love for me, I understand it, and you are expressing it with a leaf. Not that I want a leaf. But in your mind there is love for me.

Sw. Nirmalanand: Just as we offer laddus for Guru Dev at Samadhi Mandir.

Sw. K.: Yes! Yes!

Vis.: When we start loving spiritual life, the world distracts us. Why should it do so?

Sw. K.: [*joking*] Are you saying that God has made a blunder in creating the world? That is what it amounts to. You are telling God, 'I want you only, and why have you created the world?'

Vis.: Yes! Yes!

Sw. K.: He will tell you, my dear man, I have created nothing. I am a simple man and unnecessarily you are blaming me for the things I have not done [*peals of laughter from the gathering and Swamiji*.] He has not created the world. You see this chair I am sitting on is made of fine electromagnetic waves. Eh? But there is no such thing as a chair from the point of view of physics. Can you say that the electrons have manufactured this chair? In a conference held one day did the electrons pass a resolution, 'Let us become a chair?'

A Voice: Their perfect order is distributed into this form of chair.

Sw. K.: They are in perfect order even as this chair. If you see the chair with a powerful microscope, you will not see a chair there, you understand? So it does not mean that the chair has been created. It doesn't exist. If it is really there, you must be able to see it even with the microscope. Your imputation that

God has created the world is like that. He has not created the world even as the atoms have not created the chair. As I said, God is a poor man, sitting always as He was! He has done nothing but you unnecessarily say He has done this and that. So it means some defect in the perception of man who says God has created the world. Do you understand?

Questioner: That is what He has done—given a defective perception?

Sw. K.: There is no He. You are part of Him—you are blaming somebody of whom you are yourself a part. Your doubts arise because you are not seeing things properly. Can you say, when I think of God, my mind rises to God? If it does, then you will be able to do your official work in the world, and not feel you are debarred from it. Your spiritual life will not be contradictory to your official life. Once you see that point better, you can work better—now because you are not seeing clearly, you are fumbling. You come in to conflict because you do not see things in their right context. When you see things clearly, no conflict arises and your efficiency increases. When you do meditation, you will do more work, instead of allowing meditation to prevent you from doing work. Will you say that Lord Krishna did not meditate or that He did less work than you? [*The lunch bell rings.*] There! Enough food for thought. Now go and feed your stomach, which is crying for food. God bless you—Namaskar!

A: Why is the spiritual path so difficult? What makes it so?

Sw. K.: The emotions and sentiments don't go hand in hand with logic and intellect of mankind. Your logic may impel you and force you in the direction of an aspirant. But the sentiments which are human and sometimes sub-human are against this logic of the intellect and there is conflict in one's conceptionality. All this is very well known to people like the Lamas and Jesus. Though very rare, there are few souls that can understand this mystery. It is not easy to understand it; it is a mystery and it is a mystery because it is not accessible to human understanding. It is not like two and two make four. We are in a realm where two and two do not make four. If something is said which is not acceptable to the human mathematical mind and the social way of thinking, nobody accepts it. We are immersed in social decorum and social norm of thought, and we want to press even God into that norm and if He is not amenable to that norm of our social way of thinking, we are not prepared to accept that God. So we must be clear what it is that we are asking for. Be prepared to get to such extremes as sacrificing your ego and your social relationships and accepted social norms, this may be demanded of you at some stage of your progress. You are unable to go there, because the logic and arithmetic there are quite different; so we arrive at a conflict. We cannot displease the world. We cannot displease God either. We are trying to please God by pleasing the world also at one and the same time. But it so happens that they are not in harmony with each other. And in the blunt way Jesus said God and Mammon cannot be pleased at the same time. Mammon is the extrovert mind which moves towards objects of the senses. It does not mean gold merely; it is only a symbol of the peculiar extrovert way of thinking, which directs itself towards sense objects and sense only, including everything and anything that you see with your eyes or think of in the mind. Man is accustomed to think only in terms of objects which include society, which include everything that you regard as worthwhile and valuable in this life. But the value that you are unconsciously or subconsciously seeing as the special ideal is something transcendent, which is a very significant word. It simply oversteps the limits of mathemetics and human logic where your calculations do not hold good. Parallel lines may meet, the three angles of a triangle may not be equal to two right angles. All this is absurd from the human point of view. But that is the truth in some other realm. You may call it the D-IV-dimension or multi-dimension or whatever it is and that is what you are exactly asking for. You have got yet another prejudice which compels you to think in terms of the world of objects; you cannot forget it, because you are born into it. I am giving you an idea of how hard it is to find a person who can teach you, and even if you find such a person, how difficult it is to assimilate into your personality what is taught. It is impossible—almost impossible. After considering these difficulties in the way, if you are prepared and ready to go through the ordeal, I think there is no problem. But ordeal is the word, one cannot easily enter in and get into it. You have to crush your ego and demolish all your ordinary norms of thinking. It is almost like death itself. It is like dying to the empirical life. There are two kinds of prejudices; social and personal. We think in terms of society and also in terms of personality. We cannot get out of this twin situation. What will happen to this body? And what will people say about me? You are frightened about these. These two difficulties have to be overcome with great caution. And the caution you have to exercise in this path is all the problem there is. That is the subtlety of the path. You should not go to any extreme. You have to seize the golden mean in such a manner, with such concentration and caution, that you don't get kicks from either side. Go slowly causing displeasure neither to your body nor to the outside society nor to God. You are to please everything by harmonising everything. The most difficult experience one has is that of being in harmony with everything. When you are in harmony with one thing see that you are not in disharmony with another thing. So go very slowly and cautiously, and if even you take only one step see that it does mean progress, provided it is a firm step so that you do not regret it afterwards. It takes time, patience and force of will, coupled with understanding. Aurobindo was a great man—you must have heard of him. Someone at his deathbed asked "Master, what is your message to the world"? He said, "It seems that the world is not ready for it." Maybe it is true in some sense because the world is ready for what is pleasant, while it isn't ready for any unpleasant truth. It doesn't want it and says let us wait [*laughs*], keep it a while! How can we forget that we are so and so, that we belong to this country or that country? How can we forget all these things? It is not easy to give up these ideas. But just imagine! How wrong these ideas are! It is not ultimately true that you are a man, a woman, Western, Eastern, tall or short. These are all gross empirical ways of thinking and they are not ultimately true in the evaluation of things. Yet these are such hard-boiled thoughts that we cannot easily get rid of them, especially when we try to get out of the personal and step into the realm of the impersonal. Then it is that you realise your status as a speak in the universal set-up. You are not a man or a woman, not even a human being, you are a speck of dust! A drop in the ocean of spirit or in the ocean of the Universal! It cannot have sex and nationality—it cannot be designated in any way whatsoever. When such connection enters your very being, I think you will enter the path of the spirit. Then alone the actual progress starts. Till that time you are only struggling against the current to swim against it.

The Lord's Lila—What is it?

Dr. A.: What is Lila (as we see in the war of Kurukshetra)?

Sw. K.: What we cannot understand we simply call 'Lila'.

S.D.: Can we say that it is the cause and effect of the cosmic in the Lilas because in Lord Krishna's life we discern Lilas; he never directly does anything. He always causes things to be done.

Sw. K.: He directly does also.

S.D.: Which one?

Sw. K.: Perhaps His directions produce the feeling that He is causing them. When I push you and you fall on somebody, it does not mean that you have done something. I make you fall on that person. But if you are not conscious that I pushed you, you think you have done it yourself. Ultimately He only does.

S.D.: He does not want an instrument to do it.

Sw. K.: And when you are not aware that you have done it, you say He has caused and caused it to be done by somebody else.

S.D.: It was even so in the case of the man who was led by Lord Krishna into the cave so that the sleeping man, when waking up from slumber, would see him and the former would by the power of the latter be burnt up.

Sw. K.: That man was not led by him into the cave; he was forced to go there on his own accord by the will of Krishna and that man thought he went on his own accord like the hypnotised man not knowing that he was hypnotised.

S.D.: No. Swamiji seems to think that I am bringing down God's capacity to cause....

Sw. K.: He does not cause anything to be done through an instrument because He has no instrument outside Him.

S.D.: Then, why does He tell Arjuna, "Be my instrument"?

Sw. K.: He is not Arjuna for Him. Arjuna is His own limbs working. But from your point of view it is Arjuna. He simply showed the Cosmic form and Arjuna vanished in it in one second. He said, "I have done everything Myself. Now, from your point of view let it be that you do it as it were. Already what has to be done has been done." The future has taken place in the present itself because He has no time. For you, the war has not taken place. For Him, it has already taken place and the matter is over. But still, from your point of view, it is a future. In Eternity, there is no future. What you are going to have or what process you are going to undergo in the future has already taken place in the

Eternal Mind. So it is not a future for it. What has not taken place for you has already taken place there.

S.D.: But except in the case of Sisupala, He does not war with anyone. And he always...causes wars.

Sw. K.: This is all your way of looking at it.

S.D.: [*Bursting into laughter*] Yes, that is true.

Sw. K.: But it may not be correct. He might have willed it.

S.D.: I am not objecting to it. I am only asking if it is the correct interpretation.

Sw. K.: If you think that your interpretation is correct, how do you know that—He has no instrument and He does everything Himself from His point of view. But from your point of view, He has done it through somebody.

Dr. A.: Lord Krishna was in the human form only, when he performed all His lilas.

Sw. K.: No no.... If you think of 'ma' as a human being you are thinking wrongly. He said, "Foolish to think that I am a human being". It is mentioned there in the Bhagavad Gita *Anjananti Ma moodha manusham*... "Not knowing Me really if you think that I am a human being"—he has made that point there.

Dr. A.: Even when He shows Himself He conceals His *prabhava*.

Sw. K.: He says, "You have not understood Me."

Kn.: He is known as *kapata nataka sutradhara*.

Sw. K.: You have not understood Him. Because He has concealed Himself, perhaps you are not able to understand Him still.

Kn.: Yes, He will never allow you to understand Him. Not that you cannot understand. In that also He is *kapata nataka sutradhara*.

Dr. A.: But what is the idea in appearing like that? He could have retained His *prabhava?*

Sw. K.: Why are you commanding Him like that? [*Laughter all round.*] The moment you command Him, He ceases to be free. But He is free [*laughs*].

Dr. A.: It is not that we are commanding Him. We are only trying to understand Him.

Sw. K.: When you understand Him, you become Him, eh?

Dr. A.: Where is the harm in trying...?

Sw. K.: There are the gopis. They became Krishna when they behaved like Him.

Dr. A.: They never bothered to understand...

Sw. K.: They played flute like this [*imitates*]. They took broomstick and played like this [*laughter all around*], and somebody killed Putana. The gopis are doing that. Another gopi killed Bakasura. They were playing all his drama because they became one home with Him.

Dr. P.K. Rao: Mira also behaved like that.

Dr. A.: Mira became one with Him. What I am saying is: why does He conceal His cosmic personality and reveal it only occasionally?

Kn.: Even to Arjuna, He did not reveal it always. Arjuna could not have contained it.

Sw. K.: "Everything is in Me and nothing is in Me," He said. "And yet everything is in Me, look at my wonder. Look at this great yoga of mine!" Now what is His yoga? Hatha Yoga? Or what is it? He said, "*Pasya-me yoga maiswaryam*". Look at my yoga. What is the yoga He is telling about? Raja Yoga? Hatha Yoga?

Kn.: That is what I was saying. Though it may not be intellectually understandable for us, it is quite possible for God to be the world also simultaneously.

Sw. K.: But He is not calling it the world at that time. He Himself is that. It is something He is doing within Himself. Even the process of His doing is Himself.

Dr. A.: Why does He conceal it from us?

Sw. K.: He never concealed it. Even that you can call it Lila, His way of concealing it. Why did He vanish from the Gopis for a few minutes?

Dr. A.: They say that Viraha is the highest state...

Sw. K.: Well, that is why He is doing it for you so that you may create viraha in you. He is troubling you very much, otherwise, why will He do it, Unless he wants you?

Dr. A.: No. I am saying why does He......?

Sw. K.: Only to create *viraha* in you. Otherwise, if you understand Him, what viraha is there? Then you will keep quiet and sleep very well because you understand Him very well. You won't aspire for Him.

Dr. A.: No, no. There must be some difficulties in revealing your inherent nature.

Sw. K.: He has no difficulty. What difficulty has He?

Dr. A.: The world. Why does not He reveal Himself. The world is not ready for Him? Or they will injure Him?

Sw. K.: What is the difficulty for a child to keep quiet without being naughty? It is building a mud-house and playing with it. God is looking at us like a child. He builds a house and plays with it. What is the harm in keeping quiet? Why does He not keep quiet?

Dr. A.: For 114 years He did this; for everything......

Sw. K.: I am not talking of time limit, but of facts. Why does He create the world? This is what you have been asking in a sense again and again and putting various questions. This is your question, isn't it? The very same thing you are putting in difficult words whenever you ask God, "Why is He doing something? Why has He created the world"? Why did He create the world? You tell me that first. Then I will answer other questions.

Dr. A.: I am not bothered about it.

Sw. K.: [*laughing*]. The questions are all interrelated. When you cannot ask one why, you cannot ask another why also. Otherwise, you should not ask why at all. You are trying to subject Him to some logical analysis.

Dr. A.: You must understand why I am asking.

Sw. K.: That is called logical analysis. Again you are coming to the same point. You are trying to understand through intellect, through logic. And first of all cutting Him off from you, you have done it already. You have already separated yourself from Him and then put this question which is why it is not permissible. You have taken Him as an outsider and then put questions about Him. Otherwise, why this question? How does it arise if He is not outside you? You are judging Him as a person judging another person. The moment you become an organic entity involved in Him you will never speak. You will say "well I understand everything". Because you know yourself, you do not put questions to your own self.

Dr. A.: I can speak of Him as Him only because....

Sw. K.: What Him? You have separated yourself from Him. He will never answer questions about Himself. You don't put questions about yourself, such as Why I am asking you? You don't ask me this question. Or why do I put questions? You have got a justification for your own point of view. You have no doubt about the validity or the justifiability of your own questions because you are one with your question. But you can't give so much concession in respect of a thing outside you. The whole problem is of dichotomy between the subject and the object as the philosophers tell us which is the trouble with everything up to the downmost atom. No scientist can understand the world even today, because he sees the world outside him. No philosopher can understand, because he thinks God is outside him. Creation is outside him, etc. etc. And no Sadhaka can understand God's ways, because he thinks God is outside him. He is a future being, or transcendent or whatever it is. Though He is temporarily and tentatively justified in thinking like that, under the present circumstances you cannot find fault with Him.

Dr. A.: As a child He is never concealing......

Sw. K.: Again you are putting the same question. Who told you He is concealing Himself? It is your own interpretation and you are justifying your interpretation, I am saying He is not concealing Himself.

Dr. A.: I want to know the secret. And you are not telling me that, Swamiji?

Sw. K.: [*laughs*] Why should you say that He is concealing, because it is not clear to your mind. You are saying He is concealing.

Dr. A.: He takes efforts to see that it is not clear to my mind.

Sw. K.: He says, "I never do anything. [*Quotes the verse "Na......"*.] I neither give anything nor take anything nor am I concerned with your merits and demerits."

Dr. A.: But He has given all authority to Maya. It is the same as He is doing it.

Sw. K.: Again you have brought in another thing for the same question [*laughs.*]

Dr. A.: He tells Arjuna, "This is your duty. Go and do it."

Kn.: And yet He says, "I take birth for punishing the wicked..." And then He says, "I do nothing...."

Dr. A.: He is very shy!

Sw. K.: This is another, a greater glory you are giving to Him (*laughs*). The highest credit that you can give Him is that He is the greatest liar. To say, "I create the world without creating it," is the greatest lie He is telling. Isn't it? Eh?

S.D.: But does He say that?

Sw. K.: Well, you see, it looks like that.

Dr. A.: He tells lies which are truth and speaks truth that are lies! [*Hearty laugh all around.*]

Dr. P.K. Rao: You are strongly confused with Him.

Sw. K.: This is the devotee who speaks.

Kn.: Devotees and non-devotees, both speak like this.

Sw. K.: What you are doing is *ninda stuti* "you fellow, you think you know everything. You don't know your own father!" This is what a devotee cries out. "When you don't know your own father, how do you say you are omniscient. I deny this", he said.

Dr. P.K. Rao: Yes, *ninda stuti.*

Sw. K.: "You fellow," one man cried, "when Buddhists denied your existence, I established you and you have no pity on me. You are not giving me a morsel of food." He wrote a book in Sanskrit, called Kusumanjali. He wrote a book in which he established the existence of God on various grounds against Buddhists' denial. But he was a poverty-stricken Brahmin. He had no food to eat. He just cried, I established your existence when the Buddhists completely denied your existence. And see what I get for it! This is all devotion. Devotion takes various forms which are inscrutable. Devotion is as inscrutable as God Himself. And the devotee also becomes as inscrutable. Afterwards he is not in any way less than God. And they say that the devotee becomes so great that he simply pockets God afterwards! God starts dancing to his tune behind him. What do you say for this? If he speaks, then God speaks—only then.

Dr. P.K. Rao: God becomes afraid of him!

Sw. K.: Yes, yes. "I am *Bhakta-paradhina*" "I am helpless", Narayana told Durvasa, "I cannot do anything". Narayana said that He cannot do anything. When Durvasa says "withdraw your Chakra", He says "I never did anything. Don't insult me like this. I am helpless in this matter. I am *Bhakta-paradhina*". Metaphysical philosophy can't explain all this. There is a transcendent truth in it. There is something transcendent which overcomes the limits of intellect and surpasses in every way and takes you to the realm where you are flooded with what you may call devotion or Bliss or Ananda or whatever you call it, it doesn't matter. You get flooded with it and your philosophy goes into thin air. It demonstrates the limitations of philosophy, ultimately. When philosophy has known its own limits, then it has transcended itself. But if it thinks itself to be powerful and proud, then it won't understand anything. Reason is helpful only to the extent that it can tell you where its limits are. And when it loses its own limits, it has become humble at once. And then you are taken by some other force. Limitations of reason must be realised and reason helps you understand its own limitations. When scientists like Einstein have realised the limitations of science itself they are the greatest scientists. And they have understood the limitations of science and know why it is limited. And because they know the limitations of science, they are more than mere scientists. They are almost mystics. When you know the reason why you cannot understand a thing you have understood it to some extent (*laughs.*)

S.D.: You have got your answer! Is that what Swamiji means?

Sw. K.: Because you must be knowing why you have not understood it. That is the reason. That is wisdom. There is some flaw in the way of your thinking itself and you understood the flaw. Then you have overcome that flaw immediately, you have transcended it and gone to another realm beyond human level. There you become a real devotee.

Dr. P.K. Rao: Beyond reason......

Sw. K.: No, transcend it. Then you are possessed by a force and care-taking element which is superhuman. Then it is that you become a real instrument of God. You are crying about instrumentality. The real instrument you become at that time. When you have completely overstepped the limits of your own capacity, and you know that you have no capacity except that you have become a humble instrument of a Power which is completely in charge of you. This is what the devotees realised. And they are most care-free people, most helpless, most happy and no botheration at all for them.

Dr. P.K. Rao: Is it not called intuitive perception?

Sw. K.: Well, call it whatever you like. They go beyond your intuitive and logical and scientific understanding and your social law. They behave like fools and idiots and you cannot understand them. They have no ethical or moral principle, nothing of the kind, their law is quite different.

Ay.: Swamiji, in Gita they say that knowledge is higher than......

Sw. K.: Well, that knowledge is of no use. That knowledge is not your book of knowledge—no Plato, Kant or Hegel. It is not that knowledge.

Ay.: It is not......

Sw. K.: Knowledge is greater than devotion. That knowledge is interpreted in one way. Devotion is greater than knowledge. You have to interpret it in another way. And yoga is the greatest. He is saying Karma is the greatest, yoga is the greatest, knowledge is the greatest, Bhakti is the greatest—in different places. But he puts it in different contexts. And they appear greatest at that time. "None like you," Swami Sivanandaji Maharaj used to say. You don't know what he means by that.

S.D.: What is it, Swamiji, that you said just now?

Sw. K.: "Nobody can work like Swami Krishnananda. Nobody can speak like Swami Chidananda," Swami Sivananda would say this in their presence and they wouldn't know how to take it.

Visitors: Gita has 700 slokas and Vyasa has written all the 700 or was it composed by three different authors as some say?

Sw. K.: A 'Somebody' cannot say that. Why? If Vyasa has written the Mahabharata, he has written the 700 slokas also. If you think he has not written the whole Mahabharata, then you can omit some. If he has not written, who else has? Nobody else. Isn't it? Who is that somebody, otherwise? Well, "Sanjaya said". And Sanjaya himself could not have written that sentence.

A Visitor: And it takes 1½ hours to recite the slokas.

Sw. K.: No, no. He has not recited them. He was not singing the slokas. He only spoke as He spoke. The poet wrote it in slokas. What can he do for that? You think the same slokas when he spoke? He spoke ordinary language like 'get up'. But when you sing music [*Here Swamiji puts the words 'get up' into a musical and literally sang: 'G......e......t......u......p' to the hilarious delight of all present and he himself rejoiced when his singing was over.*] But Vyasa did not say like that. They say he took a few minutes, not 1½ hours. We do not know exactly. Some say it was a conversation for 1½ hours and some say it was 48 minutes, etc. There are various versions. We do not know exactly. Anyhow there was sufficient time. They were not in a hurry to attack because after the Gita was over, war did not take place suddenly. Yudhisthira had something to say and he went and prostrated before all people and something took place.

Question: What is Dharma and what is Rita?

Sw. K.: The effect of Rita is said to be the Dharma of the cosmos. 'Rita' is cosmic law, order of things....Says the Rig Veda [*Swamiji recited it in the exact orthodox cadence in which it is* *meant to be recited.*] It manifests itself as the first order of things. That is the Dharma of the universe. The law which is operating in the universe is called the Rita. And the basis for it is the Absolute. That is the 'Satya'.

Sadhak Disciple: Swamiji, 'Namaha' is said to be self-surrender. How does it mean so? Does the word mean that?

Sw. K.: No, the word does not mean that, but that's its significance! When you say 'Namaha', at that time you are in union with and united to the deity you say 'Namaha' to.

S.D.: I have a few doubts in the Mahabharata, doubts which refer to a particular English translation of it by a certain author. Swamiji has also read this book, I think?

Sw. K.: This is not a good translation. She, the authoress, writes like a woman. The Mahabharata is a virile epic, but she renders it in a very sentimental way.

S.D.: You mean she emphasises the sentimental aspects?

Sw. K.: Yes! She has omitted many important passages also. I think she has omitted sage Durvasa coming for Bhiksha and Lord Krishna saving the situation by eating a wee morsel sticking to the Akshaya Patra. This book was published in 1965, more than a decade ago.

S.D.: Swamiji seems to have read it with great attention and, very unlike him, made a large number of marginal notes to fill in the omissions in the printed passages of the translation.

Sw. K.: Her language also is not good. She writes softening the atmosphere. She misses the virility as a result of which the epic loses its impact in her way of writing it. Rajagopalachari's translation is good. It is a smaller book but it is written very well. [*Addressing a new comer*] Well, so now, what is your problem?

Visitor comes close to Swamiji and relates his problem which appears to be a psychological one.]

Sw. K.: Does anyone else in your family have this problem?

Visitor: Yes, my father.

Sw. K.: I see! Now you have told me a secret. Rest and reduction in the intake of food will help you. Are you reading any literature now! First, give up all pills, and sleep as well as you can. Don't read before going to bed. Till 12 midnight you read! No, you should not do that.

Visitor: Cannot get sleep.

Sw. K.: Does not matter, go to bed by about 9 at night. Just lie down and rest, even if you do not get sleep. No, don't go on a year's leave. It will do you harm. You have not trained yourself to keep your mind at rest. You do not know what to do with yourself. So take a week's leave, that is enough. Keep working. Stop trying to find answers to useless questions like the ones you have been trying to solve. Will the sky fall on my head? What will I do, if the planets dash against each other or the sun burns up the earth? These have no answers. Even so, the questions you have been trying to solve have no answers. Don't bother about them. They have nothing to do with you. I will give you medicine from the Sivananda Pharmacy—our Ashram's. You ask Panditji there to tell you how to use them. Do you come to Delhi sometimes? Go and see an Ayurvedic Vaid there. I will give you the address of the Vaid, and you can tell him that Swamiji has asked me to go to you. He is good in the profession. He will help you. (*After sometime*) Have you been meeting any other Sadhu?

Visitor: Yes, One.

Sw. K.: What did he tell you?

[*As their conversation became confidential, it could not be recorded.*]

Dr. N.S. Rao: What is Truth, Swamiji?

Sw. K.: Jesus was asked, what is Truth? There was no time for him to answer it. Before he could answer he was condemned to be crucified. Truth—the Ultimate Reality—is that which cannot be contradicted. That is what they call the Absolute. When you say the Absolute, you mean it is not related to something else. And it can't be defined by characteristics other than itself. You can't say, it is like this:. . .When you say it is like this, you are referring to something else in comparison. And you can't. I am so-and-so's son. You are defining yourself in terms of somebody else. But you have no definition of your own. Eh? But THAT is not like that. You cannot define It in terms of somebody else, that somebody else also is within It—not outside It.

Dr. N.S.R.: It may mean limiting it.

Sw. K.: Yes, yes, denying it almost, defining it is denying it, they say. All determination is a negation—that is what Theresa said. Definition is determination; determination is negation, almost so in the ultimate sense.

Dr. N.S.R.: In defining the soul, we say I am not the body; I am not the mind, I am the knowledge and the Brahman of this knowledge—why can't it be said like this? I am this also and that also instead! Not this, not this!

Sw. K.: It means the same thing. They are not different statements when you say I am not this. What is it that you are denying? You are denying something. Isn't it? What are you denying?

Dr. N.S.R.: I am not this body, I am not this mind....

Sw. K.: Why do you deny the body when you say it is a part of Brahman?

Dr. N.S.R.: That's what I am asking.

Sw. K.: There's a point in it. Not so simple as you say. There's a point in that denial also. Your idea that something is outside is denied. Even the idea of the body is the idea of externality. Any idea is the popular man's idea of something external. And you deny everything external. And together with this, it is not denying the body as such but as the externalised existence of it. And when it is non-externalised it ceases to be the body. This is as good as denying it. So that you are actually including it.

Dr. N.S.R.: That's why I said...

Sw. K.: To say that you are everything is the same as saying you've nothing. They are not two different things, for to say it is everything, you must be able to comprehend that state. You can't conceive everything that statement asks you to and therefore such statements have no meaning.

The moment you say everything, you have some preconceived idea about it. The totality of many things, or something like that. Even the idea of totality can't be there unless you have some idea of space etc. And even the idea of space is not permitted because it is an idea of externality. So ultimately you are reducing yourself to the same predicament. There are two methods, *Yoga-Vasistha* mentions, either you affirm that you are nothing or affirm that you are everything. But don't affirm that you are something. That, it says, is the only cause of bondage. But nobody can affirm like that; you can neither say I am nothing because you have got an element of existence which affirms itself. And it can't deny itself. It is very hard to deny anything like that when it does exist. Nor can you include everything in yourself. There are many problems in it. You think over it and see the idea of your individuality and everything is different from yourself, is so inveterate that you can't say I am a cobra, I am a frog and the like. You may say that in a linguistic manner, but actually the feelings will not permit such an affirmation of universality unless you are a super-normal person. That is what I explained to you yesterday also. You can't affirm a thing which belongs to a state of reality in which you are not at present. You understand? I am the President of India. What is the use of affirming this? You are not in that set of circumstances that can give meaning to this affirmation and so on. So you are not in that level of consciousness where universal affirmations, or such an affirmation, can be made; it is a particular level. You may become the President of India, there's no objection to that, but at present that affirmation is irrelevant. And so if you make a statement, it is but a grammatical sentence, there is no correlation of reality behind it. Likewise, if you say I am Brahman, you must be fit to conceive such an idea, then it will have meaning, for it will be actually from that level of your life that you speak. Otherwise, it will merely be a grammatical statement that you make. It has a subject and an object and a predicate—no practical connotation. So you should never make affirmations beyond your capacity. Your capacity is comprehensive in the present level of experience. So they are good as far as they go. But you must be sure whether any statement you make is fit for that state we are in—whether the prescription is fit for your ailment or not, then only the next question arises.

Dr. N.S.R.: When the sun is rising over one half of the world that half is illumined but the other half is in darkness. So when you say 'illumined intellect' that is...

Sw. K.: It is not illumined intellect if it is only partially illumined. You don't mean that half the intellect is in darkness?

Dr. N.S.R.: Yes, that's what I am coming to. Are we to take it as a sort of a transparent layer which gets illumined or......?

Sw. K.: It depends upon your concept of the intellect. If you think that intellect is a material substance, naturally you will give it a shape—square, round, tall, short, thick or thin or whatever it is, transparent or opaque—you've to add all these adjectives to your definition of it. What is your definition of intellect? Is it made of matter? If so, what is its size? All these questions arise.

Dr. N.S.R.: This is only putting it academically, what is intellect, what is intelligence?

Sw. K.: Intelligence is that which illumines the intellect. It is the energy that makes the intellect shine in respect of itself as well as in respect of others. The electric energy is the source of the illumination of the bulb. The bulb you can say is intellect. It is *jada*—lifeless. It has no consciousness. It can't shine on its own, just as that the bulb can't shine unless the power is charged into it. Here the illuminating power is the intelligence.

Dr. N.S.R.: When, for example, you say intellectual curiosity, what is that?

Sw. K.: That is a psychological state.

Dr. N.S.R.: It has nothing tc do with this question of an illumined intellect?

Sw. K.: The intellect has its own functions and one of its functions is 'curiosity'. It understands, it doubts, it is curious. Curiosity is eagerness to know something. And that is a condition.

Dr. Aruna: It has to be shunned.

Sw. K.: Why? why do you shun it? I have a curiosity to know the Absolute. I will not shun that idea! Why should I?

Dr. N.S.R.: When you put the question which is to know the transcendent, we do not call it curiosity. Otherwise, don't put questions out of mere curiosity, we say.

Sw. K.: That is so, every question is not transcendent. When you put a question which can't be answered at the present level of your understanding, it is called transcendental. And you should not put it. But curiosity is permissible in certain circumstances. It becomes a curiosity when the answer cannot help you in any practical way and is irrelevant or meaningless. When it is out of a practical desire which can be implemented, you need not call it curiosity, you can call it a natural aspiration for understanding. But when it is impractical, you call it curiosity; for, then it becomes unnecessarily asking about something you can't understand.

S.D.: But it is the urge to evolve—curiosity?

Sw. K.: No. no. Curiosity is a desire which can't be implemented—that is what Dr.'s meaning is. Otherwise, you don't shun it.

Dr. N.S.R.: Is it *Chitta*, the sub-conscious?

Visitor: The sub-conscious or the un-conscious? You can call it both put together. All of them have the same function. But...

Sw. K.: No. They do not carry out the same functions. The *chitta* remembers—memory is the function of the *chitta*. Understanding is the function of the intellect. Thinking and doubting are the functions of the mind.

Dr. N.S.R.: Desiring also?

Sw. K.: Yes, desiring is also a function of the mind.

Vis.: Is mind consciousness?

Sw. K.: Consciousness is the background of the function of all psychic apparatus. It is the light behind the total consciousness of the psyche.

Voice: Can it also be called. . . .

Sw. K.: It is called the *Atman*. What you call the *Atman* is the Supreme.

Nal: Mind is *Atman?*

Sw. K.: No, mind is only the instrument of the *Atman*.

Nal: Is consciousness the *Atman?*

Sw. K.: Yes, yes. That's how we define it for all practical purposes.

Nal: Then what are the functions of the mind?

Sw. K.: Thinking and doubting.

Dr. N.S.R.: Mind is *jada*, 'un-conscious' matter?

Sw. K.: It is like a mirror. Does the mirror shine or not? It can't shine itself. But it shines when the light falls on it. So the mind can't think if it does not have the consciousness of the *Atman* behind it. It reflects the consciousness of the Atman; it shines as if it were its own light.

Dr. N.S.R.: Like the *Atman?*

Sw. K.: Yes, yes. It behaves like a glass when the light passes through the glass. You can't see the glass, it is so transparent. But it is still there as a material substance.

Nal: Then *chitta* is the un-conscious?

Sw. K.: The sub-conscious and un-conscious have to be combined. It has the character of un-consciousness and it has the character of the sub-conscious also. They work in different ways at different times. It is a total mass which works in different ways under different types of pressure. It is a big conglomeration. They are only names for the different functions of your individual way of thinking. And it includes understanding, discrimination, doubting, etc., etc.—hundreds of things.

Nal: Judgement is the function of—?

Sw. K.: The intellect. 'Buddhi' is the Sanskrit word and 'intellect' is its English equivalent.

Dr. N.S.R.: Then there is a question on Brahmacharya. We are asked to observe Brahmacharya, for it reserves energy for higher purpose.

Sw. K.: Yes.

Dr. N.S.R.: If everyone were to observe Brahmacharya, how could you get a Sankara, a Ramanuja, a Krishnananda?

Sw. K.: Why do you want a Sankara or a Ramanuja when every one has gone to Brahman? [*laughter in the gathering.*] When everybody has gone to Brahman, why do you want a Sankara, a Ramanuja?

Dr. N.S.R.: For example—

Sw. K.: Why do you want them? Why?

Dr. N.S.R.: For the ordinary men.

Sw. K.: Where are the ordinary men when you have gone to Brahman?

Dr. R.: Such people as are in ignorance of Brahman and such matters.

Sw. K.: Where are they? I cannot see them!

Dr. R.: They are the average men—'jivas'......

Sw. K.: They do not exist before the Brahman. So you are talking from a lower-level point of view and contradicting it by bringing in a question of the higher level which is only curiosity, as you said first. This is called curiosity—you bring about an impractical ideal in conjunction with the practical reality. See?

Dr. R.: These are questions that are asked of us by our branch-members of the Divine Life Society and by the other people also. I must give them proper answers.

Sw. K.: If you can give an answer to your own self, you can give an answer to others also. But it is not clear to you. How will you clear it for them?

Dr. R.: That's why I am asking you.

Sw. K.: You see, no one should just use some words whose meaning is not clear to the mind. What is Brahmacharya? You first define it to me. If you tell me what you mean by it, then I will tell you if I have got some commentary on it.

Dr. R.: Preservation of that fluid—

Sw. K.: Why do you want to preserve it? What for?

Dr. R.: Er, Hmm! I mean...

Sw. K.: What is your purpose, what is the higher purpose, tell me.

Dr. R.: For God realisation.

Sw. K.: How do you get realisation by the preservation of it? What connection does it have with realisation?

Dr. R.: That is what I want to know.

Sw. K.: So everything is doubtful. You are not clear. So you are putting doubts without knowing their meaning yourself. Unless the thoughts are clear from bottom to top, you can't proceed along any line. It may be Brahmacharya. It may be cooking food. Even in cooking, the entire process of cooking you must first know, from beginning to end. But if doubt comes to the mind, is this the method or is it some kind of a crochet in the mind of people? The method should be very clear to you, the entire scientific basis—in such and such a manner, in such and such a way. Then you will not put questions of doubts, and will be very clear on everything about it. Your question is like asking if everybody in the world should take medicine or not. You tell me, should everybody in the world take medicine? Everybody should take medicine only if everybody is sick. Again should everybody take the same medicine? The answer is 'Yes' only if everybody has the same disease. But not otherwise. Brahma means the Absolute, Carya is the attitude. The attitude that the Absolute has is called Brahmacarya ultimately. What is its attitude, tell me? What does it think? To have the same attitude as the Absolute is Brahmacarya. Well this is an ultimate definition. But there are lower grades of it also. To the extent this attitude can be implemented in your lower level of experience, to that extent you are a Brahmacari. Even the first step is a necessary step. Inasmuch as even the first step is the lowest and the most insignificant perhaps, it has also a connection with the highest step. It is a necessary step. And inasmuch as it is necessary for you, it is necessary for everybody else also. So why are you dragging in Sankara and others unnecessarily onto this level of these poor people on the very first step? If anything is good for you, why should it not be good for others? Under the same circumstances, of course. If the circumstances are similar for you and the other person, what is good for you is equally good for the other person also. If everybody realises Brahma, what will happen to the world? The world will go to the dogs? What an unfortunate thing! You are suggesting that everybody will die—in one stroke—this is what you are thinking!

Dr. R.: It is good if all people go to God. It is better if everybody doesn't go! Somebody should be there to take care of the world! The Bhagavad Gita says that perhaps out of the millions, few try to and out of the few, perhaps one achieves God Realisation.

Sw. K.: Dear friend, scriptures will not help us; our intellect also will not help us. You have to serve a Guru, they say. These difficulties arise in our mind because we don't serve a Guru. Now we don't live under a Guru. And we don't follow the advice of a Guru.

You have no question arising in your mind at that time, if you simply do what the Guru says. You don't ask him why I should do all that. What he says you do, but if he says don't do this, you don't do this. Because you can't use your intellect for everything just like that. Now you started using our intellect and you are in a turmoil. Nothing, no question can be answered like that. That is to be understood. Otherwise everybody can read a book or purchase the whole set of 108 and more Upanishads, read them and reach Brahman. How is that possible? The difficulties become more and more insurmountable as you go further and further on the path of spirituality. In the beginning the difficulties are simple and they don't look complicated. It looks as if it is a simple path. But afterwards when the difficulties become so very great and nebulous and incapable of comprehension, you require personal guidance. And therefore on this path, a Guru is absolutely essential and you are not to worry your head with any question. And if you have any difficulty you simply say, this is my difficulty at this time, what shall I do? The Guru will say, 'Do this' in one sentence. You do it. There ends the matter—If he says, 'Go away' or asks you to stay on you do that; if he says, 'Sleep', you sleep. If he says, 'Have your food', you eat: If he says don't eat today, you should not ask him why, and all that. He has a better understanding of your difficulty than your ownself. So you have no problem under a guide. Sometimes even *japa* cannot be done. Not that every day you do no *japa*. Your mind is upset and there is tremendous worry and tension. At that time, you should not do *japa*. You will be thinking in your mind, because the scriptures enjoin do *japa*—I do *japa*. Guru may say at this time—please sleep. Take rest, go and sleep. So there is an exception to every rule.

Meditation or japa should bring satisfaction and clarity. That is the test of the correctness of your approach. You should not be depressed, moody, mentally troubled and in a state of assailing doubts; that would mean you have not followed the technique correctly.

It is not because we have only read from books that we are what we are today. Perhaps there are people who have read more books than I. That is different. If we, the disciples of Gurudev Swami Sivananda are alive today it is because of Him. Otherwise we would have died of worry. For my part, I can never forget Him. Master Sivananda is my father and mother, even today,—not merely many years back, even today. It is not the Upanishads that help me, it is He. [*Swamiji's voice is choked perhaps with feeling and recollection.*] And I can clearly feel that he is helping us—even to day. He is very kind. I have never seen a Guru like him, and I can never hope to see another like him. The greatest person I have ever seen in this world is he. And because we had the opportunity of living with him, we feel like crying sometimes now that he is no more with us. We weep (actually sniffs). Such a great person we have never seen—great in every respect. He was a baby, child like and also like Brahma, Visnu, Siva, so high and god like—whatever you can think of as the best and the greatest. What I am today is because I could stay with such a Guru and thus blessed by serving him as I would serve God. Thank you for your *satsanga*. Namaskar!

November 26, 1978

A typical November morning, hesitating warmth and chill. A bit misty. This kind of weather had laid down Rev. Swamiji with severe attack of asthma for the whole previous week or ten days. He was continuing to wheeze and cough through the hours of the morning *darshan* for which there were 15-20 persons waiting longingly for refreshing conversations.

Swami Krishnananda: [*Sees Dr. P.K. Rao reading a book.*] That book discusses the metaphysics of a very absolute logic. And finally the whole logic comes to nothing because you are lost in the forest of words. He says, for example, that similarity it is where two objects are essentially the same. And comparison does not arise between them when they are dis-similar; if similar, comparison is possible, if they are not similar there is nothing to compare.

Dr. P.K. Rao: Is it 'nyaya......'

Sw. K.: Yes, it is 'nyaya' all right, but too subtle and advanced for a sadhak. It speaks from a very high level. Ultimately, he says also what Socrates said. Socrates questions the existing value of things of his time. The value of all things was taken for granted by the philosophers of his time who ruled the people's thoughts. Das. Gupta in his Studies in the Philosophy of Madhusudana Saraswati takes the view that Nagarjuna negates the world and God. It is all only in the imagination. It is just a 'void'. Of course that is the view Buddha also takes. He calls the Absolute state 'void'. The Hindu philosophy says it is 'purnam' —plenum—completeness. In a way, they are both saying the same thing. When there is nothing but completeness, there is nothing other than ONE; it is void. The two views ultimately meet at the same point. Socrates also states that there is neither this (world) nor that (God). And he is right. We are fools imagining that the world exists and is related to God. What is relationship? Something else must also exist to be related to. Then what can be the relationship of the non existing thing to that which is? We are all putting ourselves on the back thinking we are very wise. That is not so. That is what Socrates' Dialectics tell. How can A be related to B? It cannot be because A is A. The very fact that you are saying A is related to B shows A is not B, is it not?

Dr. P.K.R.: It is like Nyaya Vaiseshika.

Sw. K.: If he is not B, how can there be any relationship? You have already said there is no connection. And what do you mean by relationship of A to B? You are floored in one sentence. What is the meaning? And yet we are getting on. He argues like this and you get fed up. But look at the point raised. It is a very interesting subject. It is not a joke. And it is one on which everything hangs. Your entire life is hanging on this little concept of relationship. Neither you are one with That, nor different from That. What else are you! Neither this nor that!

Dr. P.K.R.: He does not give the answer.

Sw. K.: No, No! He simply has stunned you. By that he has proved the unreality of the relationship; it does not exist at all. By which also he proves that the world also does not exist; because the world is nothing but relationship. So the whole world vanishes into thin air in one second by this argument, and you are in a delirium of thinking that there are relationship and things. Are you sleeping?

Dr. P.K.R.: I got taste of that kind of logic from Sankara Muni's Atma Puranam. He goes into this Nyaya Vaiseshika argument, Paksha and then......

Sw. K.: No, no. This is Vedantic argument. Not Nyaya Vaiseshika. Of course all these are based on Nyaya, the effect and the cause. The effect has come from the cause. It means it is different from the cause and so should have characteristics not inherent in the cause. But if they are not in the cause, from where do they come?

Dr. P.K.R.: There is no cause, rather it is modification of the cause.

Sw. K.: Again, we are in the same trouble. You cannot say something comes from nothing. So there must have been something existing there. So the effect is already in the cause. Then why do you say it is different from the cause? I am giving you a taste of all these arguments of Vedanta. Either you never go near it or you understand it! [*Laughs heartily.*]

Dr. P.K.R.: I think it is best to stay away from it.

Sw. K.: [*Still laughing.*] Socrates used to put questions to the Greeks like that and debunk all their so-called wisdom. They were sophists. They thought they were very clever people. And this man's work was only to show that it was not so. They could not define even one idea—Truth. What is truth? You tell me what is truth. You all say, truth, truth, truth. Unless you know what is truth, how can you speak of truth? Let me first of all learn from you what is truth. Then I will speak the 'truth'. Now, you cannot answer this question, you cannot tell me what is truth. Then, why do you tell me to tell the truth? Your instructions are useless. Why do you tom-tom around, speak the truth, when you do not know what truth is?

And finally he said; there is only one thing I know: I know nothing! A very profound statement, that! Truth is what corresponds to facts. But how do you know what is fact? Then only the question of correspondence comes.

Dr. P.K.R: If Socrates wanted to tell people that what they were saying was not anything correct....

Sw. K.: But his point is you cannot define things like that. Your logic cannot help you in defining things. Nothing can be defined in this world; everything is undefinable—*anirvacaniya*. This is what Sankaracharya said finally. It is undefinable because every characteristic is definable only in terms of another characteristic. If you say something is red, there is some-non-red. Otherwise it cannot be said to be red. But how do you know it is non-red? Because it is red! Wonderful definition you are giving [*laughing*.] You are hanging on non-red for red, and on red for non-red. Do you call this a positive definition? [*pause*] And, this goes up to the limit, to the definition of God, Reality, the Absolute, the ultimate value of life, everything! And everything falls to the ground, everything is undefinable. The whole structure of philosophical thinking cracks and falls in a second, if you pursue this logic to the ultimate limits. And it cracks your existence also finally as you are a part of this world, and nothing exists. Then what remains? There was a man called Sriharsa, who wrote a big book called *Khandana Kavyam.* Everything falls and cracks because of this invincible logic which does not allow anything to exist and stand on its own legs. But he says—he has got a saving factor; everything fails, everything has gone; nothing is, but at least you have awareness that nothing is! That is sufficient for you, he says. You cannot say the awareness also is gone because if awareness is gone, there must be an awareness that awareness is gone! So anyhow you cannot get out of the fact that you have awareness that awareness is. That awareness itself cannot be denied. So again there is a basic minimum of positivity if at all you can call it so. That is TRUTH.

S.D.: Nihilists, they say there is nothing. They destroy. Is it not so?

Sw. K.: No, no. They destroy the idea that your definitions are correct. The ideas are all destroyed. You are right. They are called vaiseshikas, destructive critics who do not accept the validity of anything. Everything is invalid—even what he says! That is another thing. Nagarjuna in India, Sriharsha in Vedanta and Bradley in England, they are of this type.

Sw. K.: [*Now turning to the Italian visitor.*] How are you? Happy? Comfortable? You want to tell me anything?

Italian visitor: [*Through the interpreter*] Yes. She is very happy. She asks what is soul? Because you talk about it in the book you have given her—which I am translating, as per your instructions, into Italian for her.

Sw. K: The soul is the ultimate irreducible minimum of existence of anything The soul is the ultimate essence of existence of anything. Everything can be reduced to something else. You can reduce matter to molecules, molecules to atoms, atoms to electrons, and so on. Finally there is a state beyond which you cannot go down. That is the last barest minimum of reality. That is the soul of things.

Q.: Do we make distinctions between the spirit and the soul?

Sw. K.: You need not make a distinction. There is no necessity —they mean the same thing.

Q.: Just one thing. Oh yes, spirit is the essence—the soul is the essence—so they are the same. It is the ultimate reality. That is the soul. You use another word—Atman is it different?

Sw. K.: Soul is English. Atman is Sanskrit. So in what language would you like me to speak? There is a Latin word *Anima Mundi.* That is maternal soul. When you say my soul, you don't mean the absolute self—you mean your physical personality, psychological individuality—that is what they call *Anima Mundi* —the corporal self. But ultimately even that is not the reality. Because that also can be reduced to further ultimate state. There is an absolute reality which is the true spirit.

Q.: What is the spiritual path?

Sw. K.: Spiritual path is the way to the Infinite. It simply means the way to the realisation of the spirit—the path.

Q.: What is spiritual life?

Sw. K.: The dialect for this realisation is spiritual life. It is in stages, from one step to another step. The law of the spirit is quite different from the law that we apply in our empirical life. To that extent you can apply the laws of the spirit in your daily life, to that extent your life is spiritual. It is integration, unity and harmony, whereas empirical life is the opposite of it.

Q.: If you follow the spiritual path you must now be very kind and very good to others. Just leave people going their way or....

Sw. K.: Listen, listen: these words, kindness, etc. are traditional and they have to be understood in their scientific spirit. You cannot be kind by merely uttering the word kind and taking its dictionary meaning. If a particular attitude which you call kindness is in consonance with the law of the spirit, it is necessary to be kind. It is a false idea of kindness if it is contrary to the fact and then it may not work—A mother has great care and kindness for her own child, but that kindness may be unkindness to others. If kindness to one becomes unkindness to others, you cannot call it kindness. So I am giving you an example where a traditional meaning has to work. If the mother gives a bitter medicine to her child to cure the illness, it is kindness. But if she takes away the sweet from another child's hand and gives it to her son, it is unkindness.

Q.: So you must take the whole?

Sw. K.: You must take the whole and spirituality is nothing but that. You cannot rob Peter and pay Paul. That is not charity, Rita?

Rita: No.

Sw. K.: Though charity is good—ethical instructions have a limitation of their own because they have only local value, not of absolute nature—so they have to be understood from the point of view of civics in which they operate—not in a general manner.

Q.: There are people dressed in rags and they don't look after their body. Why do they do like that? Aiming at something? Or, when they are so badly dressed, are they aiming at realisation and negating the body?

Sw. K.: They do it as a kind of austerity to control the mind and develop will-power. The practice of this kind of discipline is itself not spirituality. But it has a negative value in the sense that it helps in the development of will-power for the purpose of higher religious practices. I will give you an example. You fast on the *ekadasi* day. Now that fasting itself has no spiritual value. But by that you develop a control over the mind and mastery of the physical instincts to some extent. This will-power that you develop is helpful to you for the purpose of applying that very same will for meditation. Your making money by itself has no value, but it is done for another purpose which has value. So is this austerity—it has a secondary value, though not an absolute value.

Rita: She thinks it is not a very good choice....

Sw. K.: Which one?

Rita: Wearing rags.

Sw. K.: They are having a type of psychological mind. But it does not mean it is necessary for everybody. It is not necessary for all, but necessary for a particular type of psychological condition. If you understand this—it is human psychology—and that human psychology is the same everywhere—East or West, South or North—It makes no difference.

Rita: It is lacking in human dignity. It is madness.

Sw. K.: Human dignity also is a part of human psychology. Unless you become identical in feeling, you lack understanding. And East or West makes no difference. You cannot think like a monkey unless you yourself become a monkey! You think of them differently because you have not entered their mind. And the others similarly think about you that you are mad to wear the dress you do! To judge anything from one's own point of view is not wisdom. There is always a necessity for giving due consideration to the others' point of view also.

Visitor: What is the standard?

Sw. K.: Every standard is correct from that level. No standard is wrong. You must take it at that level.

Visitor: But then what is wisdom?

Sw. K.: Wisdom is not negation of anything. Everything is O.K. from His point of view. That is why God does not interfere with anything. Everything is O.K. for Him, because every point of view is His point of view.

S.D.: You are the Greatest Advocate for God, Swamiji. For all that He does, you excuse Him and let him out!

Sw. K.: God's point of view is all points of views.

Kartikeyan: But He does not spare the wrong-doer. But according to God, there is nothing wrong!

Sw. K.: He is not saying He is a wrong-doer, he will say, well, that is another way of doing it.

Kartikeyan: But we are vicious people still! And we are punished.

Sw. K.: He will never call it punishment. It is a thing which He himself does within himself.

S.D.: Even death, Swamiji explains, is evolution.

Visitor: But by that (punishment) man suffers.

Sw. K.: Suffering is only an ethical word you are using. It is your way of looking at things. When you are dipped in the Ganges it is suffering for you, but the fish does not call it a suffering.

Someone: But is it suffering or not?

Sw. K.: You ask the fish if it is suffering. It will say I don't know what you are saying? Again, when you are thinking of suffering, you are cutting off some aspects of it in your mind and calling it suffering. If it does not agree with you, it is suffering. It is a question of whether it is agreeable to your constitution;—again it is a subjective point of view. When your viewpoint does not tally with certain situations then you call it suffering. That is all!

Someone: Is it a path?

Sw. K.: Which path? Don't interfere with other people's path. Each path is correct from its own point of view. You follow your own path. We should not interfere with other's path and say it is wrong.

Someone: There must be a standard.

Sw. K.: Standard? Your standard is good for you, that is all. My standard may not suit you.

S. D.: Mind your business, in short?

Sw. K.: Ah, yes. My standard may suit you when you come to my standard and your standard will suit me when I come to your standard (*laughs*).

Dr. N.S. Rao: That means standards are not static?

Sw. K.: That is for your convenience. They have no absolute validity. When you have acidity in the stomach you give sodium bicarbonate. This is a standard. But you cannot give that to everybody, unless there is acidity. What do you say? It is a standard prescription and you give it to everybody because it is a standard prescription.

S.D.: But a prescription is given for a specific ailment.

Sw. K.: But not for every ailment. You won't give it for every purpose. So all standards are conditional and relative. Absolute standards do not exist. Otherwise, everybody can have the same prescription for all conditions. Time, place and circumstances —these are conditional factors. For example, if you may take a bath in Kerala, 5 times, but in the North India, Kedarnath also five times? How is that possible? In Kerala it is necessary, because the climate is such. You will fall sick if you don't take bath—it is warm and perspiring—you can't go with a coat in Guruvayur temple, they will tell that you are a stupid. But a man with a coat does and then pooja in Kedarnath. So it is the place and the time also; suppose you have got typhoid fever what will the pujari in the Kedarnath Temple advise as to how you will do the puja, tell me. Either you do not do puja or take a bath in the Ganga? You want to take bath in the Ganga with Typhoid? That will be something made. It is just commonsense.

Actually, it also happened once; the poor man had typhoid and they want to kill him, emphasising only the tradition, that he is to take bath with his typhoid in the Alaknanda. He cannot do the Puja without a bath. What is the verdict? A meaningless verdict of death. Time, place and circumstances and the prevailing condition—these should give the verdict. If there is a war taking place, what do you do at that time?

S.D.: There is a hot spring in Kedarnath? He can perhaps...

Sw. K.: No, no, they will not allow him to bathe in the hot spring. God does not want comforts [*laughs and so also the gathering*]. How do you do Puja? At that time? You do *archana*, with Sahasranama and so on. But sometimes it may not be possible also. There is a hubbub all around—floods, cyclone, wind, somebody is dying, and what not. Do you sit and do *archana* while all this is an? Conditions and circumstances must be taken into consideration in deciding on what action is to be taken in the context of *desa*, *kala*, *vastu*, *sambandha*. You must live and let others live. You might have to lower your standard sometimes to let others live. If you do not raise your standard of living beyond a certain limit, it may not enable others to live. That is a great point in social sciences. But if you do not want others to live, you only want to live, then you keep your standard!

S.D.: Then there is no system as pulling up to the standard?

Sw. K.: Yes. If you can pull upto the standard, good. But in pulling up the standard you pull up your standard and pull down others. Qualitatively, comparatively, you must raise up others.

Dr. N.S. Rao: There is no absolute standard?

Sw. K.: What do you mean by absolute standard? I cannot understand what you are saying—I am telling you, the world is empirical and relative. Everything is hanging on something else. How can you have an absolute standard in the circumstances of such inter-dependence?

Dr. N.S. Rao: Was there never an absolute standard?

Sw. K.: They say there was absolute standard—in mythology at least—Krita Yuga, when everyone was like every one else. Government did not exist. There was no government—no use. What is the Government for?

Dr. N.S. Rao: To do justice to everyone.

Sw. K.: Yes, that time was called Krita Yuga. They say that a millenium of that type prevailed; Bhisma mentioned this in the Mahabharata. There was no caste and no distinction of any kind. And Vedas also did not exist! Only Pranava—"OMEKARA eva pura veda praneva sarvang mayaha." This is what Krisna tells Udhava. There was only one Veda—it was called Om—The Rig Veda, Sama Veda started afterwards. There was only one caste called Brahma. Not Brahmana Kshatriya, Vaishya, etc. No Government, because everybody knew his duty. So that was an ideal, it is to be known as Krita Yuga, and they say it will come again.

Dr. N.S.R.: Krita Yuga will come?

Sw. K.: Well, they say it will come. You have got now Kali Yuga and all that. After 4 lakhs of years. The wheel will move and the spokes that are down will come up again.

Dr. N.S.R.: The cycle will go on rotating?

Sw. K.: Well, it has happened so many times—28th Kaliyuga is now going on. The wheel has rotated 28 times they say—eh?—Yes, twenty-eight. There are one thousand cycles like this in a Brahmas Day. And that does not include his night. Night is an equal period—same length—one thousand four cycles must take place—28th is going on. So, after Brahma's birth, now it is not even 1/2 a day [*laughter all around*]; even mid-day has not come —it is about 11 o'clock or something like that: Well, all this is the theory of Puranas and Manu Smriti and Mahabharata. Now even the Western Scientists have accepted it. They don't base their arguments on scriptures.

Dr. N.S.R.: But all by men...

Sw. K.: But men with scientific minds. This earth has come from the Sun. How do you know this? You have not seen the sun splitting in some parts. But you have got some facts based on some observations, etc. Light travels at one lakh eighty thousand miles. How do you know this? You have got some calculations on which it depends. Likewise this also. There are some calculations and observations made by which they have come to the conclusion that there is recurrence of the cycle—And in Christianity the miracle, when Christ will come and rule. And this is called Krita Yuga in our terminology. They say it will happen. So we have to wait and see unless you reach the absolute before that [*laughter*.] Then you don't have to bother.

S.D.: Is it possible to reach the Absolute in the Kaliyuga?

Sw. K.: I don't know if there is Kaliyuga for the Absolute! It doesn't exist for it, poor thing! The Absolute doesn't know what you are talking. It is like talking to the...

S.D.: I know what I am talking...

Sw. K.: It is like talking to the Sun about night. What is night? He says what is night! [*laughter*]. He doesn't know what you are talking about. "I have never seen it," the Sun will say.

S.D.: Can the jivas attain the Absolute in Kaliyuga?

Sw. K.: Kaliyuga is nothing but the condition when you feel that you cannot reach the Absolute [*S.D. laughs*]. That is called Kaliyuga. When you feel it is possible, Krita Yuga has some to you in a second. This is another revealing and solacing factor for you.

Dr. P.K. Rao: It is a condition of the mind.

Sw. K.: You need not worry about the cycle, it will come automatically and in one second though the Puranas say it is four lakhs of years.

Dr. P.K.R.: It amounts to that. It is an attitude of the mind Swamiji.

Sw. K.: Yes, ultimately the Yoga Vasistha will tell you all this. All these terrifying doctrines will vanish in a second before another greater truth. They are terrifying. When understood they are nothing. Otherwise who can bear these four lakhs of Kali Yuga —You will die by hearing it. But there is also another teaching that it is not so terrifying if you can understand it—you can simply melt it like the snow melts before the light of the sun. The whole Kali Yuga—mass will melt before the light of enlightenment—in one second—so Bhagyalakshmi. Mataji, don't cry unnecessarily once you believe God exists. But a clause has to be added to it: God exists and nothing else exists. Then it would be a complete statement. But you can imagine what consequences will follow from that doctrine of nothing existing. You will vanish in a second and be finished.

Dr. N.S.R.: Then what is the meaning of 'All-pervasive'?

Sw. K.: Nothing, nothing! When everything has vanished, then where is the question of pervasiveness? Again you are implying that something else exists when you are diminishing. By saying He is all-pervasive, you have implied that God is different from the world. Then only you would use 'pervading'; that would make him a second-grade God! First you deny God, then you say He is staying far above, then you say he is related—you see the Bhagavad Gita. All the 18 chapters will tell you all these various stages. First, know God—the Gita never talks of God in the beginning; afterwards He is slowly beginning to tell that He is above, then He will say He is below also, then He will say relationship—He is everywhere—yes, he takes you like that gradually. Religion has various stages of approach like that, but you should not say "That only", in the beginning itself. So gradually take the mind up [*laughs.*]

Dr. N.S.R.: To the ultimate truth?

Sw. K.: Ah, yes! When you are prepared, when the vessel is prepared to contain the substance, then only you can fill it with the substance. Otherwise a pot of mercury poured into a mud the pot will crack. So the chapters of the Gita prepare the mind gradually for the reception of higher knowledge. In the beginning it was such a catastrophe simply crying. It started with crying —slowly you know [*to Dr. N.S. Rao*] who has been writing a serial in the DLS Magazine on Bhagavad Gita, how it goes. Strategic method is adopted, step by step, until there is a cataclysm, the flood of God coming. There's nothing like the Gita. It is everything, if it is properly appreciated. God comes and attacks you like a cyclone. In the beginning it is frightening. Oh! oh! Sufficient! Enough! Arjuna says, cyclone I don't want. Even a God-cyclone is terrifying. Is it not?

S.D.: Yes, Arjuna cried like that.

Dr. A.: Is idealism not a mania?

Sw. K.: A normal thing you don't call mania. If you have desire to eat food, you don't call it a mania. But a desire to commit suicide can be called mania.

Dr. A.: I mean martyrdom?

Sw. K.: Martyrdom is...

Dr. P.K. Rao: Martyrdom is done for a good cause.

Sw. K.: That is a different matter, now you are interpreting something. She is talking as it is. All martyrs are so for a good cause only, not otherwise. Nobody calls it martyrdom for a bad cause.

Dr. A.: But that is a mania.

Sw. K.: Why do you call it mania if it is a good cause? Martyrdom is not a mania because a martyr is aware of every sequel of consequences and is prepared for it. So there is no shock for him and he is the master of emotions. If you push a man into the Ganges, he gets a shock. But if he himself dives into the Ganges, he gets no shock—he is prepared for the cold and the force of water—But a person who commits suicide, you call a maniac—He is not prepared for the consequences—his being gets a shock.

S.D.: But the man committing suidide is prepared for the consequences. He knows he will end and will go into the unknown...

Sw. K.: That is only at his conscious level, but not at that subconscious level which gets a shock because it is not prepared for it. What is the time? Nearly twelve? Go, go all of you, you will be late for the second batch even if you do not go now. Thank you, God bless you all!

A visitor from Australia asked Swamiji whether a seeker should search for a Guru.

Sw. K.: Who told you about Gurus? How did this idea come into your mind?

Vis.: A certain friend told me that I must search for a Guru.

Sw. K.: Take him as your Guru. For you believe that you should do what he has told you. Otherwise you would not have listened to his words. If there was no need for a Guru in your mind you would never have put this question. Unless you felt a need that you should receive guidance at such supernormal levels you would never have put this question: should I or should I not search for a Guru. That this question has come into your mind means that you want a Guru. Your friend who told you that you must search for a Guru, has cut the ground from under his feet by saying you must look for a Guru. Guru is one who gives advice and guidance. Your friend has given you both and has therefore become your Guru.

There were visitors from Italy, England and other places. Swamiji enquired in great detail and concern about their comforts in the Ashram and gave advice concerning matters of their Visa and health, pointing out the great differences in diet, climate, etc. which, he said, they must have been experiencing.

Sw. K.: So you have come today. You are not afraid? [*Laughs, others too laugh.*] I want to talk to you about your people, your house, home your plans, etc., etc. These are all very important matters which must be clearly understood before you take any decision regarding your future plans. Casually in the emotion of the moment you should not decide matters which have long-time effects. Your decisions are not to be taken before all these aspects are examined thoroughly so that all the aspects are correctly understood before taking the next step.

Ch.: I have written to them all.

Sw. K.: Send a telegram. Letters take a long time to reach.

S.D.: What does 'Trayi Marga Pradarshakaya' mean? Is it what Gurudev used to call the 'Trisul'?

Sw. K.: You are mixing up the meanings. 'Trayi Marga Pradarshakaya' means the one who directs you on the path of the three Vedas—the Rig, Yajur and Sama. The 'Trisul' means, the three disciplines by which you control the mind: (1) the daily fixed routine, (2) the resolve you take to improve virtues and eradicate your weaknesses, (3) and spiritual diary. These three are like the three points of the Trisul.

Kn.: The statement 'Truth is that which has no contradiction' is unsound logic. The world then has to be negated. And that cannot be because God is the world.

Sw. K.: So long as the two words, world and God, are not used, this point is correct. Well if you must have it, what you call the world is what I call God. There should be no duality. Hence the statement that Truth is that which has no contradiction has to be accepted; it comes to that. Of course Goudapada also takes this view. And the Nasadiya Suktam also says "Does God know that He has created the world?" The idea is that the world is a part of God. He Himself is the world; it is like the sun-light, which is just a natural feature of the sun. The world too is a natural part of God, so to say.

Kn.: Even in the state of the Final Deluge (*mahalaya*) the world exists in its involute form and so cannot be neglected—no, not at all.

Sw. K.: Despite this fact, Mula Prakriti is not independent of God. It is just one aspect of His, so we come back to the point that there is only ONE, no two, no one person. And truth is that which has no contradiction to it. You can have the world provided you first state that God alone is.

S.D.: If I see only God in *idli* and *dosai* (cookies) like pan cake and the like), I cannot enjoy them! What is the point of my eating them?

Sw. K.: When you see God, you would not want to eat *idli* and *dosai* as such. You will find the joy in God which you see in them. He is every kind of joy and all joy.

S.D.: I know it sounds like that man who said that if there is no sense of hunger or sleep, he did not want to go there to God.

Sw. K.: It is said that after taking Varaha Avatara, the Lord got so one with its own Avatara, that he forgot His Real Self. And when Mahalakshmi said, "My Lord! We have been here so long and it is over-due for thyself to return to thy true divinity," the Lord is supposed to have asked "Do we get this food we now live on there also?" And when the reply was negative, it is said, the Lord observed, "In that case, let us remain here only." And if you want to enjoy *idli* and *dosai*, you do not need to see God in them!

S.D.: The point I wish to get to is that the Rishis have lived on dry leaves for their sustenance—did they taste the dry leaves.

Sw. K.: Their mind was not on what they ate; the biological need was satisfied by the act of eating the dry leaves. Their state of evolution was such that they could digest them. You cannot eat them and live. You will fall sick. There was no question of taste or of the mind contacting what it ate. You too become unconscious of the taste of the food or of what you eat when your mind is preoccupied with something else. You eat merely as an act that must be finished to be able to get on the next thing on hand.

S.D.: Swami Chitbhavananda has written a commentary on Saint Thayumanavar's Guru in Tamil. In this, he says that *siddha-purusas* who have attained such a *siddhi* as to be able to preserve their physical body for any number of years as they wish to, have an object in so preserving it. And to illustrate this, he cites the example of the saint of our own century whose name was Tipin-linga Swamigal. It is authentic information, he says, that this Swamigal lived as recently as only 500 years ago and had achieved this *kaya-kalpa-siddhi*. And this saint had preserved his physical body (he was born with) for over one hundred years. The object in view was that with this single body, without further merging with the Absolute, he could experience in this single body the terrors of *grabha vasha* and reducing them thereby to this single physical birth. It is not *prarabha* that gives a physical body to the Jiva. How can all the *prarabdhas* of the different births be experienced and exhausted in this single birth itself?

Sw. K.: That also has been pre-determined by his previous *prarabdha*. That he should strive for or that he should achieve success in thus exhausting all his *prarabdha* in the *kaya-kalpa-siddhi* of this same body—all this is due to his *prarabdha* only; it is this *prarabdha* that has determined that all this shall be so. You can keep this body for 500 years or so, as long as you have willed it should and after that time only it will disintegrate. This is possible, but it needs a very highly developed evolution of the soul and hard work for years after which you can attain *kaya-kalpa-siddhi*. Now, as for the questions. Who gives this urge to acquire this *siddhi*? Who gives this urge to know God? Who told you to tread the spiritual path? Who gives the knowledge of God the Absolute? No one knows how all these come or from where. Sankaracharya the great simply gives up further probe at this point and urges that it is God's Grace alone that can induce the urge, this knowledge that there is a higher knowledge [*quotes a Sanskrit line from Sankara*]. If this were not so, everybody, even the buffalo, could have knowledge of the Absolute.

S.D.: This grace which God gives, which He alone can give—how does He give it? Like the rain? As a boon? Or......

Sw. K.: It is just His nature to shower grace on whom He wills, without any motive; not giving it so that you might return it. God is not mindful of your gratitude about it. It is His own being. God has no motive or discrimination. A blind man was going to the temple to see God. Someone told him, "since you are blind and you cannot see, what is the use of your going to the temple for the Lord's *darsan?*" And that blind man replied. "I may not be able to see God, but He will see me!" That is how God behaves. He has no motive or discrimination. He showers His grace upon all, at all times, on all occasions.

S.D.: Are we not now qualifying God with some characteristics—a mode? The Absolute has neither.

Sw. K.: It is His nature.

S.D.: If every bit is pre-determined as explained in the case of the *kaya-kalpa-siddhi prarabdha*, it gives one more leg for fatalism.

Sw. K.: There is no such thing as fatalism. Fatalism is not a blind mechanical action or reaction. You are unable to understand the whole truth of it and are unable to analyse the cause and its effect—that's all. Every single aspiration or desire, every single impulse or urge leaves its impression upon your *prarabdha* which works accordingly. Nothing happens outside these impressions.

S.D.: Swamiji often says that in God there is no dirt, no ugliness, no ugly sights. Is it because they undergo a chemical change in God and so dirt and unsightly matter becomes pure and non-ugly?

Sw. K.: Is it chemical change when the sun shines upon you? Is it undergoing a chemical change in its rays when it lights you? It is just its nature to shine, and give warmth and light. Everything is perfect in God. It is when you isolate a thing from God, isolate yourself from things, and see them in a variety of ways that all imperfections come in. There is nothing but perfection in God. And when you are with Him, your consciousness is that of God only, and you see also everything in its perfection. Everything becomes yours when you enter God. There is nothing outside you. At that stage of God-consciousness, nothing exists but yourself. And what is Samadhi. [*All this is said with the passion of a mother defending her beloved child against a false accusation.*] You push people and objects outside your being and then become filled with criticisms of them. People whom you consider your own are always good in your eyes. It is people whom you consider outside you that you find so much to blame for. Nothing is outside God, and nothing is dirty or ugly in Him. Gurudev never found in anyone anything bad. A certain man abused Gurudev, and it made the General Secretary very angry. So he reported the matter to Gurudev, who merely remarked, "The poor man is angry. Take some *badam* and milk to him." The General Secretary again got annoyed and grumbled that Swamiji always spoilt people like this! But the *badam* and milk were given to the man who abused Gurudev. The man was *thunderstruck*! And that act of Gurudev truly made him repent and he turned a new leaf in his life. That is what is called seeing everyone in yourself and not as external to you. Sivananda Maharaj thus answered a question, saying his disciples should see everyone with equal vision.

What do you understand by 'equal vision'?

Dr. A.: The Bhagavad Gita says you must look upon a dog and a Brahmin with the same eye.

Sw. K.: What does it mean? The elephant eats grass, cows eat straw. Will you feed the Brahmin with grass and straw, because you must see him as you do the animals? Seeing all this with equal vision means seeing everyone in and as your own self, not externally as 'the other', as an 'outsider'. And I told you how Gurudev gave *badam* and milk to the man who abused him merely because that man was angry and so abused Gurudev! That is what is called seeing everyone with the same eyes. A disciple should just be guided by the Guru. If he understands and obeys, well and good. If there is no understanding, at least he should obey, in the knowledge that the Guru has told him why he sould or should not do a thing, because the Guru understands why he is instructing him in that way—although the Guru has not told the desciple of it, the why of it. Gurudev, Swami Sivananda, has written a poem; in the form of that poem he has said all that which he would call being his disciple would mean. The book is in the library. And Gurudev's poems are much better than his other writings, though some may seem to have beenwritt en in a light vein. The disciple should be concerned with only what he is told, This is what Jesus said, "Tomorrow's will be told tomorrow." Now we are concerned with the today, the present. Now I work or chat with you all as my way to God.

* * *

S.D.: When a person fights for justice and gets angry at the injustice, it is called righteous anger and as such is justifiable. Still it is not permitted for a seeker. Why?

Sw. K.: To follow a principle is not getting attached to the principle. A principle is not an attachment. It is only when you get attached to an idea that you want to fight. Anger is emotion. Righteous anger is therefore meaningless.

[*A visitor from abroad and a keen seeker after Truth plies Sw. Krishnanandaji with his questions.*]

Visitor: How to see God as everything?

Sw. K.: If you can be independent of the world, then you can see God in everything. The difference of opposites is the obstacle that prevents you from seeing God in everything, because the opposites do not exist in God; they cease to be opposites in God. God is positive in its entirety.

Visitor: What is the distinction between male and female?

Sw. K.: It cannot be of the psyche. The psyche is not involved in the physiology of the body......

Visitor: What is meditation as part of yoga?

Sw. K.: The yogic meditation is the summing up of all our activities. The purpose of all our activities is to be one with everything. But even in meditation Space and Time come in and this is the tragedy which our activities try to overcome; our activities split up the purpose of unifying the activities in view as 'desires'. Hence no desire is contradictory to any other.

Another Seeker: What is free will and what is (God's) grace?

Sw. K.: When God's will passes through your personality, it is your 'free will' and when the cosmic urge manifests itself through you, your personality takes 'effort' and that is the meaning of free will to act and effort one makes to act. Effort from the lay man's point of view ordinarily appears to mean that activities are isolated. When you are writing, is it the nib writing? The eyes are unable to see what is behind the visible form. Hence the sense of isolation of activities. When the little finger moves, the child thinks that only the little finger is moving. But mature minds with knowledge of the working of human body know that the whole physiology of the human system is behind the movement of the little finger.

Visitor: Is *Prana* the Ultimate Truth?

Sw. K.: It is not, because a vibration, a motion is trancient and this is not the characteristic of the unchanging Truth. But tentatively you can call it Truth inasmuch as it is the subtle essence of the cosmos. It is, relatively, Truth, but not actually Truth.

Q.: What is its origin? And is it from Prakriti?

Sw. K.: The origin is the Atman, the Supreme Being itself. It is the breath of the Supreme Being. Prakriti is also *Prana* itself. Prakriti is a potential condition of *Prana*. Prakriti is a philosophical term in Sankhya and ultimately means the same thing as what the Upanisadic language terms as *Prana*. The two terms are two different ways of expressing the same thing.

Q.: Are *Gunas* dependent on the power of *Prana*?

Sw. K.: The answer is the same as for the above (last) question. The three Gunas are the three ways in which the universal *Prana* operates. When it works by way of division, destruction and isolation of one thing from another, it is *Rajasic*, when it works by way of stability of static-forms of energy of things, it is *Tamasic*, when it becomes subtle enough to become transparent and therefore capable of revealing the harmony of things, it is *Satva* and is superior to the other two gunas and hence called *Satva*.

Q.: Is *Prana* identical with Existence?

Sw. K.: Since *Prana* is an expression of existence, how then can you say they are identical? *Prana* is an expression, a vibration, a motion, a manifestation relatively of the Reality and, therefore, we should not call it existence as such because it is manifestation of the Eternal Being, and it is not the Eternal Being itself.

Q.: If its existence is Existence itself, is it co-related with the will of God as the originator of the universe?

Sw. K.: Yes. The will of God manifests itself as the cosmic *Prana* in its grosser form. But the cosmic *Prana* itself is on a higher level called the will of God.

Q.: Is *Prana* "Mrityu" or Death Principle in this universe itself to some extent?

Sw. K.: It is the Principle of Death only in the individual and not in the cosmos, because the cosmos does not die as the individual dies. There is death in the individual but not in the universal, it can withdraw itself from the physical embodiment called the body. At the time of death the *Prana* in the individual withdraws itself from the physical body, and gets absorbed in the mind and it is this phycho-physiological complex called the blend of Prana, senses, the mind, the intellect etc. which is called the subtle body that re-incarnates itself in a new existence. So *Prana* is not 'Mrityu' or death by itself, but it is what causes death by an extrication of itself from the physical body when the purpose of the physical body is completed.

Q.: Is *Prana* playing with *Prana* whichis present in all manifestations though *Prana* is *Shakti* itself? What else can it be? Other than the substance of everything? Can it be thought and matter also?

Sw. K.: The answer is not different from what has already been said. *Prana*, thought, matter—they are inter-connected and convertible. The subtler thought and the grosser form of thought are *Prana*. The movement of thought is *Prana* and the thinking aspect of *Prana* is thought; and matter, of course, is something grosser than *Prana*; It is the visible individualisation of things that we call *Prana*, but the energy that is behind matter is called *Prana*. Higher than *Prana* is thought which is the cosmic thinking principle of thought.

Q.: What is *Prana* in relation to the Consciousness of the Absolute?

Sw. K.: Consciousness co-vibrating with and through space and time is called *Prana*, whether it is vibrating universally or individually.

Q.: Has *Prana* a place to merge in the Absolute?

Sw. K.: The *Prana* being the manifestation of the Absolute; naturally gets absorbed in the Absolute at the time of the dissolution of the universe and also at the time of the liberation of the individual.

Q.: Would......even the attempt at meditation to realise the identity with *Prana* be bound to the cosmic consciousness or is there a passage to the Absolute transcending the universe and its *Shakti*?

Sw. K.: Everything is cosmic ultimately; because, everything is correlated inter-connected. Whenever you breathe, naturally you get connected with cosmic *Prana*. The intention of meditation is to connect one's *Prana* with cosmic Prana. Only then it becomes a passage to Eternal. It is not only the *Prana* that is trying to connect with the cosmic *Prana* but everything also that is also in us For example, the mind, intellect etc. are also being connected. The individual *Prana* in us by means of Pranayama or harmonised breathing should get connected with cosmic *Prana* which neither inhales nor exhales. Similarly you must connect your individual thought with the cosmic will or the universal thought. So also we have to connect our individual understanding with the cosmic intellect which is called Hiranyagarbha.

Q.: Why did the substratum or Cosmic *Prana* vanish as the Lord of the mind, Indra, appeared? Are the cosmic mind and the cosmic *Prana* inseparable?

Sw. K.: They are not inseparable because the cosmic mind is the internal condition of cosmic *Prana* and the cosmic *Prana* is a grosser manifestation of the cosmic mind. The substratum or the Cosmic *Prana* vanished because Indra is the principle of the ego. While speech can express by means of fire which is a principle of nature and of health and which is symbolised in *agni* as its deity, and while we can act in consonance with the universal being, by means of the expression of the *Prana* which is symbolised by the deity Vayu approaching Supreme Being, Indra cannot approach the Being for Indra is the Ego. When the ego approached God, God vanished because God and Ego are polar opposite. So it is that Indra could not see the Absolute. Even so, even thought speech and *Prana* could visualise the Absolute Being, they could not understand the nature of the Absolute. Similarly, even in our practice of harmonised activity like philanthropic works and social service, we are unable to understand the nature of Reality, though by such harmonised activity, we are trying to diminish our ego. But Indra is the principle of the Ego itself in direct opposition to God, which is why when he approaches, the Absolute vanishes. This is a lesson to us as well. We should not meditate with our Ego. It is worse than merely studying the scriptures and giving discourses on the nature of God, etc. or doing social service which to some extent is good. But when the Ego contemplates, God vanishes because He is inclusive of the Ego principle also. The meditating principle is not the Ego. It is the universal being itself. It is God meditating on God ultimately. So if you consider yourself Mr. so-and-so and then start meditating on God, God does not come to you because He is inclusive of your being also. The concept of the universal means the affirmation of the idea that other than the object of meditation, nothing exists. That is called universalisation. When you think of something, you should not think of something else at the same time—that is the essence of concentration. If you believe God is all, you should not think of non-God at the same time. That is another way of defining universalisation. If a thing exists—and only that exists and nothing else—and your objective in meditation is so complete in itself that other than it cannot be, that is called a universal concept. What you think is not important. But are you thinking something else at the same time? That is the whole point. Are we able to concentrate upon it exclusively? You should not think anything except that. That is called concentration. How can something be outside of that object of your concentration? First of all you have to convince yourself that the object of your meditation is all-prevading and it is all-existence. It should be the only thing that exists. It should not be one of the things in the world. Then there would be no valid reason for the mind or the ego to think of other objects outside it. Spiritual life is not easy. It requires a little of effort of thought. We have to think in a new way altogether. Now the time has come to think of only one thing and not of anything else. The other things we consider to be outside are a part of what you have been thinking of. So the essence of concentration is exclusive absorption in the object of an Omnipresent Reality. That is the essence of meditation. Everything which upto now you have been regarding as a little finite being becomes an integral part of the Cosmic Being. It is an awakening into the true relationship of things to reality. When you realise your integral connection with the Absolute, you will realise in every sand particle, in every dust particle, everywhere God himself. That is meditation. You need not close your eyes and sit in the meditation hall. The moment you are aware of this, you are in a state of meditation. That is the way to be happy. Otherwise you are happy inside the meditation hall and unhappy outside. You must be happy in the street, in the market-place, in the bath-room and not only in the temple, etc. That is what is described as your 'travelling in space' by Yogic practice. You must travel in consciousness first. The whole point is, we require some guidance from a guru until such time as we are able to live in this kind of living awareness.

S.D.: What is Time? There is a confusion in giving different meanings to it.

Sw. K.: Time is consciousness of the succession of events. It is not the time factor of this world of ours. Time was the first creation. Jiva with reference to creation is both the animate and innanimate mass of creation as a whole. In the evolution of Prakriti, the rocks and other innanimate objects by re-arrangement of their internal atomic, neutronic structure evolved into trees and the like of the planned kingdom in the evolution of Time.

S.D.: It is again said that the Jiva, Maya and Time (to which reference is made in the Bhagavad Purana) were lying meaninglessly around untill the Supreme Being entered them simultaneously when creation began. How does Time make Maha Satva, the Ego and the five gross elements cohere? Is it by sequence? Can it be said that up to now the evolution was something like a chemical action and Time a manufacturing factor giving meaning to the chemical actions?

Sw. K.: A poor anology but it is something like that and of a much more complex and deeper nature.

S.D.: Is Time equal to, I mean, the same as consciousness?

Sw. K.: Time is consciousness of succession of events. This is different from the Time-spirit which is Narayana himself, The hub and the wheel and the spokes is a constant figure of speech to explain this differentiation between Time and Time Spirit. It is a cliche of the sacred texts, even as is the anology of black rat and white rat eating the thread which means time, that is day and night which are heirarchy of time. If you see the stone in the statue of a dog, you don't see the dog. But if you see the dog, stone does not exist. Snake and the rope is such another cliche.

Q.: What is Madhu Vidya the Brihadaranyaka Upanishada expounds?

Ans : Three things are in three different places, the Absolute the Universe and the Jiva. The inter-connectedness of these are explained in this chapter. The Lord's energy is divided when the equilibrium of the three Gunas get disturbed under the force of His energy known by the name of Time. Externalised energy is Matter and Objective. Energy of the Lord and time is subjective. Mimamsa speaks of Him as Karma, Charuvakas speak of Him as nature. Some speak of Him as Kama.

Dr. X.: Why is the Anandamaya Kosa a sense of darkness? There is no awareness of anything in deep sleep which is, because it is resting in the Anandamaya Kosa.

Sw. K.: There is no such thing as "Kosa" for the Anandamaya. It is only a way of putting it, for there are no Vrittis in Anandamaya Kosa. Vrittis arise only with reference to objects that are externalised as objects outside. This is what happens even in dream and since there are no objects in deep sleep which rests in Anandamaya Kosa, there are no Vrittis. The absence of Vrittis is not a state of a nescience that is darkness. Anandamaya Kosa is so brilliant, the light of the million watt bulb that it seems dark, like the sun's disc appears dark when you see it with naked eye. The mind cannot take this amount of brilliance that is in the Anandamaya Kosa. Hence the Jiva gets the sense of nothingness. Also there is no such thing as "entering" bliss. It is not pulled up or down as happens in the case of a satelite entering the orbit of the moon. The pull in the state of bliss, if you so wish to put it, will be from all sides. You just become merged into it, one with this Existence-Knowledge-Bliss.

PART III

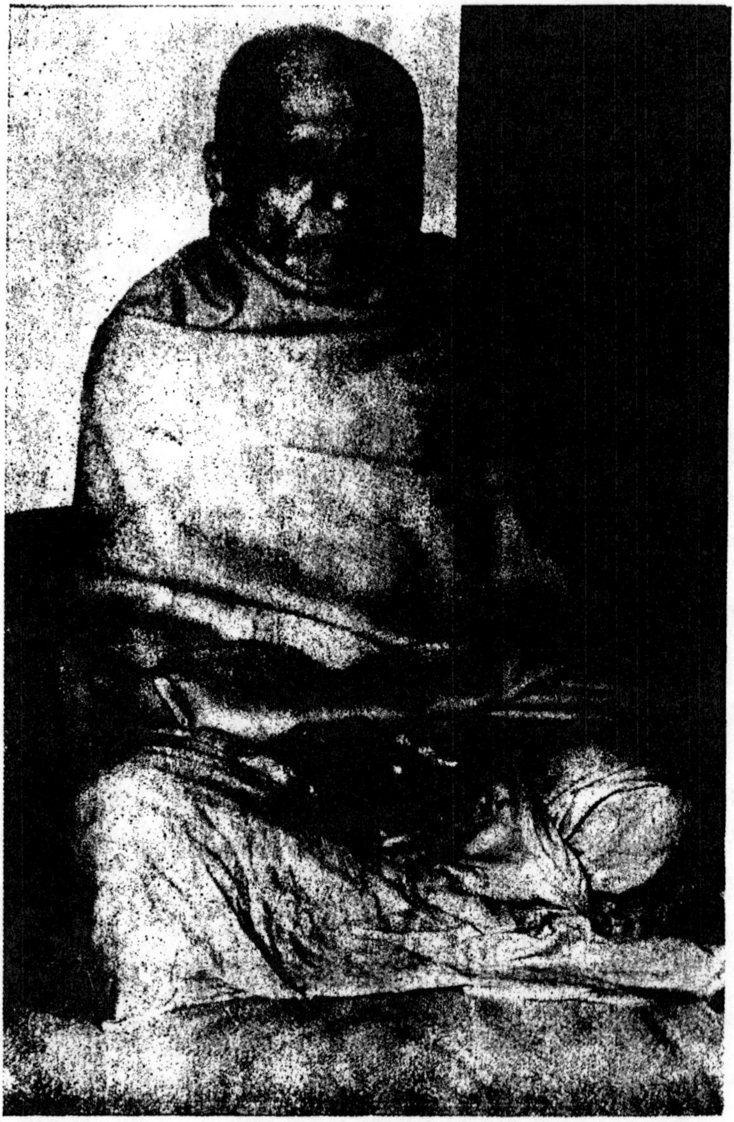

Swami Krishnananda—The Philosopher

Practical Hints on Sadhana

1. First of all, there should be a clear conception of the aim of one's life.

2. The aim should be such that it should not be subject to subsequent change of opinion or transcendence by some other thought, feeling or experience. It means, the aim should be ultimate, and there should be nothing beyond that.

3. It will be clear that, since the ultimate aim is single, and set clearly before one's mind, everything else in the world becomes merely an instrument, an auxiliary or an accessory to the fulfilment of this aim.

4. It is possible to make the mistake that only certain things in the world are aids in the realisation of one's aim of life, and that others are obstacles. But this is not true, because everything in the world is interconnected, and it is not possible to divide the necessary from the unnecessary, the good from the bad, etc., except in a purely relative sense. The so-called unnecessary items or the useless ones are those whose subtle connection with our central purpose in life is not clear to our minds. This happens when our minds are carried away by sudden emotions or spurts of enthusiasm.

5. All this would mean that it is neither advisable nor practicable to ignore any aspect of life totally, as if it was completely irrelevant to the purpose of one's life.. But here begins the difficulty in the practice of Sadhana, because it is not humanly possible to consider every aspect of a situation when one tries to understand it.

6. The solution for this is the training which one has to receive under a competent Guru, who alone can suggest methods of entertaining such a comprehensive vision of things, which is the precondition of a true spiritual life, or a life of higher meditation.

7. There are economic and material needs as well as vital long-

ings of human nature which have to be paid their due at the proper time and in the porper proportion, not with the intention of acquiring comfort and satisfaction to one's self, but with a view to the sublimation of all personal desires or urges, whether physical, vital or psychological. An utter ignorance of this fact may prove to be a sort of hindrance in one's further practice on the path of sadhana.

8. It is, of course, necessary that one should live a life of reasonable seclusion under the guidance of a Master until such time when one can stand on one's own legs and think independently without any aid from anyone.

9. But one should, now and then, test one's ability to counteract one's reactions to the atmosphere even when one is in the midst of intractable and irreconcilable surroundings. Seclusion should not mean a kind of self-hypnotism or hibdernation and an incapacity to face the atmosphere around.

10. It should not also mean that one should be incapable of living in seclusion alone by oneself when the occasion for it comes. In short, the ideal should be the achievement of an equanimous attitude to circumstances, whether one is alone or in the midst of an irreconcilable social atmosphere.

11. While in seclusion, the mind should not be allowed to go back to the circumstances of one's family life, official career or to problems which are likely to disturb the concentration of the mind in God, because the pressure of these earlier experiences may sometimes prove itself to be greater in intensity than one's love for God.

12. It is impossible to concentrate on God unless one has a firm conviction and faith that whatever one expects from this world can also be had from God; nay much more than all these things, which the world has as its treasures and values.

13. It is difficult to have the visions of one's aim of life when the mind goes out of meditation to whatever it longs for in the world. Hence, a deep study of the upanishads and the Bhagavad Gita, the Srimad Bhagavata and such other scriptures is necessary to drive into the mind the conviction about the supremacy of God.

14. Study of Svadhyaya, Japa of Mantras, and Meditation are the three main aspects of spiritual sadhana.

15. Svadhyaya does not mean study of any book that one may find anywhere at any time. It means a continued and regular

study, daily, of slected holy texts, or even of a single text, from among those that have been suggested above. A study done at a fixed time, every day, for a fixed duration, will field the expected result.

16. The Japa of the mantra should, in the beginning, be done with a little sound in the mouth so that the mind may not ramble towards different things. The loud chant of the Mantra will bring the mind back to the point of concentration. Later on, the Japa can be only with movement of lips, but without making any sound. In the end, the Japa can only be mental, provided that the mind does not wander during the mental Japa.

17. A convenient duration, say, half an hour, or one hour, should be set up at different times, so that daily sadhana should be at least for three hours a day, and not less. It can be increased according to one's capacity as days pass.

18. During Japa, the mind should think of the meaning of the mantra, the surrender of oneself to the deity of the mantra, and finally the communion of oneself with that great deity. Effort should be made to entertain this deep feeling during Japa every day.

19. Meditation can be either combined with Japa or it can be independent of Japa. Meditation with Japa means the mental repetition of the mantra and, also, at the same time, meditating deeply on the meaning of the mantra, as mentioned above.

20. Meditation without Japa is a higher stage where the mind gets so much absorbed in the thought of God, surrender to God and union with God, that in this meditation, Japa automatically stops. This is the highest stage of Meditation.

21. Throughout one's sadhana, it is necessary to feel the oneness of oneself and the universe with God.

A Talk delivered on the concluding day of Sadhana week on 7 July 1977.

Hints for the Practice of Yoga

First of all, you must love God from the very bottom of your heart. Be very careful to be true to your ownself. Yoga is not for anybody's sake, neither for your friends or relations, nor for the sake of your Guru, nor for the sake of telling others, "I am also doing Yoga". You do it for your own self. Be sure that you want God, and nothing else, when you close your eyes and sit for meditation. Be sure that you are not doing so merely for becoming a student of Yoga or start with an intention of building an institution of Yoga. These are terrible travesties. If such are your motives, you are not going to succeed in Yoga. Be honest to yourself. You can deceive others many times but not yourself. You know very well what is behind your mind. You cannot put God in your pocket and say, I can come to you through Yoga, but my motive is something different, something else; that will not work. Honesty is the gateway to success; it is indeed fifty per cent of success. Learning is not necessary, no need to be learned. All that you have to do is to be sure and sincere that you are crying for God only and nothing else. Let the aim of life be clear in your mind, first. I repeat, your aim should be nothing other than the Ultimate Reality.

The world is also real, this idea may come to your mind. I am not saying that the world is unreal. I am only talking about your misconception about the nature of the world: that it is outside you. It is not really outside you. The world is real, but it is not outside you. You are not outside it, but a part of it. You also are in the world. The exclusion of the world from you is your problem and then many questions arise. Is the world real? Is God real or not? etc. Let the world be real. We have no objection. But it is not real in the sense of its being outside you in space and time; it is connected with you. Is the hand of your body real or unreal? If it is a part of your body, then it is real; if it is cut off and thrown out or is paralysed, then it is unreal. In Yoga, we identify consciousness with the being of the world, with the self-hood of the world. Again, to come to the point, the Self-hood is in everything. But when we think of the world as an entity outside us, then we have removed this Self-hood from the world, divested it of its Self-hood and placed it as an object, an instrument or tool of utility for our satisfaction and then we place ourselves in the position of 'the self'. 'I am the self, you are the objects!' Anything that you look upon as outside you is an object. The object also is a subject from its own point of view, and you are its object; if I am an object for you, so are you an object for me. And this, that, everything is an object. There are, then, only objects, and no 'subject' anywhere. This situation is called *Samsara* or bondage; these are materialistic ways of looking at the world. Everything is external. Now turn the argument the other way and look at everything from its own point of view. It is true I am an object to you, you are an object to me, everything is an object to everything. But I am also a subject from my own point of view.

So, if you take everything from its own point of view, there is no object, everything is subject only everywhere. This realisation is freedom. So in one moment of time, you can be in bondage or freedom by merely shifting the mind from one view to another: from subject to object or the other way round. If you can extract the selfhood of things, it does not matter whether the world exists or not; you will yourself understand that it exists. But if you look upon it as an object, you are also looked upon as an object by it. Now you are turned out. The exile of Adam and Eve from the Garden of Eden is nothing but the isolation and externalisation of the individual from God. You also have been exiled and alienated in this manner. You are cut off from the Whole. The five elements are in your body; the same five elements are in the world. From this point of view, at least, you should not think that the world is outside you. Yet we think so. The space, air, fire, water and earth principles, which are the constituents of the world, are also what constitute your body. Then where comes the question of the world being outside you? That space, that which has separated you from your object is also within you. It is only in thinking spatially, that the world is separated from you. Nothing has happened. It is only a kind in your way of thinking. In the ultimate analysis, creation has not taken place.

The creation of the world is an experience that has been introduced into our mind by the projection of the principle of externality, which is described as the so-called "Maya" of the philosophers. And many such words are used to designate the mystery. If the world has been really created and really externalised and projected and we have been thrown out, then there would be no going back. That such a thing (going back to the Real) is possible, that Yoga is practicable, that Samadhi is a real experience, that God-consciousness can be had even today, shows that there has been no such a catastrophe as we imagine. The catastrophe is psychological, mental, inward; it is created by our own self. So from this point of view, at least, you must be sure that the aim of life is God-Realisation, realisation of the Absolute, Brahman. It is not things we are asking for, it is happiness that we are seeking. And the happiness you are asking for is in the Selfhood of things, the Self which is the Absolute. Even the greatest fool is therefore asking for that only; he wants nothing else. It requires a little bit of understanding to know this difficulty. Hence be clear in your mind that when you practise Yoga, you want only that and your heart is fixed on that.

Be in an atmosphere suitable for this practice. Be in the company of people who think alike, not in that of people who think the opposite way. Be in an atmosphere holy and sacred; and to the extent possible, from your own point of view, have friends of this nature. Either have good friends or no friends. But don't have bad friends. Bad friends will distract your mind, shake your faith by saying things contrary and illogical.

Find a suitable time for sitting silently, though everybody is busy no doubt. In the 24 hours of work, you have to find time for two to three hours a day, which can not be difficult to find, if you use your will, despite the fact that all of us are busy with our own work all day. And, in those two-three hours, you must find time to sit unseen by people. Even if you are in a family, you must find time for this. Have a separate room for meditation. If you cannot afford to do this, then go away to such a place as will help you to be alone. When in your room, shut the door and for three hours don't see anyone. Don't lift the phone, don't have newspapers and suchlike things in that room. But you should have good books like the Upanishads, the Gita etc. Have, if possible, elevating pictures or portraits of worthy people, spiritual or philosophical people. Then be seated. Every day you should sit at the same fixed time and this should not be changed. Changing this to different hours of the day is like taking lunch at different times of the day and thus spoiling your health. You should have the same fixed time for every activity that you do. If it is 6 P.M. that you have chosen, you should stick to it. If any other time is decided upon, stick to that hour alone.

Be seated in one posture. When fatigued in this posture, you can relax a little and stretch your legs and again sit in meditation. You can even stand and move about and sit again. Try to control your body, muscles and mind. Then recite "OM" to create a vibration in your system. And implant in your mind the idea and the feeling 'I am in search of God'. Then try to analyse the nature of God. Yesterday someone asked me, what is God. It is just that which is before you; but divest it of the name and form complex. And then, what you see before your eyes is God Himself. He comes in a masquerade. He has put on a mask upon His body in the form of space-time, and then He looks like the world, 'playing' a drama before our eyes. God is not outside. He is just here. What you see with your eyes is just that minus space and time. This is very important to remember. So just analyse this for yourself. Take the help of the Bhagavad Gita, the Upanishads, the Sermon on the Mount or any other such elevating scripture and bring your mind back to the point of being able to think of God as being of the same nature of the Self that you are seeking. Chant a Mantra, repeat a formula, so that the ideas contained in the Mantra can help you to create an idea in your mind of what God is.

Fix the attention of the mind on this concept and then identify yourself with the selfhood of all things. You will immediately see a vibration taking place. You must know that everything is alive, full of vitality. In the world, nothing is dead. Even the walls will speak to you, if you actually identify yourself with them and all things. So feel the presence of things in yourself and yourself in things. *Atmavat Sarva Bhutani*, Feel this.

After a protracted time in this practice, you will begin to realise that there is some sort of a vital connection between you and others, which was absent till now. You can't see any connection between you and the actions of others because your mind is conscious of the physical body only. Gradually the mind should be allowed to go higher from the physical to the vital, from the vital to the mental, from the mental to the intellectual, as is said in the Upanishads. Then, when you go higher and higher into the deeper layers of your personality, you begin to feel the relationship with others in greater and greater intimacy. The more internal you go, the greater is the relationship you feel with others. Outside on the surface of the waters every wave is different, but when you go deeper into the ocean, they are the one and the same ocean. We are different from one another on account of our identification with our body. We are really one internally; there is a vibration connecting one with the other. Even now the ether of the waves is moving from one place to another place. There is a connection which is not felt on account of the identification of the mind with the body. So dehypnotise yourself. You are not this body but something different; you are not the Prana; you are not the mind; you are not the intellect; you are one with the Cosmic Intellect in the end, Hiranyagarbha. Then move higher and higher untill you begin to feel yourself in the Self of all beings. These are the Samadhis or Samapattis as Patanjali calls them and these are the various experiences you will have in meditation when you go deeper and deeper into the practice.

But this would be a very hard task indeed. So you don't find time to sit and sit as per the strict discipline. You should sit for meditation at the same fixed time. Today at this time, tomorrow another, and then the thread is broken. Even if you are on a railway train, you should sit for a few minutes. It is the train that is moving, what does it matter to you? You sit and control the mind. The mind is not moving along with the train. Why can't you practise Yoga? So, don't miss any opportunity. Every day, the mind should be trained to think in this manner, and afterwards, even in the ordinary life of day-to-day routine you must create the habit of continuing this practice. Even when talking you must have this practice. It is not that you can talk some nonsense and then go and sit for meditation. It is not like that; that will not work. What happens is that the greater part of the day is spent in irrational thinking and only a few hours are given to meditation. The former will spoil the latter practice. So in the more advanced stages of practice, you must cultivate this dehypnotising type of thinking and practise to think only in this way even when engaged in office work or in the ordinary business in life. This work in the office or in buisness in the ordinary way of life is not contrary to the practice of Yoga. All (this) work should be vitalised, i.e., charged with meditational consciousness, so that your background becomes only that. There is a story of the ayah looking after her mistress's child. Ayahs are people who take care of other people's children; they go to a stranger's house and fondle and take care of the child in that house with such love that it seems as if she is the mother. But her mind is not there. Her mind is on her own child at home. Her thoughts are centred on her own child's activities. Is it safely playing? Has it had its feed properly? I must go home at 5 o'clock in the evening and see what is happening to it, etc. etc. Such is the background of her thoughts. Her mind and love is only for her child at home, though outwardly she is lovingly looking after the child under her care. But the outward work she is engaged in, earns her salary; and she is working as an ayah. This outward appearance is not a real fact. You cannot at once make out this fact, its being an outward appearance, this distinction between her outward act and the thoughts in her mind. For all outward appearances, it looks as if it is her own child now in her care. This is the way it is said that you should conduct yourself in the world. When in office or in ordinary business of life, you are like the ayah, looking after your work as she does her work in all good will for the salary it brings. She seems to be looking after her own child even when she is only an ayah looking after someone else's child. Her mind is somewhere else—on her own child at home. You are working for the sake of somebody, for some other purpose or intention in your mind. Your intention and purpose in the background, as already pointed out, is to maintain a meditative habit so that all work is charged and vitalised with the meditative consciousness. Your work is only the training ground for orienting all your activities to this meditative consciousness. Hence, all your office work etc. should be done only to the extent necessary and indispensable, not beyond this limit, not to amass wealth, not to become rich or make a name or gain power; that is not the intention behind your work in the world. It is only to that extent necessary and indispensable—your office work; the purpose is that it is the training-ground for the mind towards the higher aim you have in your mind. This is the true picture of things. Understand that you should not go beyond this amount of work in the world, beyond this limited purpose. The higher purpose is something internal, the true Yoga. All work becomes Yoga only then. Work should not be opposed to it. In this way, then, you will find gradually that work becomes natural. You do not need to bring into play any stress or strain in doing your work. The concentration also becomes better. Swami Sivanandaji Maharaj used to say that if the Yogi does the work of a sweeper, he does it better than anybody else; if he washes vessels, it is cleaner than an ordinary man cleaning them. Whatever work he does, it will be perfect, because his concentration is so much on his work and his love for things is equal to the love he has for God! Because he sees no distinction; he has begun to see the universal in the particular. The name and form are gone. The substance is seen; the potness of the pot is gone, only the clay remains and there is only universality, and Karma-Yoga becomes practicable. It is this great art that is taught in the Bhagavad Gita. The whole gospel of the Gita is only a sermon of the seeing of divinity in things and transforming activity into yoga by visualising the Ultimate Substance in name-and-form. The name-and-form has completely gone from the substance; it does not exist at all. It is only spatiality and temporality that is called a pot; what you see is actually clay. So that what I see is not the wall; I see the Reality behind it, in fact, but invest it with a name-and-form which I give to it on account of the spatiality gone into it.

The Substance is the Absolute Itself. What does it then matter If I touch the wall, it is not the brick wall that I touch but my own Self extended in space and time? This is a very advanced condition in Yoga; all cannot visualise this state. I am merely mentioning it to you that this is possible. This state of experience where you live in the world with the consciousness of the Substance of things, free from the externality characterised by name and form, space and time, is called *Jivan-Mukti* or liberation even while living in this world. There is no harm in living in this world. The world is not the devil it looks. It looks like a devil because it is outside. The non-Self has got identified with the Self. The devil is the non-Self; the Self is God. So, the moment the non-Self is identified with the Self, the devilness in it goes! How the evil of things in the personality can be obviated and how even the worst of things can be converted into the best of things is another subject.

I have no doubt that all of you will strive hard in the practice of Yoga, you have set your minds on, and focus all your attention and energy on it, all through the Sadhana. May God bless you all. May Gurudev Swami Sivananda's grace be upon you all is my prayer.

SIGNIFICANCE OF JAPA AND PRAYER

Many of you, as spiritual seekers, would be practising Japa,—repetition of the Lord's Names. When you were initiated you would have been told that you should do Japa, chanting of the Divine Name. *Tat Japath Tadarthabhavanam*—the recitation, chanting or Japa of the Mantra is to be accompanied by a contemplation on its import or meaning. As a matter of fact, Japa, according to Sage Patanjali, is not merely a mechanical chanting of the Divine Name, though chanting is also Japa, but is it *Tadartha-Bhavana* or the contemplation on the meaning of the Mantra. To give an instance, *Om Namo Bhagavate Vasu devaya* is a Mantra. Chanting this is Japa. There is external verbal Japa, as well as internal Manasika Japa, or mental Japa. Japa is the repetition of a Mantra, which is a mysterious group of letters or phrases so connected with one another that when the Mantra is chanted a peculiar sensation or vibration is generated in the entire system. That is the difference between the ordinary words or sentences or groups of phrases and a Mantra. A Mantra is the result of a vision of a seer and it is the concrete manifestation, in the world of language, of the deity or Devata, which is made to manifest in the Mantra. When you chant a Mantra correctly and systematically with proper intonation, there is immediately set up a vibration in the nervous system in such a manner that a harmony is established in the whole world. Different Mantras produce different vibrations and they involke different Devatas. *Om Namo Bhagavate Vasudevaya* is a Mantra of Bhagavan Sri Krishna. It means literally: 'Om prostration to Bhagavan Vasudeva'. Surrender to Sri Vasudeva is implied therein. Now, the prostration, salutation, is an external symbol of the internal union. When we do 'Namaskara' to a deity in the temple, to a friend or any person, we join both the palms and bend ourselves low. This Namaskara, and the joining of the palms, is indicative of the feeling of union of oneself with the other. 'I and you are one'; that is prostration, that is Namaskara. "Bhagavan, I am one with you," is a spirit of surrender, and here begins meditation on Bhagavan Vasudeva. When the Mantra is chanted you have also the requisite atmoshpere created in the mind for contemplation on Bhagavan Vasudeva, to begin meditation and to feel His presence. This rule applies to all other Mantras, also.

There is a little difference between the recitation of a Mantra in Japa and the offering of prayer (Prarthana). While the Japa is always a fixed form of utterance of words or formulae, as in a Mantra, prayer can be an expression on one's feelings in any language and in any manner one would like. Prayer is primarily supplication to God for his grace. In ordinary forms of prayer, it can be directed to an ulterior end, such as acquisition of material objects, recovery from ill-health, and the like. But the truly spiritual form of prayer asks for nothing from God; it asks for God alone. Though prayer may be expressed in words, phrases or sentences, it need not always be so; for prayer can also be mental and the devotee can inwardly solicit the grace of God by an act of deep concentration of mind and a feeling of union with him in love and adoration. The scriptures abound in prayers of various kinds addressed to the various gods of the pantheon, but often directly to the Supreme Being. Usually, it is the practice to regard one's chosen deity (Ishta-Devata) as the highest divinity and exalt it to the state of the Absolute, so that the devotee has no idea in his mind other than that of his deity. This is indicative of the truth that there is ultimately one God whose forms are all the deities adored in worship. Prayer can draw in grace by a spiritual attunement of one's being in the intensity of feeling, which is the motive power behind prayer. Feelings that rise from the deepest recesses of one's heart can produce immediate results, because of their proximity to reality. Japa and prayer are regarded as the best forms of worship (Puja) and sacrifice (Yajna) as they do not involve dependence on external objects or circumstances. The purpose of this special rite is to grow into the likeness of the deity, whether by attunement of personality through Mantra-Japa or self-surrender by prayer.

The thought of God is like a fire which will burn all desires. The highest knowledge is nothing but the deep feeling of the presence of God everywhere. That is the highest wisdom and that will give a death-blow to other desires of the world. The desire for God is a desire to destroy all desires. It is not a desire in the ordinary sense of the term. As a single match-stick can reduce to ashes a huge mountain of straw, a single thought of the Omnipresence of God, the immanence of God and the Omnipotence of God is enough to burn up all desires pertaining to this world, because God is the fulfilment of our aspiration and when we feel His presence, there need be no other desire. A single moment of honest, genuine deep thought of God is more than equal to the performance of several *Asvamedha sacrifices*, *Agnishtomas*, *Rajasuyas* and so on. It is the highest sacrifice, the highest Yajna and the greatest truth. In one sense, through Japa and prayer you should be in a meditative mood, at all times, which is the purpose of spiritual practices.

ON REASON AND HIGHER LIFE*

First of all, it has to be remembered that reason is not everything, and it is futile to work up an apotheosis of reason. This itself is contrary to reason, and it is a prejudiced faith of the human mind which makes it imagine that reason is all. You ask, 'On what is faith based?', but I ask, 'On what is reason based?' 'Who told you that reason itself is reasonable?' Don't you think that this itself is a faith that you have inherited due to your social circumstances which you yourself condemn on another occasion? That the human mind unquestionably clings to the doctrine of a reason for everything and does not want to accept anything which cannot have a reason shows that the mind is prejudiced; and do you call this rationality?

Secondly, it is not true that everything in creation can be explained by reason, and I do not believe that you will again subscribe to the prejudice that the visible alone is real and there is nothing above what the human mind can visualise. The culture of our land is not based merely on reason, though it is not contrary to reason. The greatness of our culture lies in a super-rational faith,—mark super-rational,—on which even reason is based; because reason is an offshoot of experience, as inference is based on perception. Our culture is primarily rooted in the great gospel of unselfishness for which you want a reason now. Yes, there is a reason, and this reason is our philosophy. This is our religion, this our aim, and this the fond ideal of all humanity. Without going deep into the reason behind things too much, it is not difficult for us to discover, with even a little of common-sense, that we belong to a wider environment of which we are *integral* parts, and we do not exhaust ourselves in the shell of our personalities. Emphasise again, we belong to a wider environment, we are constituents of this environment, and we cannot exist if we are disloyal to the law of this environment to which we belong. To cite an example, a limb of the body cannot exist if it wishes to revolt against the law of the body taken as a whole, because the limb is an integral part of the body. Now, unselfishness or selflessness, as you wish to understand, is nothing but the way or the mode in which the part belongs to the whole, by which it surrenders itself

*A letter addressed in reply to certain queries from a modernistic mind.

to the fulfilment of the law of the whole, through which the lower is transfigured in the higher. Are you satisfied that there is a reason in unselfishness? In an unseltish act we do not do something unreasonable, but the only reasonable thing possible, for unselfishness is the discovery of oneself in the larger whole. I believe this is sufficient reason.

Now, about the question of money which you have raised: No one says that money as such is evil, as nothing in God's creation *as such* can be called evil. Taking money or giving money as such are not evils. But the evil lies in clinging to anything, getting disturbed by the absence of it, being in an emotional tension when deprived of it,—in short, being attached to it. All attachment is evil,—not money or gold, or anything for that matter. As to why attachment is evil is a different subject altogether, which I would like you to study in detail by going through standard texts written by geniuses. But this does not mean that we should necessarily accept money for our services. I do not mean to say that taking money is always an evil. But not to take money is noble and is a mark of greatness. Not to accept money is not in any manner the denial of one's ability to produce, as you put it, for though money is a measure of one's ability to produce, as you say, it is not necessary that the ability should always be measured. Let it be there unmeasured. What is the harm? No harm happens to the sun if there is no one to measure the intensity of its heat or light. One may lose money by not accepting it, but thereby one does not lose one's ability to produce, because money is not the ability,—it is ability that brings money.

Further, as I have pointed out above, our existence is to be dedicated to the larger whole to which we belong, and in not accepting money for services rendered, you are only asserting your participation in the larger whole, while simultaneously diminishing the importance of the part, taken independently, in the light of the whole. That is it love of money which is evil does not mean that it is not evil when it is *coveted* by one who is able to produce it. Whether one is able to produce anything or not, all earthly love is bad insofar as it binds one to a limited life of a very narrow perception. Earning money honestly is one thing, and coveting it is another thing. There is nothing wrong in earning it, but there is something wrong in coveting. Earning has a spontaneity of naturalness, while coveting is deliberate and artificially construed. However, it has to be reiterated that things themselves are not evil but attachment is evil, for all attachment is a bar to the onward progress of the human individual towards a larger reality of which it is a part, as already stated.

Whether it is moral to accept something for nothing is a digression from the point at issue, for unselfish service and accepting something for nothing are two different standpoints. Do you think that people accept money merely because they do not want the other to receive something for nothing? Is it the consideration of the morality of the others that makes us accept money from them? Have you seen one individual in this world who thinks like this? You know, legal quibbles do not always touch the core of truth. Take the matter as it is, on its face. Do we accept money from others so that others may be benefited by the morality thereof? Definitely not. We want the money for ourselves. And the morality in regard to the other is irrelevant to the matter. I am reminded of a man who, in anger, thrashed some poor fellow and when queried later on answered that he thrashed the other to instil into him the lesson of 'bearing insult and injury', which is supposed to be a spiritual virtue. You can imagine how untrue the man's answer is, though it is true that it is good to bear insult and injury. Similar is the case with receiving and giving money, the point that you have raised. Giving is considered as good and taking not so good merely for the reason that giving unfolds our real personality while taking encumbers it. This is simple enough to understand. The question of the morality about giving and taking is clear to your mind, I believe.

Sacrifice is the voluntary surrendering of a value, it is true, without thought of reward. You say that sacrifice of the nature of dedication of oneself or one's values to total strangers, especially those whom we despise, is not possible. But there are many other impossible things in the world from the point of view of the ordinary mind, but all possible with some effort and understanding. The reason behind sacrifice is the same as the reason behind unselfishness, which I have touched to some extental ready. It is not based on blind faith as you think, nor on other's saying it, and it is not beyond one's power of reasoning, as you surmise. It is also not impossible as you seem to think. You are right when you say that to make a *true* sacrifice is death, but it is death of the false personality and not the real one. It is the death of our prejudices and erroneous notions. It is the death of what is to be cast off one day or the other. It is not the death of the real *we*. Suicide is not the solution, for suicide is not the death of the personality but its affirmation in stronger terms than one would do when alive. Suicide is the clumination of attachment to oneself and one's own pleasures, which is foolishly affirmed with the wrong notion that by the cutting off of oneself from circumstances which are painful one can attain the desired end. This is not the solution because the effect cannot be destroyed without removing the cause.

Giving one's body for scientific study may be some sort of unselfishness,—there is no denial. But this is again attachment to humanity as a corporate body, which is not in consonance with truth. There is something more real than humanity as a group, which cannot be forgotten.

It all, in the end, hinges upon whether an act is done for one's personal pleasure or for the good of a larger existence. But no sacrifice should involve pain or injury to others. This is another condition to be borne in mind, barring of course the pains of the nature of the operation performed by the doctor for the good of the patient. To perform a sacrifice it is not always necessary that there should be a 'taker', for sacrifice is not always material. Sacrifice is possible even if you alone exist in the world and there is none else, for sacrifice is more a psychological act of self-dedication to a higher existence than a mere parting with material objects, though the giving away of material things also is a part of sacrifice of a lower order. Remember again that sacrifice is not giving where it is not needed but the giving for the sake of wiping out of the encrustation of one's egoism and attachment. You seem to be thinking of only a horizontal sacrifice where someone takes something but there is a vertical one where the higher one consumes the lower. The gigantic fraud that you speak of is not the moral principle of giving but the ignorance with which we deny its meaning and value due to insufficient enlightenment about the truth of things. The principle of giving is based on the principle of the relinquishment of the narrower personality in the larger good which is the eternal reality.

We do not 'give' merely because another man's need is identical with his lack of ability. This is not the reason behind giving. We give because thereby we evolve, and there is the end of it. In this world there is always someone who has a larger ability and some other who has a lesser one. There is no point in mentioning it in the interpretation of the psychology of giving. In the performance of duty the result is not the motive. The motive is the psychological process that is going on in the act of giving. What you *think* and *feel* is important. The end beyond it is not the consideration. Our philosophy of *Karma Yoga*, which is the philosophy of the Bhagavad Gita, is one of emphasis on the essential value of active duty and not the passive existence of its remote end. It would be a poor philosophy that identifies this with the dogma or those who, in their inability, what to share the bounty of others. The question of 'others' has no relevance to the act of giving. As I mentioned above, giving is a psychological process and there is no psychology except in the subject which thinks. There is no use tagging on to it the object which is an extraneous element to all thinking. This inability to distinguish between the true subject and its false object, which is only a notion of its, is itself the outcome of a muddle in our thinking, for the person that we see outside is not the object. The person standing outside us as a subject *in his or her own capacity* is not the object of our thought. The real object is the *objectness* that we associate with that subject. We have to think over this is little deeply.

There is no use merely being a skeptic. One who doubts everything should also doubt one's own conclusions in order to be a consistent skeptic. That would be a wonderful state of affairs, isn't it? What is your standard of judgement, and what is the standard on which you base this standard? Can you doubt that standard? Can you be a skeptic about it? All doubt has a reference to a standard which itself is not doubted. We cannot live with doubts. Life itself is a negation of all doubt, for life *is* and doubt negates all existence.

Your queries regarding selflessness have been adequately answered, and your point concerning the one who imagines he has no self as he borrows from others should have also been answered. Borrowing is not effacement of ego but a strengthening of it, which is not difficult to understand. A shameless man is not an egoless man. We always distinguish between *Sattva* and *Tamas*.

Our highest wisdom is expressed in the great sentence of the Veda: 'Reality is One and undivided, though it is envisaged in variegated forms.'

THE PATH OF DEVOTION IN THE EPICS AND PURANAS

Devotion, or love of God, is a renowned way of the saints and sages who could speak to God as one could speak to a human being. While all saints and sages were of this special character throughout the world, India, especially, has been known for ages for the practicality of its religion and the very intimate relationship that a devotee can maintain with God. Always, in most of the religions, God has remained a distant object of reverence and obedience to the divine law. We have, here, a religion that has come to the homes of people and become a part of the daily life of the individual; and religion becomes a living feature in the world only when God becomes something vital in one's daily life;—for religion is love of God. The daily contact that we inwardly establish with God is religion. Our personal relationship with what really is, is religion. And while cultures of the past in different countries had towering philosophies and scientific achievements of their own, it is rarely that we find God coming to the hearts of people and speaking in the language of man. The lives of saints and sages are a more elaborate commentary on the nature of the working of God than all the scriptures and revelations that we hear of, because the saints bring God to the world in a living flame of experience rather than through the vehicle of language and words, textbooks or even scriptures.

It is this interesting theme which is dear to the heart of man, rather than to the intellect, that is the preoccupation of a very interesting and prominent set of religious literature in this country, known as the Epics and Puranas. The country is filled with people who adore God in terms of the description in this type of religious literature. We have always a name given to God. We have always a heart-to-heart feeling of relationship with the God that we worship, whether in temples or in our homes. We can cry before God. We can sob and weep before Him. We can represent our petitions before Him, and we need not merely fear Him. This is what the Puranas tell us. While it is often said that religion commences with the fear of God, we may also say that religion culminates in the love of God. It is not merely a philosophic love that the Puranas and Epics speak of: rarely do we find love being philosophical. It has, of course, a philosophy of its own, which rationalistic philosophy cannot understand. All our loves are super-rational. A mystical feature characterises all affection in the world, mystical in the sense that they are purely private, and we will not explain, or can explain, this feeling of ours to other people in the world. All love, whatever be its nature, is inexplicable. The moment it becomes explicable in a scientific language, it ceases to be affection charged with vitality. It has this very uncanny feature, which also is the characteristic of the love of God.

The way in which we contact God in our life—*in our life* is a phrase to be underlined,—is our practical religion. That which the scriptures speak of, is one kind of religion, which only keeps us in a state of reverence and awe, and creates in us a particular type of Bhakti called *Aisvarya-Pradhana-Bhakti*, that is, the love of God as Creator, Father and Sovereign Supreme, the love of God as Isvara or the Master of all Creation. *Aisvarya-Pradhana-Bhakti* is one type of devotion which is especially to be noticed in the later Sri Vaisnava literature of the South, initiated by the Great Vaisnava theologian, Ramanuja; but we have another type of internal contact that the devotee establishes with God, more intimate, we may say, in one sense. Sometimes, it goes by the name of *Madhurya-Pradhana-Bhakti*, the devotion which was emphasised by certain other teachers of the Bhakti schools, especially Nimbarka, Vallabha and Gauranga Mahaprabhu, as well as the Tamil saints, the Alvars, who preceded Ramanuja. Here all intellectuality, ratiocination and analytical approach cease, and the soul speaks to God in its own language. It contacts God in the vitality of being, rather than the words which the tongue speaks. As already mentioned, love does not want any philosophy, nor does devotion to God. It can feel the presence of God. Why should we try to analyse Him? When I can touch Him, hear Him, contact Him, and imbibe whatever He has, why should I try to subject Him to scientific analysis or philosophical disputation?

Thus, it is that in a symbolic language, the Puranas speak of such saints as Narada going to all the worlds including Vaikuntha, Satyaloka and Kailasa. These analogies of saints like Narada penetrating through all the realms of the cosmos, contacting God on one side and meeting man and even the demons on the other side, is a representation of the significance of divine devotion—the extent to which devotion can reach in practical life. One of the peculiarities of the representation of God's activity in the cosmos, in the Puranas and Epics, is that creation is said to be constituted of different layers,—the fourteen worlds, realms, or *lokas* as they are called; and to make the theme interesting, catching and vibrating to the soul, to make you have a stir in your personality and to make your hair stand on end even by listening to the glories of God, the Puranas employ a technique of making God a personality similar to your own. He also lives in a realm as you do. He has certain features as you also have, and He sees you. Not only that, He sees through you. He sees your past, your present and your future. Not merely that; God is the repository of supreme compassion, pity and mercy. He is not merely a judge who is pitiless to your representations, who reads only the textbooks of law and says, 'I am not concerned with justice but only with law,' as some of our judges may say today.

God is concerned not only with law but also with justice. There was an Englishman, a Chief Justice of the Calcutta High Court. It is said that one of the advocates stood up and said: "Your Lordship is, after all, bound to do justice." The Chief Justice remarked: "Far from it, I am here to dispense law". This shows the way in which man's mind works, and the way Dharma works in the world. Dharma is not law merely; it is also justice. If there are five hundred witnesses against an innocent man, he can be hanged though he has committed no crime. This is law working, but it is not justice. And this actually happened. This is not merely an illustration. A poor man was once hanged during the British regime and the mistake was realised much later, some ten years afterwards, that an innocent man had been hanged; and the then Government, in order to hush up the fuss that people might create, paid a sum to the wife of the victim and asked her to go to Bangalore and settle down there. But there was no mistake on the part of the judge, because he had evidence.

Well, the point is that God is justice, it is true, not merely law; but He has also a very tender feeling for man. This is what the Puranas want to make out, which even the Vedas and the Upanishads do not properly explain. Your heart begins to melt when you think of God in terms of how the Puranas describe Him. Nothing can be more effective than the method which touches your heart. If I speak to you in a way which your heart responds, you are mine at the very moment: but if I speak to you as a lawyer, as a scientist or a metaphysician, you may nod your heard, but then, to your way.

This psychology of the human mind was very quickly realised by the authors of the Púranas who were not just interested in telling you something which is not a fact, as there are people who will merely cajole you by non-factual information. The Puranas tell you of the factual relationship that you have with God and which you have forgotten. It is not that the Puranas recount only grandmother's stories, as our so-called educated, modern youth might think. Not so. It is not a sweet lie that they tell us. It is a new type of truth which you have forgotten in your pride of intellectuality through a wrong type of education into which you have been introduced and which began to instruct your intelligence with an erroneous logic of God being subject to understanding and intelligence and having nothing to do with the private life and the emotions of the human being.

The special emphasis of the Epics and Puranas is that God can hear you and speak to you, and you can speak to God. All the stories, analogies and symbols that these scriptures employ for describing man's relations with God and vice versa, signify that God is nearer to us than we imagine; and He will help us even if we do not know Him. This is another speciality which this religious literature reveals to us. Even if you forget God, God will help you. It is not that He thinks of you only if you think of Him. That would be a very legal way of looking at Him. God is not merely a legal man. He is, therefore, portrayed as not merely Pitamaha (grandfather) or Pita (father) but also Mata (mother) and Dhata (supporter). I am the Saviour, the Protector, the Generator, the Withdrawer, the Sustainer, the Onlooker, the Supervisor, and many other things of that nature,—these are magnificently described in the pregnant words of the Bhagavad Gita.

What God is man is not supposed to know; but enough it is if you understand that it is easier to contact God than any other thing in the world. This is what the Puranas and the Epics want to tell you. Other scriptures of a more logical character may argue that God is difficult of approach, more difficult of approach than anything else in the world; but here you are told that other things are more difficult of approach than God. Other things may be far away from you, but God is nearer to you than they. Your own wife and children may be very near you, but God is nearer still. Even such relations who are your own kith and kin may not help you in your difficulty, but God helps you instantaneously. People help you even when you do not ask for help, because God is one who knows what you want. You are not always in a position to understand what your needs are. Mostly you are in a confused state of mind. You cannot ask for what you want, but God's speciality is that He can know what you would need even after hundreds of years, and those things are provided for even now. Provisions are made for your journey that has not yet commenced—whatever you may call Him. He is more than all the people, who only show a lip-sympathy to you. His love for you is more than your love for Him. This is another speciality of the divine devotion portrayed in the Puranas. God's love for man is much more than man's love for God. He wants you more than you want Him. Who can understand this mystery? It is also said with great meaning and significance that when a devotee takes one step towards God, walking, God takes one hundred steps towards the devotee, running. While the devotee walks one step, God runs one hundred steps towards the devotee!

The stories of the Puranas and the Epics illustrate this important point of the divine relationship that eternally subsists between God and man. No one can read this literature without a stir of one's nerves and a rapture in one's mind. No one can read this wondrous literature without tears in one's eyes, because here it is that you know how to touch God through your soul, through your feelings, through your affection. When do you shed a tear? When your feelings are stirred, not even the best scientific argument can make you shed a single drop of tear. The heart should be shaken from its very roots, and then even the philosopher kneels down on the floor.

This is how God is brought to the home of man by the Puranas. A very interesting incident is recorded in the Drona-Parva of the Mahabharata, which must simply strike you with wonder, and actually make you sob for the love that God has for man. During the war, after Jayadratha is slain, Arjuna is speaking to Bhagawan Vedavyasa on many a matter. One of the surprises which Arjuna expressed to Maharsi Vyasa was: "O Maharsi! Can you explain to me one interesting thing? Whenever I was up in arms in battle, I used to see some mysterious figure moving in front of me, which I could not decipher properly, sometimes visible, sometimes invisible, but not touching the ground. I saw a figure like that of a human being, now coming out of the mist as it were, making himself slightly visible to my eyes, now going into the background of the misty atmosphere of the war-field, but his feet were not touching the ground. He was just a few feet above the ground level. He was doing nothing, just looking this way and that way, moving to this corner and that corner. The only speciality that I observed in his appearance was that he had a trident in his hand, a knot of hair on his head, and I saw some snakes round his neck. These were all the things I could see of his personality. I could not understand what it was, who he was, and what was the meaning behind it." Vyasa smiled and replied: "O Arjuna! It is very good that you spoke to me about this mystery that you saw, and I shall take this opportunity to tell you something of this miracle, which you cannot understand, nor can any man understand. Do you know who fought this war, and who it was that worked through your arms? Do you know that you have, yourself, no power to stand before ferocious warriors like Bhisma, Drona and Karna? Do you know the power of Bhisma? Not all the three worlds can stand before him, not to talk of the Pandavas! Arjuna! Can you stand before this mighty ferocity of Bhisma who could defeat Parasurama, who learnt the art of warfare from Vasistha himself? Is there a man in all the three worlds who can stand before Drona? Who defeated these warriors? Well! It is the greatness of those beings whom you cannot see with your eyes. They have worked this miracle for your sake, Arjuna, and remained always in the background. Do you know whom you saw? It was Lord Siva. You are indeed blessed. He knew the pitiable condition in which you all were. He came down from Kailasa to help you, not telling you what His intention was; and He knew that it was humanly impossible for any person to stand before these—Bhisma, Drona and Karna. Not all of you, Pandavas, put together, can face them, even if they are to fight throughout their lives. What would be the fate of these poor children? Siva knew this, and He was moving in the midst of the Kaurava forces sucking the energy of them all, not taking any direct action. Who could stand before Him, if He were to take action; the very odour that emanated from His body was enough to paralyse all the Kauravas. Arjuna, I need not speak to you more about this wondrous being you saw. Blessed art thou that you could see Him." And after this narration, there is a beautiful prayerful description of the mighty Lord of Kailasa, which Vyasa speaks to Arjuna.

God works thus; and there are other incidents which we shall see, in what followed, to the same effect, as on occasions when Bhisma himself spoke to persons like Duryodhana many a time. Every day Duryodhana came after sunset and wept before Bhisma. "What is this? What is happening, grandsire? Thousands of my people are being slain every day, and you are yet alive!" Bhisma would say: "My dear child! Do not tease me and taunt me like this every day. You are under the impression that I am only pretending to fight. It is not so. I would have pounded all these Pandava forces, including the Pandavas themselves, in a single day, but for the presence of a single person there, who is sitting in the chariot of Arjuna. But for Him, the Pandavas would not have been there on the first day itself. I alone am sufficient; all your army is not necessary. Duryodhana! You do not know my strength. But what can I do, you do not understand the difficulty into which you have been involved. I have told you many a time that you should not engage yourself in a conflict with those people whom Krisna is helping, but you would not listen to me and now you come and taunt me. Well! Tomorrow I shall do my best." This happened twice or thrice. Bhisma did his best. He went to the extreme of his ferocity. Like fire blazing, he began to fight through the forces. Thousands were massacred by a single arrow that Bhisma shot, but not a single Pandava could be killed. Again Duryodhana cried at night: "What is all this? You could not kill even a single Pandava, grandsire, and I have depended upon you people. After so many days of battle, you could not bring down even one of the Pandavas." Again it was the same reply which Bhisma gave: "My dear child! I do not want to get angry with you, though you often irritate me. But I shall tell you the truth again. You will not win what you have in your mind as long as Govinda is on the other side." Well! This is the old story again," said Duryodhana, "and I am not here depending on you senile people. I have got my comrades like Karna." And there could have been a cutting reply from Bhisma. Bhisma held his tongue, however, because there was no use frowning on the stupid man Duryodhana.

And how does God help? Asvatthama's ferocity in the Mahabharata, again, is a case in point. We are told that Asvatthama, one day, approached his father Drona and said: "You taught everything to Arjuna whatever you have taught me. What is the difference between a disciple and a son? No difference at all? The son naturally is dearer than disciples. You teach Arjuna everything. Will you not teach me something which Arjuna does not know?" Drona thought: "This is a very foolish son, not so wise as Arjuna, and I should not teach him mysteries which may enable him to work havoc." But Asvatthama went on pressing his father with importunities: "Teach me something which Arjuna does not know, otherwise what is the good of my being your son?" Arjuna was taught to wield all the *astras*. There was nothing which he did not know because he was instructed by Drona. But on account of a fatherly affection for even a stupid son, which every father has, Drona finally yielded. "All right, come here, I shall give you something, but beware, I am giving you fire in your hands by which you can burn the worlds; but, my child, do not use it against devotees of God, because it will not work against them. It will work against real enemies. This is the Narayana-astra, the missile which is invoked with the power of Narayana. I am telling you this today, and I am initiating you into this mystery. If you release this, all the world can be reduced to ashes; but do not use this. I am warning you, lest you should be yourself in danger when you misuse it." Yet Drona was cautious. He did not tell him how to withdraw the missile, because if he could withdraw it, he would go on using it again and again. He knew the lack of understanding which Asvatthama suffered from and his eagerness to use it one day or the other! So he could use it only once. Once it is let off, it is let off for ever. It could not come back for a second use. But there is a method of withdrawing it also, which in this particular case, Drona never told Asvatthama.

And you know, the occasion came for it. When Drona left his mortal coil, the fury of Asvatthama knew no bounds. He said: "I know the secret; today the Pandavas shall not be in this world. My father has told me something; and today there shall be none remaining on the Pandavas' side, not Yudhisthira, not Bhima, not Arjuna; and he took out his 'cat out of the bag', and he let it out with the invocation of Narayana-mantra. Well! You know what happened? Not even an atomic bomb can work such a havoc. It multiplied itself into millionfold. Everywhere, the whole sky was filled with burning missiles; and there were no stars, no sun, no moon, no sky. It was all fire. That was all. And when Arjuna saw that sight, Krisna was accosted: "O Lord! What is this that is coming? I cannot understand it. Some new thing is coming which I have not had occasion to see." Krisna said: "I know what it is, and there is no remedy for this. No one can stand up against this. The best thing for you all is to stop fighting. It shall not do any harm to those who will not fight it. It is destructive only to the enemies. Those who prostrate themselves before it are not its enemies, and so the best thing for you would be to cast down your arms and lie prostrate before it, and then it shall exhaust itself." Nobody knew what this mystery was, what it was that was coming; but then Krisna said that there was no use fighting with it; and to all it was proclaimed loudly: "Cast down your arms; prostrate yourself before this fire that is coming; that is the only way of saving yourself." And all did this except Bhima. He retorted: "I am not a coward. I, a Kshatriya, to cast down arms,—nothing doing! I shall see to it." He took up his mace and began brandishing it. Krisna and Arjuna went there and told him: "This is not the time to show your valour, friend, please listen to us." But he would not listen, then he was pulled down by Krisna and Arjuna. "Come down, stupid man, you do not know what you are doing." And there was nobody to fight; and the *astra* went here, there, everywhere, seeing and looking for a single enemy. Nobody was there to fight with it, and so, finally, it extinguished itself. Thereafter, the flame entered the body of Krisna, because He was Narayana Himself. It entered the body of Narayana.

Asvatthama was gazing from the top of a tree to see what was happening, to see the heap of ashes of the Pandavas. But no such thing happened. He saw no ashes anywhere! They were all fighting as before, "What is this? What is the matter? My father also told a lie, Rishis tell lies, God tells lies, the whole world is a lie, fie upon all things, fie upon even parents, fie upon truth—there is no truth in this world," He cried and went back cursing everyone. And he met Vyasa on the way. "Whom are you cursing? What is the matter?" asked Vyasa. "What is the use of saying anything? The earth is not worth living on when even a father can tell a lie; my father told me a falsehood that he initiated me into a mystery which Arjuna did not know, but when I used it, it proved futile. Can there be anything worth-depending upon in this world? Is there such a thing as truth in this world?" wailed Asvatthama. Vyasa said: "Your father did not tell you a lie. He initiated you into a tremendous mystery regarding which he had already given you a warning—not to use it against the devotees of God. You used it against Narayana Himself. It has gone to Him from whom it came. It was the *astra* of Narayana and it has gone back to Him. You have used it against Krisna and Arjuna who are the manifestations of Narayana and Nara in this world."

Use not your power against God. You may be wondering why these stories, these histories are recorded in the Epics and Puranas. Yes, it is to stir your feelings as to how God can help you and save you. Krisna had a private conversation with Arjuna: they were very good friends, you know, they used to go for walks together, to dine together, sleep together, work together. And in comradeship, when Arjuna talked about the mighty beings that were felled down in the war and the mysteries about such people like Karna and others who had powers and weapons which were invincible, Krisna spoke: "My dear friend! Do you know how anxious I was as long as Bhisma, Drona and Karna were alive? Do you know that I did not sleep properly as long as these three were alive in the world? And do you know what I did? Do you know why Karna did not use his missile against you? If he had used it, it would have been difficult for you to face it. He had a sakti which he was daily worshipping for your destruction. He would tell himself: "Tomorrow it shall be used." Many tomorrows passed; every day he used to say, "What had happened to me? I forget about it. Tomorrow morning I shall use it." Arjuna enquired: "Krisna, why did he not use it for so many days?" He actually never used it against him. It was used against a wrong person later on due to a mishap that took place. "Do you know, Arjuna, why he did not use it? Every day, in the morning, when he was to face you in battle, the first person he would look at was myself. I was in front of you, and the moment he looked at me, I hypnotised him, and his mind got muddled. He would not remember anything, and until I foiled his sakti, I did this work of hypnotising him every day, so that he would not remember anything. And I know that you have no idea as to why I sent Ghatotkaca. But you know the sakti was used against him, though it was kept for a different end. Not knowing all this, you and your brothers were weeping that your man was killed." If you read the Mahabharata you will know how the incident happened. Draupadi called out: "Krisna! Krisna!" When in the court of the Kauravas, Dushasana was after stripping her of her clothes. The Supreme Lord at once saved her modesty by willing the apparel on her person to be endless! It is said Dushasana fell down in a faint with the fatigue of unsuccessfully disrobing her. It is also believed that Krisna Himself became the unending garment.

Again, egged on by Duryodhana, Durvasa, the great *tapasvin*, would have reduced the whole clan of the Pandavas to ashes with his anger, but Lord Krisna saved them. Durvasa came with his eighty thousand disciples to the Pandavas and asked for *bhiksha* for all of them after they had their bath and returned for it. The Pandavas had just finished their mid-day meal and Draupadi had washed clean the Akshaya-Patra (the inexhaustible dishing bowl) which would keep filling as it was emptied in serving the food out of it. But this could be so only once, and once the *patra* (vessel) was cleaned after Draupadi had finished her meal, this miracle would not happen. So Draupadi was in the greatest fix. And she turned to her Saviour and prayed to Lord Krisna. There was a knock at the door in a few minutes, and, Krisna was there most unexpectedly. Suddenly He wanted something: "Oh! I am terribly hungry! Give me food! Quick, I am dying of hunger." "But, Krisna, we have finished our meal and I have washed the vessel. That is why..." "Oh! Bring me the vessel. I know there is food in it." It was vain to keep protesting, and Draupadi brought the vessel. Under the rim of the vessel there was a leaf, left out of the vegetable, sticking to it. The Lord ate that; ate it as the Virat that He was, and the whole Cosmos was fed! Durvasa and his disciples mysteriously felt their bellies full! When Bhima went to invite them at Yudhisthira's behest, for their meal, they vanished in fright, lest they should incur the displeasure of Yudhisthira for not being able to accede to his request. No one could know the mystery. Such miracles the Lord works to save the devotees.

The Pandavas had been exiled to spend twelve years in the forests as the result of the game of dice which they had lost. When in the forests Krisna came to enquire after their welfare, Draupadi shed burning tears relating to Him the humiliation she had been submitted to at the Kauravas' court and how none of the husbands had stood up to avenge the wrong, nor had any of the elders present there. Krisna wiped her tears and it was He who took the vow to destroy the herd of the Kauravas and avenge the wrong she had suffered. And He did this without lifting a single weapon against them! Who but He can save His devotees in His unbounded mercy and love for them!

It is again Krisna that defends Bhima who had to use a so-called unfair means to kill Duryodhana by splitting his thighs. Yudhisthira accused Bhima in the name of Dharma that a true warrior does not win by unfair means. Then Lord Krisna points out how time and again Duryodhana had been most meanly unfair, why Yudhisthira himself was unfair in playing dice and in his attitude of letting the Kauravas humiliate Draupadi and preventing the other Pandavas from acting. Bhima had taken an oath to avenge the wrong done to Draupadi by killing Duryodhana. In avenging a wrong, the end justifies the means, He hinted. When God becomes fire. He burns; when He is ice, He freezes. He is war and peace, the worst and the best, for opposites get reconciled in universality.

Galore are such instances in the great epic, the Mahabharata; and all these incidents related now are detailed variously in the Sabha, Aranya, Bhisma, Drona, Karna and Salya Parvas.

And now, behold the Srimad-Bhagavata Purana. Look at how the Lord rescued Ambarisa from Durvasa's anger. You will find it narrated in this Purana as the Ambarisa-Upakhyana. Durvasa fancied an insult and a disregard in the matter of etiquette in entertaining an honoured guest who had been invited for 'Bhiksha' on a *dvadasi* day, by king Ambarisa. Durvasa dashed on the ground one of his 'jatas' and thus created an ogre to eat up Ambarisa. Instantaneously, Sudarsana-Cakra, the Discus, came swishing like a ball of fire to destroy Durvasa. The supremely merciful Lord Narayana had sent it to save His great devotee and destroy the wrong-doer, even without being asked by the devotee himself. Durvasa ran for refuge to the three worlds and none could protect him from the Sudarsana. Finally he was advised to seek refuge at Ambarisa's feet. He did it to his great humiliation and was saved.

The Bhagavata relates the thrilling anecdote of Krisna's sports when He put Brahma in the proper place. Not a soul knew of this Lila. Brahma saw it after a whole year. He was humbled and made to realise that Krisna was no cowherd but the Supreme Being above Whom none exists. Brahma hid all the cowherds and all such things in a cave unknown to any one, telling himself that Gokula would come begging of him, the great creator. Lord Krisna quietly multiplied Himself as every calf-herd with exactly his dress, his ornaments and his mannerisms and the staff each carried with identical bends and crooks and number of knots, and every one of the calves. In the evening the calf-herds and the calves (the substitutes) returned as usual to Gokula. A cow can spot its own calf amongst a thousand of them! Yet every cow accepted the substituted calf with even greater love and affection. Every mother of the calf-herd was thrilled in a new and mysterious way at her (substituted) child, she loved him deeper, and she failed to realise that it was not of her flesh and blood. Brahma, rather mystified, came to the cave and found all he had shut in there! Yet Gokula was not the less even by a calf-herd's staff ! Brahma released all, and, falling down at Lord Krisna's feet, begged His pardon for the arrogance he had shown as the creator.

Such are His unfathomable and inimitable acts of love which He has for His devotees and for all that are His.

The point is that these miraculous occurrences, the subtle workings of God, above the ken of the human mind, physically portrayed in the Epics and the Puranas, bring out the fact that God is always conscious of what our needs are, and He takes incarnations, not merely as a four-armed Krisna or a Rama or a Narasimha or some such person, but in all necessary forms and manifestations as the occasion may demand. He works the miracles that are needed, and if you truly come to know of it, every incident of our life is a miracle. Nothing can be regarded as natural, if the truth about it is investigated. That we are breathing is a miracle. That we are alive in this world is a miracle. That the cells of our body have joined together to form this personality is a miracle. That the earth does not go and dash itself against some other planet is a miracle. That the ocean does not exceed its limits is a miracle. That the stars do not fall on our heads is a miracle. That you are able to stand on your two legs is a miracle. That your heart does not stop working is a miracle. What is not a miracle in this world? What power has man over even the smallest occurrence in this world? Have you the power to lift even your finger, if all the nerves of your body do not collaborate? Do you know what wondrous cooperation there is among the internal mechanisms of our body to make even a finger lift itself? If you have seen a huge mechanism, do you know how many parts collaborate to make a small part tick or move or touch? A very humble cog is moving somewhere, unknown, unseen perhaps, but you know what cooperation it receives from all the other parts of the machine. Do you know that all the muscles, all the nerves, all the cells have to collaborate even to enable the eye-lid to go up and down, not to talk then of breathing which is a more complicated process? Are you sure that the next early morning you will wake up? Can you say with confidence, "Tomorrow morning I shall do this"? Who keeps this heart beating? What is this miracle? Life is a miracle, indeed. It is not an equation of mathematics. It is not a formula of science. Life is a miracle, because God is a miracle, all that is connected with God is a miracle, and that is why the creation of God also is a wonder. A human being himself, being a part of this creation, is a miracle, and when man begins to know this miracle which is God and His creation, he becomes humble before this gigantic machinery of the cosmos. What is this puny, tiny human body before the relentless movement of the astronomical universe? What power had this tiny being? The purpose of the teachings of the Puranas and the Epics is to humble down man's ego before the greatness of God. God's wondrous powers are portrayed in the description of His Avataras, in the instantaneous actions that God takes, and the premonitions of man's needs that God always has in His omniscience.

It is difficult to go into the vast field of the teachings contained in the Itihasas and the Puranas, but all of them in their beautiful and grand personifications of God as Father, Friend and even Mother, speak in a single language of God's love for man. As already mentioned, it is not man's love for God that is so much emphasised as God's love for man. Yes, it is the other way round. When God starts running after you, then it is that your devotion is complete. You know Eknath Maharaj's story, wherein we are told that Sri Krisna became a servant as Srikhandia and washed the saint's clothes every day until He was discovered; and He vanished afterwards. He used to grind wheat for Sant Sakkubai. Such instances are countless as sung in the Epics and the Puranas.

Sceptics may laugh at these stories, but what is scepticism but ignorance of the mystery of God? You will easily believe me if I tell you that God shall see to it that even a spoon of sugar is supplied for your tea when it is needed. This is not a joke or an exaggeration. Even the smallest needs shall be looked to. Your cup of tea shall come to you at the proper hour, if God sees to it, and He does. It is not human effort that works in the end, God's grace it is that works, so proclaim the Puranas, which is another way of saying that God alone works. Nobody else can work, because nobody else really is. The others are only secondary existences who exist only by sufferance. The real existence is God's. While the portrayal of God existing in Vaikuntha, Kailasa, Satya-Loka, etc., and many other descriptions of this nature, are available in the Puranas and the Epics, they tell us, too, that God can reduce Himself to the level of human relationship also, if need be, and it is futile to think that God is only supra-rational, transcendent and qualityless.

There are some philosophers who say that God is only Nirguna, an abstract attributeless being. How can He become Saguna, endowed with attributes? How can He become man? How can He take an Avatara or incarnate Himself? Why do you ask, 'How He can', when you hold that He is omnipotent? To say that He is only Nirguna, that He is only this or that, is to limit God. You say that God is limitless in every respect. You have to look upon God only with awe and love. You should not try to describe Him through your logic. Some say: "There are no fourteen worlds. There are no hells and heavens. This is all a fiction of the brain." Someone said that Ganga flows only through the nose,—perhaps in the rainy season when we catch a cold! People have such stupid notions that the river Ganga is only the Susumna nerve and Yamuna and Saraswati are Ida and Pingala nerve-currents. There is no Ganga outside. This is extreme mysticism which misses its point. Mysticism is the truth of all things, but when it misses its aim and takes only one side of the issue, it goes wrong. As long as the external bread can satisfy your external hunger, the external Ganga also exists in which you can take an external bath. If the bread is purely mystical and you take only psychological bread and pulse every day, which is only flowing through the Susumna, then of course, Ganga also does not exist outside. But there is an error in the application of logic many a time, though logic is good by itself. Mostly, we go to extremes in our application of the logical categories to principles of life. It is not that rationality is bad or logic is futile, but it should be properly applied by a properly trained mind. Then it is that we take both the sides of an issue into consideration. God is inside as well as outside, and you must speak only in the logic of the given realm in which you are, the state of evolution in which you find yourself. And in the dream condition you must speak and use only the dream logic. So, to say that God is this or God is that, that God cannot take Avataras, or God cannot become a human being in his incarnations, would be to misapply the philosophical logic by a transcendent use of the categories, while the argument is from the lower level. There is a misapplication of the system of logic when you speak from a lower level by applying the logic of the higher level. This should not be done. What is really meant is that there is no delineating of God's powers and God's glory.

This fact of God's greatness, put in a humanised language and by a humanised application of fact, the Puranas and the Epics try to bring out in their beautiful, mellifluous style, and they speak to you in such a feasible and acceptable way that it goes into your heart. The method they apply by which the meaning enters your heart is so effective that you think in terms of what they say and there is no other way of thinking. This is how art works in a more effective manner than science and logic. The Puranas are artistic expressions of spiritual truth, and that is why they appeal to your heart more than philosophical treatises. The Harikatha Kalakshepa system (discourse by song and music), with which many of you may be familiar, is more interesting and appealing, more capable of bringing truths into your mind, than a scientific exposition of philosophy, because here there is intimacy established with your feelings rather than with your understanding. This is to say that the Puranas and Epics speak in the language of feeling and love, rather than in the rules of understanding and intellectuality. This is the speciality of the Itihasas and Puranas-God coming to man in feeling, in practice, in symbol, in art, in visualisation, in practical contact rather than merely as a possibility of the future. God is today, not only tomorrow, and He is with us just now, capable of blessing us with His bounty.

The Puranas make out that there is nothing which God cannot give us, and God does not take time to act. He does not say: "Let me see tomorrow, come afterwards". Such an excuse, God will not trot out. God has no time factor nor does he have any space factor. He does not take time to travel. He does not take time to act. And there is nothing which He cannot give us; He is the superabundance of all the blessedness that the human mind can think of. He is not merely what He can give to man, but He Himself is the embodiment of what He gives. Devotion is the way to God.

WHAT ARE THE BRAHMA SUTRAS?

On the Asadha Purnima, Sri Veda-Vyasa, the Maharisi, commenced writing the celebrated sutras or aphorisms on Brahman. The Brahma-Sutras constitute a collection or a series of thoughts declaring the nature of truth and examining the possible objections against the accepted philosophy of Vedanta, the method of approaching the Reality and the fruits of meditation on Brahman.

The First Chapter describes the nature of Brahman basing its arguments on authority or scripture. This is necessary in order to convince such schools as the Mimamsa which lay great emphasis on the validity of scriptural statements. Through scripture itself, it is proved that Brahman is the Reality. All the statements of the Upanisads have a common purpose, i.e., to establish the absolute Reality of Brahman.

The First Chapter of the Brahma-Sutras is concerned with Sruti. The Second Chapter is concerned with inference, logic and argumentation. It is proved that the Upanisads have only one meaning, that is this Reality. This is the subject treated in the First Chapter of the *Brahma-Sutras*, the *Samanvaya-Adhyaya*. The opposite philosophies are refuted in the Second Chapter, *Avirodha-Adhyaya* which is devoted to arguments based on pure reason. This is done in order to meet the objections raised by schools like Buddhism which are out and out rationalistic and do not pay heed to scriptures.

The Third Chapter is called the *Sadhana-Adhyaya*. The different methods of meditation are described in this Chapter. How to reconcile the different Upasanas, the different methods of meditation which have been described in the Upanisads have been explained here. Because in the Upanisads, we have got detailed description of various kinds of Upasana dealing with various forms of Brahman, one is at a loss to know, sometimes, how to reconcile these in practice. Sometimes they do not agree with one another, sometimes they seem even to oppose one another. It is not easy for an aspirant to know how actually to put into practice these Upasanas which have been described in the Upanisads.

We have been advised in the Third Chapter that it is possible to combine some of these Upasanas into one Upasana, that though the forms may be different, they, many times, mean the same thing. When such is the case, we may take the entire process as one meditation.

The Fourth Chapter is the *Phala-Adhyaya* or the Chapter dealing with Fruit. What is the result of the practice of the presence of Brahman? What is the fruit or the consequence of these Upasanas, these meditations?—this is described in the Fourth Chapter. The fruit is an attainment from which there is the great "Non-Return".

WORSHIP THE SAINTS

(*Speech made on All-Saints' Day*, 1952)

(Excerpts from the Yoga Vedanta Forest Academy Weekly)

Today we have gathered here to observe All-Saints' Day. It is to remember the saints. It is the expression of our wish or ambition to partake of the nature of the saints, to grow into the nature of purity, of perfection which are the constituents of the personality of the saints.

A saint is one whose consciousness has spread everywhere, whose head is in heaven and whose feet are on the earth. He walks on earth as a human being; but he is here before us as a representative of that which is beyond the earth. He combines in himself the mental and the supramental, the physical and the celestial, the visible and the invisible, the finite and the infinite. It is through him that the Infinite expresses itself. It is through him that we can behold the glory of the Divine Being. He embodies in himself all the qualities and attributes which are found in the Divine Being and which are the best, the highest, which the Divine Being expresses in the universe. He is the embodiment of virtue based on knowledge. That is the very meaning of the word saint.

What is virtue? Virtue and righteousness are practically the same. We cannot have righteousness without knowledge. What is virtue one cannot know unless it is based on the highest knowledge. Others can be partially virtuous, relatively virtuous; they may err at some time or the other. But a man who is grounded on truth cannot err because he is based on that which is absolutely right. Morality and ethics should be based on the knowledge of the Reality. Ethics is based on metaphysics. Otherwise it cannot be perfect ethics. There should be an ultimate explanation of the behaviour of a saint and that explanation is his own experience or *anubhava*.

We observe this Day in order that we may understand these principles and apply them in our daily life and have direct experience of them. There is a great value in the adoration of saints. The mind is of such a nature that it imbibes the character of that which it thinks of. That is the psychology of worship, of Upasana also. When the mind contemplates something, it grows into that thing and becomes that ultimately. We can, for example, adore the great sage Vasistha. The moment the mind thinks of Vasistha, immediately all desires, all base passions are brushed aside. It is impossible to have evil thoughts in the mind together with the thoughts of Vasistha or Krisna or some other saint. I have heard it from many people here and have myself personally experienced that it is impossible to have an evil thought in the mind when we are sitting in the presence of our Gurudev because he evokes in us the virtuous qualities alone and not the others. Since he is the embodiment of virtue, of love, of knowledge, of perfection itself, so those qualities alone are evoked in us.

Similarly in the case of those whom we do not directly come into contact with, even if we think of them, it is enough. At the time of thinking of those personalities, the mind expands into the form of the qualities of which it thinks, and becomes pure. This is the value of meditation on the qualities of saints and their personalities. We should, therefore, adore the Great Ones—Vasistha, Vamadeva, Vyasa, Suka, Dakshinamurti, Dattatreya, Risabhadeva and others; because they are our Gurus, they are our Masters, they give us knowledge; and they give us knowledge even if they are not visible to us. That is very important to remember. Knowledge is not a gross thing. It is very subtle, indestructible, incorruptible. It is ever these. It can be given to us at any time.

It is eternal. The receiver (sisya) is eternal; the giver (Guru) is eternal; that which is given (knowledge) is also eternal. In the Kausitaki Upanisad, we have the illustration of how the Guru comes to help the disciple even after death, where it is said that before reaching Brahma-Loka, the aspirant comes into contact with the Guru. The Guru may be on earth; but he is not only there; he is beyond the earth also. The Guru is not confined to a body. Being a realised soul, he pervades the universe and as he is like God Himself, he can help the aspirant wherever he goes.

These saints do help us continuously and their grace is flowing to us even now. Therefore, we must be receptive to that descent of Grace. We must open our hearts when we worship the saints. We must remember that we must remove all those qualities in us which are obstacles to the reception of the knowledge which the saint gives us. It is no use trying to approach an emperor without the proper qualifications. When we try to do something, we must be sure that we would be able to do that thing, and the proper qualifications should be there.

It is said in the scriptures that the aspirant comes in contact with a particular kind of Guru suited to him at that particular stage of evolution. People frequently ask the question: "Why does not Lord Krisna move on earth even now? He can take a body as He is omnipresent." A similar question is: "We hear that obstacles are placed before the aspirant by the gods; for example we hear that Indra sends Menaka, Rambha and others to tempt him. Why are not such things experienced these days?" These things are not experienced always. The difficulties of that kind will be experienced by the aspirant in a different degree, not with the same intensity. When a person experiences a particular condition of his mind, he will come in contact with a Guru and an obstacle of the same kind. This is the psychology of Sadhana.

The saints, the Risis and Avataras should be worshipped by us in order to grow into perfection, to become that. When we worship God, we aspire thereby to come into contact with God, to realise God. We do *namaskara*; and we become one with That. When we say "Om Namo Narayanaya" and prostrate ourselves, it means we desire to become one with Narayana. This must be our constant attitude. We must feel it in our heart and contemplate it. Let us meditate on saints every day. Let us become pure in heart and in thought, word and deed. Let us become saints so that we may fulfil the goal of existence.

THE CHRIST TO THE SPIRITUAL ASPIRANT

(Excerpts from the Yoga Vedanta Forest University Weekly December 1952)

Jesus, the Christ, the Light of the World, the Supreme Logos made visible to the human eye, stands as an unparalleled example and pattern of sacrifice, love, knowledge and realisation of Truth. To the sadhaka or the spiritual aspirant, the person of Jesus reflects the art of the inner life, life in the spirit. Christ, the Son of Man, representing the life and voice of humanity and forming as it were the sum and substance of the essence of man, is the Son of God, the incarnate effulgence of the Sovereign of the Universe. It is the crystallisation of Spirit that we call the Mystic Christ, the Light that is born to save the world of darkness. As the darkness of the world is not an outward phenomenon, so is the remover of this darkness not a mere physical personality. Great men are not seen from their bodies. It is not the form or the body that is the great man. The great man is the behaviour, the conduct, the character, the speech, the thought and conscious expression. From these special characteristics, the presence of the great man is inferred and directly perceived. He is great who has comprehended that stupendous ocean of Spirit, the Great God, that twinkles in all eyes, that resides in the hearts of all beings.

We have in Christ the great man of the Spirit, and his life is a picturesque drama of Adhyatmika Sadhana or spiritual living. From his manifestation to his re-absorption, he displayed the magnificence of God and established His Glory on earth. When the spiritual child is about to be born, the Ruler of the empire of darkness will try to slay it and the child has to be protected with great difficulty. Once the child grows up, it shall take care of itself. The individual person is the parent of the new-born spiritual boy and let him guard it against the onslaught of the ego, the king of this city where the baby is born. Just at the time when the spiritual consciousness tries to emerge by gradual steps, a natural revolt of the unspiritual forces is quite inevitable. It is true that *ghee* is burnt up when it is poured into fire, but if a maund of *ghee* is poured over a spark of fire, the spark will be extinguished. When the spark becomes a huge conflagration, any amount of *ghee* can be consumed by it. In like manner, the worldly tendencies would overpower the spiritual spark when it is in the infant stage, but the conflagration of spiritual consciousness shall burn up worldly tendencies and all evil. What is called the "dark night of the soul" in the terminology of the mystics, is a stage where the consciousness is smothered and is smouldering amidst the darkness of ignorance. The birth of Sri Krishna is involved in similar circumstances and is indicative of similar facts, and the first Chapter of the Bhagavad Gita depicting the dejection of spirit of the aspiring soul mark identical situations. The spiritual self is bound to succeed, and destroy nescience, root and branch.

The work of the manifesting Spirit is not complete even when it has begun to peep through the vesture of flesh, after managing to save itself from the attacks of the outward nature. The greater trouble arises from the higher planes of nature. Difficult enough it is, no doubt, to pass through the forest of the gross physical nature, but more difficult and hazardous is the attempt to overcome the subtler forces of the vibrant mental nature which is the pivot of outward universal activity. When the soul sheds sufficient light, enough to blind the eyes of the psychological nature, a revolt of the latter becomes the result. This revolt is now in no way advantageous to the lower nature, for it only means the revelation of the extraordinary power of spiritual knowledge and experience and the crucifixion of the flesh, the very playground of the lower nature. The individualistic vestment is cast off, the turbulent passionate nature is punished and the Son of Man re-enters the Kingdom of God which is the birthright of the Son of God.

In Christ one finds the Jivanmukta of the Indians. As one standing at noon in cool waters up to the waist experiences cold and heat simultaneously, is the illumined sage moving on earth, with a body, which experiences bliss and trouble simultaneously, with his head and heart in Heaven and feet on earth. Jesus came to make people understand and know in experience that the aim of life is not to do something else, but *to be* something else. It is not wrong action that should attract our attention and demand rectification, but the organic defect in us which is the source and the root of wrong action. Unless one is *reborn* there is no hope. To become something completely different, to change one's nature, to be initiated into the unique spiritual experience, means dying to the life of flesh and being alive to the superior awareness. It is not the ceremonial act of the Jew, but the consciousness—experience of the Christian that is the ultimate solace of the individual, that is at present confined to the narrow tabernacle, which is the abode of all corruption and pain. It is not subjection to rule and rigidity of ritual which is the law of the spirit, but perfect freedom in the Glory of God-consciousness. Man is the child of the Universe by birth, but he is the child of God by re-birth. Self-control and asceticism are the roads to inner peace. The pleasures of the world are vain, tantalizing and deceitful; they are not worth being resorted to. He who loves the world loves not the Father.

Christ was conscious of Adhikaribheda among students of spiritual knowledge and was particular to impart the higher wisdom to the initiates alone, to those who were capable of rousing the inner consciousness, while to the outwardly busy, he spoke in parables. "Unto you is given the mystery of the Kingdom of God; but unto them that are without, all things are done in parables." "And with many such parables spake he the word unto them, as they were able to hear it; and without a parable spake he not unto them; but privately to his own disciples he expounded all things." Jesus has clearly told his disciples that he had many other things which he wanted to speak to them but which they could not understand. Jesus comes close to Hindu and Buddhistic ideals in many respects, and sounds practically an echo of the ethical teachings of these older religions. The death or non-existence of the immediate personal existence is, to all these religions, the condition of the new richer life.

To merge in the satiating waters of immortality, one must first drink of the cup of death. No man on earth, generally speaking, is prepared for this ordeal. This, too, is illustrated in the life of Jesus. He wished that the cup be taken away from him,—look at the force with which the lower nature presses the soul,—but he opened his eyes and his vision became clear, and he said: "Thy will be done." The stresses of physical life entangle the higher and nobler reaches of the soul, and to keep one's balance in the face of manifest hostility is indeed a tremendous task. It is given to a very few like Jesus to dive into the depths constantly and regain the solacing consciousness which is immaterial and trans-empirical. The whole life of Jesus is one tale of the march of the soul to its destination, which is the complete unfolding of consciousness.

A life of mere negativity is not what is preached by Christ. It is not only the emptying of the soul, the selling away of whatever we have, the parting with everything that we possess, but the supreme fulfilment of Spirit through divine contemplation. But the rejection of the outward show is a necessary pre-condition of this divine fulfilment. We cannot fill a vessel with nectar when it already contains filth to the brim. Spiritual life is at once the transcending of the mundane consciousness and the saturation of oneself in the metempirical Self-consciousness or God-consciousness.

The student or aspirant who wishes to lead the life ideal should receive inspiration from the conduct of Jesus, from his life and teachings, live a life of holiness and piety, embrace humility and poverty, become a friend of the poor, love the neighbour as himself, sacrifice his all to Him, suffer and weep for His sake, cast off the flesh and its passions, and die to be born for the life eternal. It means the withdrawal of faith in things that perish, resting on the firm belief in the Omnipotence of the Maker of all things, and caring not for oneself and one's needs, for God shall take care of all, with His simultaneous knowledge of past, present and future. This reborn soul is the sage, the Rishi, the Mukta, the redeemed one, who is one with God. The Son and the Father are one. The universe produces a rare ripe fruit of a saint from its fine flower of virtue and knowledge, makes him the cream of mankind and sacrifices him to the Great Father. Here is the consummation of existence. Christ's ascension to Heaven is regaining the Consciousness of God.

Christ was the matchless spiritual teacher who pointed out that the Kingdom of Heaven is within. All his other teachings are a commentary on this text. His teaching is summed up by his statement: "I and my Father are one." The individual soul is one with the Supreme Being. *Ayamatma Brahma. Jivo Brahmaiva Naaparah.*

The Principles of the Bhagavad Gita
(An interview with a group of Christians and Pune-Ashram Nuns)

Consciousness cannot be externalised because consciousness is indivisible. If you imagine that consciousness is divisible, you have also to imagine that there is a gap between the two parts thereof. Who is conscious of this gap? Consciousness alone is conscious of this gap between the two parts. That means, consciousness is present even in the gap in between. This is another way of saying that consciousness is universal.

Everyone in this world refers to 'himself' or 'herself'. This 'selfhood' is applicable not only to organic, but inorganic bodies and objects also. If 'selfhood' is applicable to the whole world, it means the whole world is filled with selfhood alone, and since selfhood is inseparable from consciousness, it means that the whole world is filled with consciousness. But on account of ignorance, we imagine that objects are outside the self. This idea of object outside is itself a misconception. There is no object external to the self. What you call the object is self itself. Let us take the example of a dream in which a tiger chases a man. He runs in fear and finally climbs up a tree. The tree, the tiger, the chase, etc. are all a projection of his own mind and his dream-personality also is a process of his mind. So the one mind becomes everyone of these in the dream. It is subjective as well as objective. This is what is happening in the waking condition also; and, even as the one single mind became all objects in the dream, the universal mind has become all these external objects around here even in waking life. They are nothing but the universal mind ultimately. You would not know that the tiger in the dream is unreal till you wake up. Even so, there is another waking up from the present waking consciousness. That higher awakening is called God-consciousness. In that condition, you will see that all the objects of the world are your own universal self. The efforts of man for material prosperity, and the like, are an indication of his deeper urge to reach up to the universal consciousness. From social consciousness, you go to individual consciousness and from the individual consciousness to the universal consciousness, and from there, again, to the Absolute. From social aspect you go to the mind and from the mind to the intellect and from there to the universal consciousness. This is the process of universal history as well as natural evolution. Thus the whole universe is struggling to attain the self-realisation of itself. Socially, it goes through the historical process, personally through the psychological process, and naturally through evolution. The society, the individual and nature are simultaneously moving towards the Absolute. As a matter of fact, the society, the individual and the world are not three different things; they are three aspects of a single universal whole; there is only one world having only one single purpose in life. When your activities are directed to this ultimate purpose, your activities become what is called Karma-Yoga.

The main gospel of the Bhagavad Gita is Karma-Yoga, because it converts every activity into a meditation on the Absolute. The Bhagavad Gita teaches that worldly activity is itself a spiritual activity in the end, because any activity is finally inseparable from the movement of the Absolute, and, therefore, it is, in truth, spiritual activity. For the Yogi, there is no difference between worldly and spiritual activity. Everything is spiritual for him. The highest insight does not make any difference between the temporal and the spiritual, ultimately. Established religion does. So there is an apparent conflict between the sacred and the secular, the holy and the profane, the Church and the Government, each wanting to control the other. Even today, due to these misconceptions, religions are failing us. The religious teachers insist that God is above the world and blessedness is a promise of the hereafter. But God is not merely transcendent to the world; He is in the world. So everything in the world has to be considered spiritual in its ultimate essence. God is not only in the world, but is the world. He is both immanent and transcendent.

Arjuna was not yet fit for Yoga. So, Lord Krisna takes him step by step until he is qualified for Karma-Yoga. Notions have to be analysed. The senses have their own notions about things; one is, that things are outside and the other that the things are localised in time and space. That a thing can be at one place only and not at two is an inveterate notion that the senses have. They do not know that things are interconnected among themselves. If they did, they would not go for certain things only. They, thus, have a notion that things are physical, external as well as localised. But this is a misconception of the senses. In the ultimate analysis, we find that things are not diversified, but have a deeper underlying connection between them. Reality will always assert itself. It is difficult to define reality. Reality is not diversity, but coordination and unity. In the beginning, it appears that things are different, later that they are interconnected and later still, finally, that they are compounded of one and the same substance.

The Bhagavad Gita has 18 chapters and they are grouped into 6 each. The first part of the first six chapters solves the problem of the conflict of the division within the individual. The second deals with the coordination of the individual with the universal, and the third the unity of the universe with the Absolute. The solutions of the conflict of the individual, the universal and the absolute are given in these various chapters, stage by stage. The subject is very vast and a bare outline alone is given. The entire gospel will take a long time to learn.

As long as the conflict between God and man is not solved, no other conflict can be solved. The root of the trouble is the separation of the individual from the Supreme Being. The aspiration for the coordination of the individual, the social and the universal is only an indication of the individual's need to reach the Absolute. We are trying to achieve external unity through institutions like the United Nations Organization, for instance. But broken pieces of glass cannot be put together by the use of even the best gum. You have to melt the pieces and recast them to make the glass whole once again, and this is what has to be done by these organizations. We do not, however, know the secret and hope to succeed merely by conferences, etc. The individuals have to be melted into the Absolute, and only then can there be real unity. The Bhagavad Gita tells you how this can be achieved. In the beginning, you have a hasty aspiration for the Supreme, the Absolute. But this cannot materialise so easily as it requires a long period of training and discipline to mature into experience. It seems almost impossible. This is what is described in the first chapter of the Gita. You feel like doing something, but you cannot really do it. The majority of the people in the world are in this condition only. They want truth, but cannot get it because the subconscious mind revolts against the higher aspirations.

In the second chapter, the Gita tells us that this fear can be conquered through a guide or a spiritual teacher. The spiritual path is very difficult to tread without a proper guide, and this proper guide cannot be got by study of books either, because you need the guidance of a person who has already walked the path. This chapter introduces us to the great Yoga which the Master of Yoga, Sri Krisna, imparts. Here the Master tells us that all our efforts should be based on knowledge. Action without knowledge will not succeed, for what succeeds is not the activity, but the knowledge that directs the activity. As a matter of fact, the whole gospel of the Gita is nothing but the blending of knowledge and activity. We have wrong notions about both these; we assume that knowledge means no activity, while activity is divorced from knowledge. Sri Krisna tells us that neither notion is correct. It is very difficult to understand what knowledge and activity are. Action is the outward expression of knowledge and knowledge is the inner reality of action. This may be said to be the central theme of the Gita. Action is rooted in knowledge. Then you gain the requisite inner trend to conduct yourself rightly in the outer world.

In Chapters II to VI, we are told how the individual personality can be disciplined in the process of blending knowledge and action. In the blend of knowledge and action, one can enter into the state of meditation. Chapter V explains at the end what meditation is in a short aphorism. It does not mean that in your ardour for meditation, in life, you can ignore the activities of the world. Many think that meditation is an individual and private activity which has nothing to do with the world outside. But it is not so. The two go and work together, like the wings of a bird.

Chapter VII tells us that meditation is a coordination of the individual with the universe. So meditation is not a private act, but a universal process. Chapters VII to XI give the technique of gradual unification of the individual with the universal. As a matter of fact, when the individual unites itself with the universal, the spiritual manifests itself, automatically. So, in this sense, the individual, the universal and the spiritual mean one and the same thing.

Chapter XII provides the technique of the various spiritual practices to bring about this unification, the four Yogas proper. Chapters XIII to XVIII give a beautiful exposition of how you can live in the world after acquiring this universal knowledge. It is only with this knowledge that one can redeem the world and do social work for the welfare of people: *Sarvabhutahita.* All this means that one cannot do real good to the world unless one is a truly spiritual person. You need the necessary qualifications even to get a job; and to do social work worth the while you need training in the field of the spiritual, in order to succeed in the sphere of human solidarity and material prosperity. The Gita gospel, therefore, prepares you for leading a universal life in this world. The Yoga of the Gita is inclusive of social work, humanitarian service, individual peace, as well as God-realization. This is the most complete exposition of Yoga available anywhere in the world. It is a veritable ocean placed before you. Drown yourself in it; save yourself with this vitamin tablet of the Gita. The difficulty in practice arises because of old habits persisting which can be cured by everyday meditation without a break. Satya, Ahimsa, Brahmacarya, in their larger sense of freedom from tension and conservation of energy, are the pre-requisites for meditation. Whatever you do in this world is equal to an a doration of God. God is to be seen in everything visible in the world. Truth is everything, and the knowledge of the nature of Truth is at once harmony with all creations. It is an instantaneous communion of meditation and action, grace and effort, the divine and the earthly, the relative and the absolute—Krisna and Arjuna driving forward, seated in a single chariot which is this body, and this universe evolving towards perfection.

The Call of Sri Krisna

(Talk given on Janmastami)

The Gospel of Super Excellence

One important lesson of our scriptures which we have overlooked is their call to a life of glory. There are many passages in the Vedas in which the Risi prays for greatness. "O Lord, make me lustrous:" "May I be the most glorious:" "May the sun and the moon and the earth and the sea, and the sky and the heaven made by Thee, be always favourable to us for achieving greatness."

The Gita has a whole chapter—Vibhuti Yoga—in which Sri Krisna exalts the best or most outstanding specimen in each class of beings by identifying himself with it. For example, he says: "Among immovables I am the Himalaya; among rivers, the Ganga; among trees, the holy fig; among cows, the divine cow of plenty; among sages, Vyasa; among heavenly songsters, Chitraratha; among generals, Skanda; among rulers, Yama; among the celestial sages, Narada; among warriors, Rama; among men, the King. I am the glory of the glorious, the victory of the victorious, the goodness of the good-natured. I am life in all beings and austerity in ascetics."

Sri Krisna summed up the general principle of Vibhuti Yoga in these words: "Whatsoever being is glorious, good, prosperous or powerful, understand thou that to go forth from a fragment of My Splendour."

In this way Sri Krisna has commended the celebrities in all walks of life but not the mediocre of routine workers. This is the Gospel of super excellence—a clarion call to all aspirants to acquire greatness and glory by their golden deeds. As if to leave no room for doubt, the same previous lesson was taught by Sri Krisna, while showing his cosmic form to Arjuna: "Therefore, stand up! Win for thyself renown! Conquer thy foes! Enjoy the wealth-filled realm!"

Modern thinkers have made a strong plea for the cultivation of super excellence. Thus Emerson wrote: "If a man can write a better book, preach a better sermon, or make a better mouse-trap than his neighbour, though he builds his house in the woods, the world will make a beaten path to his door."

Similarly Swett Marden said: "There is a fitness in doing a thing superlatively well, because we seem to be made for expressing excellence."

In his book, "Excellence, J.W. Gardner, President of the Carnegie Foundation, writes: "Excellence implies more than competence. It implies a striving for the highest standards in every phase of life. We need individual excellence in all its forms, in every kind of creative endeavour, in political life, in education, in industry—in short, universally!"

"An effective personality," says the noted psychologist, Dr. Links, "requires not only a variety of skills but relative superiority in a few fields and distinct superiority in one. The chief superiority should be in a vocational field, the others in the fields of sports, hobbies and the social arts. The mere habit of developing superiority is a preparation for success in later life."

Seva Dharma requires hard work but mixed with brains. All work must be done efficiently. According to the Gita, efficiency in work is one of the definitions of Yoga (II/50) and the devotee who is dear to Sri Krisna is *daksha* or dexterous in whatever be does (XII/16).

Efficiency has two sides, spiritual and temporal. The essence of spiritual efficiency is selflessness or other centredness, to do the work as an offering to God or for the good of fellow beings, keeping the eye on the interests of those whom the work is intended to serve rather than one's own. Strikes, demonstration, go-slow and work-to-rule campaigns and the clamour for more pay for less work are as anti-social and unspiritual as the practice of getting richer and richer by exploiting the employees or the customers.

The performance must also be satisfactory in the worldly sense. First and foremost, it must be of good quality, neat and clean, free from errors and blemishes. Secondly, speed must be added to accuracy. The work must be completed in time. Usually a good worker is also a fast worker and slowness is a sure sign of incompetence. Nothing big can be achieved without promptness.

Another important factor in efficiency is economy in labour, money and material. A capable person can work for long hours without feeling fatigued. He uses his time and energy, in fact all resources, to best advantage. He never attempts things which his assistants can do for him. He multiplies his powers by winning the cooperation of others.

Finally, the highest ingredient of efficiency is inventiveness and originality. The really efficient man is not simply a routine worker, doing things as they were done in the past. Rather he breaks new ground, makes new, better and cheaper things, simplifies procedures and makes improvements everywhere. He leaves his organisation better than he had found it.

But the Lord of Infinite Glory is not satisfied with ordinary skill; He expects superb from His devotees.

Very noble are those who practise Karma Yoga and work efficiently for the general good. By their efforts, they maintain the world order. Even more valuable are the few who practise Vibhuti Yoga, serve as exemplars, heroes, leaders or luminaries, and make significant contributions to the knowledge, wealth or well-being of mankind.

The development of talent, which has been so much stressed in the Vedas and the Gita, is a basic principle of the doctrine of evolution. Man starts as a seed with several kinds of powers hidden in him. They must be brought out and put to good use. This is essential for the happiness and progress of the individual as well as mankind.

"Each soul is potentially divine, "said Swami Vivekananda. "The goal is to manifest this divine within by controlling nature, external and internal."

The possibilities for the development of talent are almost unlimited. Even the most learned, if they only feel humble and sincerely try, can gain deeper insights and climb to greater heights of wisdom. Similarly, age is no bar to the growth of talent. While physical development stops in middle age, intellectual development can go on even in ripe old age. Two ways to keep the mind alert and growing even in the evening of life are to apply it to touch problems and to continue learning something new all the time.

William James, the famous psychologist, used to say that the average person develops only one tenth of his latent mental ability. "Compared to what we ought to be," said he, "we are only half awake. We are making use of only a small part of our physical and mental resources. Stating the thing broadly, the human individual thus lives far within his limits. He possesses powers of various sorts which he habitually fails to use."

Alexis Carrel writes in *Reflections on Life*: "Every one should realise the full measure of his inherited mental capacities, be these great or small. This obligation is universal. All are equally capable, if they are really determined, of releasing the hidden spiritual energy in their own depths. Though consciousness develops side by side with the body, it does not stop developing when the body has finished growing. Intellect, aesthetic activity, moral strength and religious sense continue to develop even in old age."

The same lesson of super excellence was taught by an English poet who sang:

If you can't be a pine on the top of the hill,
Be a scrub in the valley—but be
The best little scrub by the side of the rill;
If you can't be a bush, be a bit of grass,
And some highway happier make;
If you can't be a highway, then just be a trail.
If you can't be the Sun, be a star;
It isn't in size that you win or you fail;
Be the best of whatever you are.

We make such extraordinary or supernatural powers which perform miracles and benefit rare individuals. Such feats, though spectacular, are of limited utility as the masses can neither imitate them, nor take advantage of them. In contrast, we take little notice of common powers developed to an exceptional degree which extend the frontiers of knowledge or make life easier and pleasanter for mankind. It should, however, be noted that Sri Krisna has identified himself with all celebrities, not only with the religious ones. All luminaries, whatever their nationality, period, and profession, reveal the splendour of God.

Worldly excellence is no less acceptable to God than spiritual excellence. Both are necessary for the maintenance and advancement of the world. Both are, in fact, one according to the Vedanta. Elucidating this point, Sister Nivedita writes in her inspiring book *Religion and Dharma*: "We cannot be satisfied till our society has produced great minds in every branch of human activity. *Advaita* can be expressed in mechanics, in engineering, in art, in letters as well as in philosophy and meditation. But it can never be expressed in half measures. The true *Advaitin* is the master of the world. He does not know a good deal of his chosen subject; he knows all there is to be known. He does not perform his particular task fairly well: he does it as well as it is possible to do it.... The highest achievements of the mind are a Sadhana.... The man who has followed any kind of knowledge to its highest point is a rishi."

Similarly Basil King writes in his book *The Conquest of Fear*: "All discovery of truth, whether by religion, science, philosophy or imaginative art must be discovery in God. When the Lord restores sight to a blind man or Peter and John cause a lame man to walk, we see manifestations of God, but we see equal manifestations of God when one man gives us the telephone, another the motor car, and another wireless telegraphy. Whatever declares His power declares Him: and whatever declares Him is a means by which we press upward to the perception of his loving almightiness."

It should be clearly understood here that 'superior power' does not necessarily mean increased spirituality. The true test of spirituality is not power, natural or supernatural, but the service rendered to mankind. Demons and devils are not dear to God, though their powers are very similar, sometimes even superior to those of the saints. "Man becomes great", said Mahatma Gandhi, "exactly in the degree in which he works for the welfare of his fellow men."

The primary condition for super excellence is a lofty aspiration of ambition, a conscious striving to know all about one's subject or to do one's work as well as it can be done. This desire appears in the form of a deep interest in one's work or the particular problem one has taken in hand. It is well-known that scientists and inventors give themselves up whole-heartedly to the object of their pursuit.

A powerful interest which dominates a man's life polarizes his mind, which then acts like a magnet and continually draws out from his stored-up experience and also from new experiences whatever is relevant and useful to the end in view. Deep interest invigorates the mind, awakens its dormant powers and is the key to super excellence, invention and discovery.

Hard work is another condition of superiority. The aspirant must master the knowledge and technique pertaining to his particular job; in fact, he must be a keen and lifelong learner, ready to pick up new ideas and new ways wherever he can find them. He must cultivate the habits of thoroughness, accuracy and reliability, he must take pains to check, revise and polish his work until it acquires as perfect a finish as possible within the limits of time available.

Inspiration only comes as a result of hard study, deep reflection and patient search for the solution. Scientific discoveries are generally preceded by a large number of different experiments, trying first one thing and then another. Edison, the wizard of inventions, made about ten thousand tests with different chemical combinations before he found the right one for his storage battery. Looking for a suitable material for the filament of his incandescent lamp, he tried more than 6,000 samples of bamboo from every corner of the earth before he found the one that made the Edison electric lamp ready for commercial use.

Similarly good writing requires not only profound knowledge but also enormous labour in writing, painstaking, revision and rewriting. Carlyle took great pains over his works and, before writing a page of his famous history books, he would consult all the well-known books on the subject. Tolstoy rewrote his *War and Peace* seven times. Adam Smith took ten years to write his

Wealth of Nations, while Gibbon spent twenty years over his masterpiece, *Decline and Fall of the Roman Empire*.

The story of the discovery of radium is a saga of patient toil in the midst of appalling poverty. It took the Curies four years to isolate a very small quantity of radium from tons of ore. All day and for months they worked together in a damp, rotting shed which they called their lab. For much of this time, Mrs. Curie had to stand stirring a boiling mixture in an enormous pot with an iron rod which was as long as she was tall. The roof of the shed leaked and they did not have enough money to get it fixed. When the rains came, streams of water fell between these two workers and their work. Their labour was indeed *tapasya* of a very high order.

Super excellence means constant improvement and innovation, thinking in straight lines instead of curves, introduction of simpler procedures, time and labour-saving devices, better and cheaper goods, making two blades of grass grow where one grew before. There is nothing in the world which cannot be improved. The best is yet to be made—whether in books or automobiles, radios or nylons, medicines or men.

The ideal of all-round excellence is very difficult to attain. Only rare persons can become versatile geniuses. But everyone can acquire mastery in some little branch of knowledge or skill. Every one can do at least some phase of his work superlatively well by developing his strong point or specialising in the part of his work in which he is most interested. And once this is done, superiority in one part of his life will stimulate superiority in other parts. Whatever a man's vocation, let him not be content to remain a mediocre; let him lift himself from the commonplace to the outstanding.

In India, we are fortunate to have excellent human raw material. But the opportunities and incentives for its development are sadly lacking. Religion has, on the whole, a blighting effect on secular professions. Even in other spheres the strong tendency is to encourage subservience and sycophancy rather than initiative and talent. Had we paid proper attention to this matter, our country would have produced giants in every field of endeavour.

We should recapture the spirit of the Vedas and the Gita. We should exalt work. We should discover and encourage talent wherever we can. We must produce not only great saints, philosophers and Yogis, but also top class men in every walk of life. We need eminent scientists, selfless rulers, farsighted statesmen, dedicated administrators, educationists, doctors, lawyers, engineers, inventors, sportsmen, artists, explorers, writers, industrialists, managers, seers, dreamers, as well as organisers and leaders. No great man has done his duty until he has made at least ten persons worthy to take his place.

"This every moment," exhorted Swami Vivekananda, "let every one of us make a staunch resolution: 'I will become a prophet. I will become a messenger of light. I will become a child of God. Nay, I will become a god.' "

"Arise! Awake! Stop not till the goal is reached!"

A PICTORIAL PHILOSOPHY OF YOGA

Imagine for a moment that the whole space is a large radiant and blazing splendour. Imagine at the same time that this blazing splendour which is filling all space and which is the space itself, is getting transmitted to everything which is within it, inside as well as outside. Stretch your imagination a little to consider the position of the little bits of things in this vast space which is brilliant, comparable with the sun, even more brilliant, and imagine that the little things in this vast space are electrical transforming stations. A transforming station receives the energy that is pumped from the power house and transmutes this energy into a particular measure of voltage either increasing it or decreasing it as the case might be. And, imagine at the same time that this transforming station is of the shape of a prism. Don't think that the station is made up of iron, steel, etc. It is a luminous body, and it is looking like a crystalline prism. So, you have to imagine many things at the same time. A great, inconceivable, all-pervading space—not the space that you see with your eyes—but a novel type of space which is all radiance and nothing but that. This radiance has its impact upon the transformer station which is of the structure of a prism. And you know what happens to light when it is projected through a prism; it gets deflected in various directions. But it is not merely a prism, it is also a power-house in a small way because it is a transformer station. Because it is a transformer, it pumps energy outward from its own container. Imagine at the same time, once again, that this transformer set has the power to throw the energy received by it outward with a great force, as water passing through a conduit pipe jets forth with an amount of pressure. Imagine that the pressure exerted by the transformer is varying in its nature, so that there are many such stations. You know the power-house can emit energy and the same can be connected to various types of transformer sets, with different forces in them to diffuse the energy received into a new type of voltage of a different intensity altogether. Now, I mentioned to you that it is not merely a station that transforms the energy into a new voltage of a higher or lower category, but that which deflects it in various directions, casts it into rays which ramify themselves even as the rays of the sun are seen to project themselves into a thousand different directions. There is a new set of energy producer, a dynamo, inside the power station, which throws the energy out with a capacity equivalent to the productive capacity of the dynamo that is placed in the transformer set. What happens? A lot of change takes place. Firstly, the vast light that is the radiance of the indivisible space has been conducted through the transformer unit which deflects it in a different way altogether. It does not merely deflect, it pumps out with a jetting energy in the direction given according to the structure or the make up of the transformer set. It is something like a person being pushed by another in one direction continuously, so that the person that is pushed is forced to move in that direction, especially if the direction is a type of a lane where one cannot move to the right or to the left and has to rush forward through the blinkers of the limitations on both sides, so that what is ahead alone is seen and what is behind cannot be seen because it is a narrow passage and what is felt is only the push given by something which cannot be seen by that which is being pushed.

This illustration which I am placing before you is to some extent comparable to the image of the "case" that you find in the *Republic* of Plato where he gives a similar analogy which is familiar to many of you. Imagine that people are thrown into a dark dungeon where it is all pitch invisibility and these captives who have been thrown into this dungeon are tied hand and foot with chains, tightly, so that they can see only the walls of the cave and not what is behind them, namely the passage through which they were driven into the cave. What do they see? They see a dark wall in front of them, the wall of the cave. Imagine, so goes Plato's illustration, that these captives are thrown there for years and years. They are born and bred, as it were, in that cave itself, so that their generation does not know what is normal life in the world. They have never seen light with their eyes. They have been living for centuries in the dark dungeon, in the cave, and they can see only the wall, and that in one position only, because they are tied hands and feet with chains, as captives in the prison house, the dungeon. Imagine, says Plato, that people are walking on the road in the sunlight and the shadows of the people walking in the sun, are cast on the wall of the cave in which the captives are tied. What do they see? They see movement of shadows. They cannot imagine who casts these shadows because they have been tied very tightly in one position, so that they can see only the wall and not what is behind, and we are also to imagine that they are there for centuries and they have never seen what is light and what is normal life in the world. They would be imagining that, that is the world of activity and that the shadows are the reality. But they do not know what casts the shadows or where they originate or the originals of the shadows.

I will give you another—a third example. Imagine there is a Parliament House; and near the House there is a pond where there are many frogs. The frogs are great scientists. They observe the movement of people around the Parliament House with powerful telescopes. The frog scientist has a microscope and also a telescope. What the scientist sees he makes a note of. And The frog scientists also make observations and note them down in their scientific study: "This building (the Parliament House) has the power of attracting people and people keep entering it." Then they observe that the people leave the building. This second observation is also noted down: "This building not only has the power of attracting people into it, it also ejects people out of it. It has, therefore, the power of attracting and repelling people." In like manner, our actions are attributed to the stimuli externally from the objects outside, like the frog scientist attributing to the building the quality of the entrance of people to and their exit from the Parliament House. The source of these actions is blotted out of perception by the disintegrated sense-perception. This is also the way in which scientists interpret the behaviour of objects by casting everything and every event in the mould of cause-and-effect relationship, under the impression that such a law operates in the universe, as an objective fact.

The impulses that we see acting within us outwardly are the action of the dynamo that is working within us which has received the energy of the power-house, whose presence is completely blotted out from the vision of the streaming rays of light, which are projected externally from the transformer set. Each one of us is a transformer set and also a prism deflecting rays of light in five different directions through the five sense organs, the eyes, the ears, etc. The senses are the rays which are deflected through the personality of ours which is a radiant transformer set but structurally patterned like a prism. Because there is a dynamo inside that pumps energy externally, we are impelled outwardly with a capacity equal to the capacity of the dynamo that is within ourselves. So different individuals that we are, we have different types of impulsion towards external contacts and we run outwardly whether we want it or not. All movements are external because of the force with which the dynamo ejects them externally into space and time. We do not merely carry this dynamo within ourselves; we, ourselves, are that. The so-called 'Me', 'You', or 'He', 'She', 'It' is nothing but this transforming dynamo which throws the energy out with a tremendous force, externally, so that, it can neither be aware of itself, nor can it be aware of the large source of light which is the infinite space from where this little jet passes through this dynamo, a little bit placed in some corner of this infinite space. So what can we say about our own selves? We cannot say anything about ourselves or about anything else. Our mouths will be shut if we are given this sharp injection, awakening us into the circumstances in which we are placed in this world of correlative actions and reactions. Hence, being buffeted from every side, inwardly and outwardly, we behave in our moods and in the actions of our psyche in different manners at different times of the day and during different days in the span of our life here and in different incarnations through which we pass. In one incarnation, we live as one species of living being, in another incarnation, we may be in another species with a sociology of its own, with a political argument and philosophical disposition applicable to the outlook available to that species. You cannot imagine what you yourself were in the series of physical existences you had had in your earlier births. But there is a connecting thread running through these recurrences of the species, though nobody can see it anywhere. But it has to exist and it exists everywhere. Either an organic connection in creation exists everywhere through the species or it (creation) does not exist at all, for creation is evolution of an organic whole, not segmented parts. But the frog-scientist has made his observation that the building, the Parliament House, has the power of attraction and repulsion. Only this much of information is available to the frog-scientist. The mind makes the same mistake and we think and act as if only human beings were the whole of creation. This peculiar situation arises on account of the organic past that has gone before us. The mind is very defective and misses the point. The mind misses the point, again, on account of its peculiar structure.

Here we are not going to tackle the problem of the first step towards God or God-Realisation, but we have to be even more cautious about the problem before us, the disease that humanity has construed as social philosophy. It is not a frog philosophy or a snake philosophy or a tiger philosophy or a honey-bee philosophy or a crow philosophy, it is only man's philosophy and it cannot be anything else because we are men, we are humans. So this peculiar pattern of the prism, that we are, can deflect the rays in one mode only. If you want, you can imagine colour prisms and also broken prisms or prisms with concave or convex effect. You can imagine what you like to pattern in your own mind the variety of species that can be possible in this infinite panorama of experience you call creation, you call experience, you call existence, you call the universe. We are running after Yoga practice with great enthusiasm with little knowledge of the difficulties in which we might be placed. The conditions which limit us in a hundred and a thousand ways are so atrocious and harrowing in their nature a little misconstrued aspiration would be a defeat of the purpose, because this is like preparing oneself for a kind of protracted warfare which can prolong itself for any length of time and which can be fought in battlefields of different areas on earth unknown to the imagination, under conditions which cannot be explained now before the beginning of the war. Such complications are before us.

We have a principal and primary problem before us, viz., that we are our own trouble-makers essentially, because through the analogy of the dynamo which is the transformer set, I mentioned to you that we are ejecting ourselves externally so that the force with which we eject ourselves outwardly compels us to be aware only of other things, other people, other conditions, and not of ourselves which are responsible for the perception of these other things, other people and other conditions. The nature of the perceptions which we regard as a totality of experience depends entirely upon the structure of this dynamo which we are. And so, in different species of incarnations, we have different worlds before us. You might have been angels, you might have been a Gabriel or a Michael, you might have been an Indra or a Brihaspati, you might have been a *Gana* of Rudra or in Vaikuntha, a *Parshada* of Lord Visnu; you might have been a Siddha in Indraloka or Tapoloka; you might have been any blessed thing in any realm of being. And those experiences of those types of beings, of individuals placed under those circumstances, were due to their being constituted in that manner, in that individuality. And now we are human beings for whom only humanity exists and nothing else can exist. The thought of any other thing is meaningless for us. We laugh at anything that is not human. We have a condescending and, what can you say?—a poor opinion of anything that is sub-human and we laugh at anything that is superhuman. How can you imagine that there can be anything else other than what your own species can contain in itself? Now, if Yoga is the power that bombards the very structure of individuality and breaks it open, so that it can connect itself to the original principle from where it receives sustenance, existence, and intelligence, naturally Yoga must be a really hard job. It cannot be an easy joke and the difficulty about it can be imagined by us, though we cannot actually pass through it at once; at least imagine in our minds, if we can place ourselves philosophically under a state of analysis of circumstances which is the legacy that we have received from great masters of yore, which legacy has come down to us in the form of the scriptures, in the form of the texts written by or spoken by these adepts, or even by messages that have been conveyed to us by word of mouth through the chain of Gurus and disciples. Various other means of communication are there, and through these means, we come to know this, the great vista that is before us, the project or enterprise of Yoga. To enter the field of Yoga is, therefore, to become a member of the comity of the whole of Creation. When you sign a membership form of the government of the universe, the law that operates there acts upon you instantaneously and they, having the power to act in multitudinous ways, have also the power to act upon you in a similar manner. We do not enter into the field of Yoga as Indians, Hindus, Brahmins or nationals of a country, or people with an affiliation to a creed or a faith. The principle of Yoga is the principle which can best be described today as wholly scientific, in the sense that it states facts for facts. With all this panoramic projection of the vista of the Light that is Yoga before us, we have to take the first step, because even if you are going to enter the ocean itself you have to place your first step on the beach, in the first waters of the ocean, and you do not place your foot in the centre of the sea. Whatever may be the distance that you may have to cover, you have to take one step at a time. Nobody takes more than one step at a time. That is impracticable. The question is, where to go and what step to take, in which direction, under the circumstances mentioned, i.e., when we are being pushed and pulled in various ways by the powers that are ahead of us and the powers that are behind us, like a person caught in the movement of a flooded river, pushed by the waters from behind and pulled also by the waters that are in front, thus being forced to move only in one direction. What solace has that person? What independence can that person have in the circumstances of the push and pull in both directions?

The ancient technique, therefore, has always been of a very cautious communication of this knowledge from the Guru to the disciples, and that to selected ones only. It was never a mass teaching, because it is of such subtlety that one has to tread it with such dexterity and with such a manipulating capacity that a generalised prescription or recipe may not have the effect desired, even as a public lecture on a particular recipe of medicine by a doctor to a large audience of sick people may prove to be of no effect at all. These days, things are different. We are living in a different century, under conditions that are quite different from the ancient conditions of the Upanisadic times. Taking for granted all these difficulties, inwardly and outwardly that we are facing, the tradition cannot be left out. The mountain that we have to scale is very high, but it was high centuries back and has not become less high because centuries have passed. Mount Everest is not going to become smaller after two hundred years. You cannot say, "Now times have changed, the mountain has to come down." Man has to gird up his energy in a different way, yet he may prepare himself according to the prevailing conditions. The prevailing conditions of the time—political, social, personal, etc.—are to be taken into consideration, even one's own physical condition. But with all these preparations, one has finally to tread the very same path that the ancient masters trod. There is only one way and no two ways. It is a part of an atom, yet spread out everywhere, says the great scripture—atomic in size but spread out everywhere. It is atomic, because invisible to the eyes. One cannot know actually what one is supposed to do at a given moment of time because when troubles come, they come like floods. You won't have only one trouble, troubles will come from all sides. You will have every blessed difficulty, inwardly and outwardly, the Adhyatmika, the Adhibhoutika and the Adhidaivika troubles. It will appear that everything is unfriendly from top to bottom. People are unfriendly, the sky is unfriendly, even the stomach is unfriendly, nothing is co-operating! These problems everyone has to face, but these are the incidental encounters and we have to bear in mind when we tread the path of Yoga, that the disciplines that we are following are capable of yielding the fruit that is desired. This is the reason why a continuous and constant vigilant observance by a Guru becomes necessary when one takes to yoga very seriously and not merely in a purely religious or social manner. Inward impulses clash with social laws. They can clash with political conditions, and your means may be something prohibited in the world. So you have clash and confrontation and rub and skirmish and a problem. Here, nobody can help you, because those who are supposed to be your helpers, become your opponents at a time when you take a step above the purely social or the conforming level of your personality.

At present we are all living at a conforming level. We have to conform to various norms of life and we look around and see who is there around us and naturally we have to conduct ourselves according to those people who are around us,—are they policemen, are they thieves, are they friends, are they men, are they women, are they children, are they what, accordingly you conduct yourself. But a time comes when you may have to brace yourself in the atmosphere of your own psychical forces which remain at present invisible to the eye. But the time may come when they alone may be visible and nobody else outside; they will become realities. You will become the perceiver of them. You will see them as if they are objects outside. At present, they are the wire-pullers inside. They operate through the individualities of people. So, when you confront people, positively or negatively, or have to deal with things in some way, you imagine that you are dealing with persons or things, not knowing that you are forced to do that by the impulses deep within you and you are guided along a stereotyped path. But a time comes when these dacoits will show their faces. When the mind withdraws itself in deeper concentration into the realms of the psyche, the wires which are pulling the individuals along will be seen; and they are the reality. Then it is that you are seized with dread and a fear takes possession of you. You do not know where you are standing. This problem you will not face when you are only telling the beads or chanting the mantra only a few minutes, or performing Yoga Asanas for only half an hour every day. Religion has not touched your skin and therefore these difficulties are not felt by you. But those of you who at least believe that they are students of Yoga, will have one day or other to face the realities and not merely the shadows on the walls. You have to see the sources which cast these shadows, and these shadows are cast by powers which are inside us, which are manipulated by our individualities according to the nature of the species into which we are born. But we have to be rid of this species-consciousness. One day we may have to stop thinking like human beings, because human beings are not the only things that are created in the world. We have other forms of life than the human and that is why you will have to forget all things that are human—every law, every regulation, everything that is human will have to be transcended, broken through. And there, God is your help, and perhaps the Guru is your help. The subject is very deep. I shall hope to touch upon it another time.

PRAYER FOR DEPARTED SOULS ITS PURPOSE AND PRE-REQUISITES

(*Forest University Lecture given on All-Soul's Day*, 1952)

Our salutations, adorations and prostrations to all those who have gone ahead of us, who have gained more experience and who are before us as ideal beacon lights in life. Today we offer our adorations to all those who are not visible to our physical eyes, but who lived on this earth-plane and who now experience a different state of consciousness. We offer our gratitude to all those who have gone before us and shown us the path.

By the remembrance of all souls, we mean the remembrance of everything that is created. It does not necessarily mean those who exist in a *Preta* condition, in the astral body; but those who have abandoned their physical body and who have taken another physical body also receive our prayers. Those who exist in Swarga Loka receive our prayers, those who live in Gandharva Loka, and all those who experience pain and suffering also receive our prayers. Our prayers reach up to Brahma Loka and the Surya Mandala, because our prayers are the expressions of our soul-consciousness.

You know there are various kinds of human beings. Similarly there are various kinds of departed souls. There are some people who feel that it is very difficult to understand how the efforts of a person in this world can influence the conditions and experiences of a person in the other world. This doubt arises on account of lack of understanding and lack of knowledge. We must know that the Universe is an organic whole. It is not a dead matter. It is vibrating with energy, life and consciousness. The Universe is one whole. If anything happens to any part of my body, the whole body feels it. So is the case with everything in this universe. Every atom of this universe is connected with every other atom in this universe. Planes are only relative; they are not absolute values. They are valid only to individuals. Hence an act or a thought or a feeling which is originated at any particular part of the universe shall influence others also with that degree of intensity with which it is generated. If the prayer is intense, it will be felt there in a corresponding degree of intensity.

The act of *Sraddha* is an example. When we offer foodstuffs or other articles which are all used in the name of the departed soul, we mean they should be received by the person "there". In this world of materialism, people who have no belief in the higher values doubt the validity of this act. How does a physical act in this world influence a subtle body that is in another world?

This may be explained by a modern analogy. Take, for example, telegraphic conveyance of money. If a person wants to send a money order, he just pays the required amount to the Post Office in his own town and wishes that this amount should be received by the person concerned at some other distant place. Now, that same money is not received by the other person. It is here itself. The Post Office in the other town receives the intelligence of the sender's wish. Only the feeling, the understanding, is conveyed, and that works wonders. The intelligence causes a corresponding action to take place there. The person receives the amount at that distant place.

The same is the case with Sraddha. The Pinda that is left here is left here. It is the symbol of an internal feeling, of a *bhava*. Sraddha is something more than mechanical action. It is an act of prayer with *bhava* and feeling. We must not underrate our thoughts and feelings. Our thoughts are omnipotent. Every thought will fructify, today or tomorrow, in this form or another form. When we do charity in the name of a departed soul, this intelligence is conveyed to him through the planes of consciousness. The pitris receive there what we give here, because we transmit an intelligence to those who are in charge of the person concerned that such and such a thing should be given to the person there. That great selfless act of sacrifice in the name of the departed soul gives wonderful benefit to him. This is possible on account of the unity of the universe, because of the omnipotence of God, because He is the Sovereign of the universe, because He is the dispenser of justice with His Supreme Wisdom.

Just as there are various kinds of men, there are various kinds of departed souls; so various prayers of different intensities are offered. Take the human beings alone. All human beings are not in the same stage of evolution. We have got "animal men"—those who have got human bodies but animal qualities. Then we have men superior to them, ordinary men, who are not bad, but are not good either. That is the second stage. Thirdly, we have got good men; they are virtuous. Superior to them we have saintly men: they are not merely good, they have started to unfold the divine consciousness. Lastly we have got divine men or God-men. These various kinds of people reach different conditions and have different experiences when they leave the physical body. Of course, those who are Self-realised are not in need of our prayers. They themselves are very powerful. Their Self-experience and Knowledge are so powerful, so great and so-valuable, that they will help themselves. But all are not saints, all are not God-men. Those who have not reached this stage require the help of others.

Soul's Journey after Death

Our Puranas and Itihasas say that the soul after death passes through different experiences. It is said that an ordinary person in whom there is a mixture of good and evil, when he dies, is taken to Yama-Loka in the beginning. If his evil traits preponderate, he will be taken to Yama-Loka. Scriptures further say that an ordinary person does not remember his past experiences. He is in a state of swoon the moment he casts off the physical body. Our prayers give him consciousness. They give him fresh energy and solace. Because he is not a virtuous man, he is suffering; our acts of sacrifice shall be beneficial to him. Even when the person goes to Yama-Loka he will be helped there by our acts of sacrifice. But a person who has read the Vedas, who has led a virtuous life, remembers his past experiences; others do not. In the latter case, the Puranas say that a Danda called the Yama-Danda is kept on the head of such a person so that he may remember his past life. It is described as a burning iron rod. At once, he remembers all his past life on earth. Then the Dispenser of Justice puts the question: "You have done so many evil deeds. What do you intend to do about them?" Then, it is said, the soul gives the reply: "I have got my relatives. They are capable of doing what is good for me. They will perform all the expiations on my behalf, and then I shall free myself from all these experiences of pain." Then it is said that the soul is sent back to the earth. It takes about 12 days. That is why we perform the ceremony on the eleventh and twelfth days here. The soul is brought back to the earth and it is made to watch what is happening there. Before that time the body should be buried or burnt. Because attachment to the body is so much that the very perception of the corpse will create a desire in the soul to enter it once again; but those who are in charge of it will not allow this—and this would be a condition of great suffering. And, so, on the 11th and 12th days we should offer prayers, perform Havanas, do charity etc.

Generally, we perform a Yagna for the peace of the soul and for the satisfaction of all those who are in charge of the soul. Otherwise, it will not be able to experience the things that are sent from here. First of all, a certain *Bali* (an offering of boiled rice, etc.) is offered, which is for the satisfaction of Yama. It is said that this act will satisfy Yama and He will free it from bondage. It is necessary that the soul should be purged of the evil deeds it has done. So Bhagavata-Saptaha, and such sacrifices and Yagnas are performed. Then we are told that the soul is released from Yama-Loka and it goes to Rudra-Loka and there it becomes one of the *Ganas* of Rudra-Loka. In order that it may be released from that place, we have to perform the Rudra-Yagna. Then Rudra releases it from the state of *Gana* and it shines in a lustrous body and goes to Brahma-Loka. It is initiated into the divine mysteries by Brahma Himself and it attains Moksha.

So gradually the soul which is not very virtuous, which has not done any good deeds on earth is also enabled to reach the higher planes of consciousness through our acts of prayers and sacrifice.

Weep not for the Dead

In this connection we must remember that the pains which are experienced by the departed souls are intensified by the sufferings and the grief expressed by those who are on earth. The scriptures emphatically say that, after the death of a person, no tear-drop of grief should fall to the ground from anybody's eyes. It does not in any way help the departed soul. On the other hand, even a soul which is about to enter heaven will be brought back if his people are crying here. No one should, therefore, weep or cry; but everyone must pray for the peace of the departed soul. The person who has left the body can be given whatever he needs from here. Study of scriptures is a great help, offering of prayers, performing *havanas* and doing charitable deeds, and even contemplation on God for his sake—all these are of great use. When a person meditates on God, for the sake of the peace of the departed soul, it is said that it will be enabled even to attain *Moksha*. The knowledge of the Guru is powerful enough to enter the heart of the disciple to dispel his ignorance; even so is the relation between the person existing here and the departed soul. For the sake of the departed soul we can meditate. It is possible to send our powerful currents of concentration and meditation to enable it to reach higher states of consciousness. For this sake, we must bear in mind that we are part and parcel of the universe, even as the departed souls are; and there is not much difference between the person who exists in a physical body and one who exists in an astral or some other kind of body.

Glory of Prayer for All Souls

Our prayers are capable of producing an effect immediately. Our prayers are expressions of soul-consciousness. The prayers should be absolutely selfless. It is necessary that the idea of personal relationship should be removed when such prayers are offered. When such relationship is kept up, the prayer becomes slightly tinged with selfishness and loses its value. We must offer prayers for all souls with an impartial attitude. Only then will it be extremely powerful and bring the desired result. We offer prayers not because we want anything in return for the prayers, but because we wish to radiate peace in the universe. When collective Sadhana is done, when all people sit together and pray for the sake of the departed souls, it brings peace to everyone in this world, even the person who has departed and taken birth again—in fact, all living people will be benefited. Everyone's life will become peaceful and everyone will lead a happy life, on account of our charitable acts. It is really praying for the peace of the whole universe. So, this offering of prayers on this sacred All-Souls' Day is our attempt to bring peace to the universe and to realise in our practical life the oneness that is at the background of all phenomena. We are all one, whether we are in the physical body or astral body; each should be grateful to the other; each should pray for the other; each should wish the good and happiness of the other, so that the whole universe will be a heaven of peace, a resting place of divine consciousness.

From "THE PANCHADASI EXPLAINED" ANALYSIS OF THE SELF*

Human consciousness is characterised by objectiveness. It is more a cognition or a perception than simple consciousness. The cognitions and perceptions are the processes of knowing through the mind and the senses. In the waking state of ordinary consciousness, the different senses receive different kinds of knowledge, and the function and knowledge of one sense is quite unconnected with those of another. For instance, the eye alone can perceive forms and the ear alone can know sounds. Knowledge differs with regard to the different senses. But, even if these different kinds of sense-knowledge are entirely cut off from one another, the person experiencing this sense-knowledge is one and the same. The person is the synthesiser of sense-perceptions which, by themselves, (are not interrelated.) The same person experiences forms, sounds, touches, tastes, smells, etc., and feels: "I am the seer, the hearer, etc." and does not feel that the seer is different from the hearer. The ultimate knower must, therefore, be an absolutely indivisible whole of consciousness. Even if there is the slightest distinction within the constitutive essence of the knower, i.e., if the knower is made up of parts, complete synthetic knowledge would never have been possible. If there is a division within the knower, what is the relation between one part and another? The question cannot be answered, as knowledge does not admit of space within itself, because knowledge is presupposed by the idea or conception of space. If these parts within the knower are not differentiated by anything other than the knower, then the knower does not become a composite whole of parts, but an undivided dense existence of pure consciousness which is absolutely identical with itself. The nature of the knower must be knowledge itself. If not, what is his nature? This question, again, cannot be answered. The most fundamental experience is consciousness or awareness, pure and simple, free from all self-contradictory divisions and fluctuations of thought. None can experience anything greater than or equal to consciousness as the ultimate basis for all experiences in life.

Hence the knower of sense-perceptions cannot be the mind,

*Excerpt from the Yoga Vedanta Forest Weekly of Feb. 2, 1950.

though the mind is able to know without the help of the senses and is able to coordinate, arrange, and systematically synthesise sense-perceptions. Thoughts differ in different places, times and conditions. Hence, there must be some other synthesising agent of even mental cognitions. Otherwise a person cannot know that he is the same individual experiencing different kinds of thought. Mental cognitions and sensuous perceptions are heterogeneous in their nature. Therefore, the possibility and the experience of a unified completeness of self-identical, absolutely immediate and direct consciousness shows that the true Self is Pure Consciousness in its essence, which is not affected by the revolting activities of the mind and the senses. The essential nature of the Knower or the Self must be simple consciousness, because in the state of deep sleep it is seen that when the body, the vital currents, the senses, the mind, the intellect, the ego, the sub-conscious, and everything that goes to make the individual gets suspended and denied its validity as an existence, the person still exists as is testified to by the following experience which, with great certainty, identifies the person who has woken up with the person who slept previously. The existence of the essential person, the Self, in the condition of deep sleep, was one of "awareness of nothing", "awareness together with nothingness," which means "mere awareness", as "nothingness" has no value whatever. Further, the existence of the experience of the Self is corroborated by the subsequent remembrances of the existence of oneself in deep sleep. A remembrance is not possible without previous experience, and as experience is never possible without consciousness, we have to conclude that the Self does exist in deep sleep as mere Consciousness. This Consciousness, therefore, exists in the waking state as the unchanging basis of the changing mind and the senses. In the dreaming state it exists as the synthesiser of mental cognitions. The objects in the waking and the dreaming states differ from one another, but the consciousness of objects is one and the same; it does not differ in relation to objects. The only difference between the waking and the dreaming states is that in the former, experience is the effect of the function of the mind with the help of the senses, whereas in the latter experience is the effect of the function of the mind alone. But the consciousness is the same, both in the waking and the dreaming states. As this consciousness is proved to exist in the deep sleep state also, it is evident that this

One Consciousness endures without even the least change in itself in all the states of experience, during all the days, nights, weeks, months and years, i.e., till eternity. It does not differ from another consciousness, nor does it differ from itself now and then, here and there, in this or that experience, as objects and mental states do. Consciousness is always one and is ever secondless. We cannot conceive of two consciousnesses, though mental states may be two or more. Hence consciousness must be eternal. Metaphysically, anything that is eternal must be infinite, unlimited. Consciousness is unlimited, for the consciousness of limitation shows that consciousness is greater than limitation. Hence, the Self is eternal, infinite, Absolute Consciousness. The ignorance that is said to exist in deep sleep cannot really exist or have any value, for, if it does, it would be an eternal antagonist of consciousness, and consciousness would be limited and perishable, and not infinite or Absolute. The illogicality of the existence of ignorance cancels its validity and posits the existence of the Absolute Consciousness. One experiences consciousness, and not ignorance, as his fundamental being or Self. This Self is, therefore, different from ignorance in the sense that consciousness is not ignorance, but it does not mean that the Self is a witness of ignorance as real existence.

The Self neither dies, nor is born, nor has any modification. If it has these changes, they have to be experienced by some consciousness. And this ultimate experiencing consciousness, we term the Self. This Self is self-luminous, non-dual, self-conscious, independent and the sole Being.

The way we should live in our own personal and Public Life

Inasmuch as you are officers, you cannot have an isolated personal life, entirely; you are socially related. In fact, there is no such thing as an absolutely isolated life for any person; everybody is socially connected. You are a social entity. You belong to the world. You cannot say that you have absolutely no relationship with anybody. So, personal life is only a tentative definition of your nature. You have a relatively personal way of living, but it is inwardly connected with various factors which are super-personal, impersonal, you may call them, social, national and international; it may even go further into the universal. You are not an individual as you may imagine yourself to be. There is an old saying of a poet: "No man is an island." An island is surrounded by the ocean and cut off from the main land from every side, but not so is a human being. He is not an island; he is not cut off from the main land of the cosmos like a piece of land in the ocean.

No man can be happy unless he discovers the sources of happiness. Happiness does not drop from the skies, suddenly. It is an expression of pefection. Wherever there is perfection, there is happiness. There is happiness in health, there is happiness in mental equilibrium, there is happiness in social solidarity, there is happiness in national security and so on and so forth. Wherever there is harmony among the constituents of a particular pattern of living, there is happiness. Happiness is only a name, a designation that we give to the perfection attained on account of a harmony brought about among the constituents of a particular set-up. You are District Collectors, for example, and you have a jurisdiction over a particular district. The jurisdiction implies your relationship with the constituents of the district. The constituents need not necessarily be human beings; they can be even geographical conditions, and so on. It is a very complicated system. So, first of all, you have to be clear in your mind as to what sort of progress or perfection you are expected to introduce in the jurisdiction over which you have control. A District Collector is an all-in-all person. He has got every kind of responsibility and is like a king without a crown on his head. He has a tremendous responsibility.

First of all, the District Collector must understand that people around him are like him. He is a representative of the people in the district, just as the President may be regarded as the representative of the whole country. You are a small President in your own district. Though it may be a smaller jurisdiction, your calibre and your responsibility are of a similar nature. What you have to understand is that people around you are not inferior to you in any way. There are also capable of being Collectors, perhaps, if the necessary circumstances and facilities are provided for them. They have aspirations like you; they have desires like you, they have weaknesses like you, and they would like to achieve what you would like to achieve. Only they are not provided with the same facilities as you have been provided with by circumstances of society, and they feel the pain of things as you feel, and what you wish they also wish. They are just like you in every respect.

You are a human being, and they are human beings. But circumstances of the society have made you the head of a group of people, towards whom you have a responsibility, and not a right. You should not think that you have a right over people. You have a responsibility, and obligation; and wherever an obligation is properly fulfilled, a kind of right also automatically comes. You need not ask for rights, they will come automatically. You shall only be careful to see that you fulfil your duties and you should not pay too much attention to your requirements. You must always pay attention to your obligations.

So, in this effort of yours, in the fulfilment of your duties, you must consider also that you are a unit of the whole country. You have to work according to its constitution. I am driving at another point altogether which is different from the merely official responsibility of a person, as the ultimate aim of every organisation is security and happiness. You do not become officers merely because you want to become officers. That is not the purpose. The purpose is to achieve an end which is superior to officership, to bring about perfection, security, happiness and prosperity, internally as well as externally.

Now, if we have a parochial outlook merely, that will defeat our purpose. Suppose a District Collector thinks: "I am concerned only with my district, the other districts may go to hell." If he starts thinking like that, you can foresee the consequences. The neighbour is connected with him in a very vital manner. It is true, in a very narrow sense, that you are concerned only with your district. But it is wholly untrue that you are concerned only with that and nothing else. Suppose the whole country is in sorrow and in a state of insecurity and everything is shaking at the bottom, what is the use of your efforts in one district merely? So you must have an eye to the larger dimension of your responsibility as a citizen of the whole nation also in addition to your responsibility as a Collector in a district. But, this, too, is not sufficient. You are in an international set-up. The country may be prosperous internally, but it may be threatened by outside dangers. So what will you do about that?

Perhaps you have no jurisdiction as wide as this: but little drops make the whole ocean. If everyone thinks that he is not concerned, well, then everything is doomed to chaos. As drops make the ocean, so individuals make the society. Each person is a unit of responsibility in the whole country. He may not be an Officer in the technical sense, but he is a centre of responsibility. Every citizen has a responsibility for the whole nation. The democratic system is nothing but a system of each one being responsible for everything. That is called democracy. But people think: "It is the Government's concern, what is my responsibility for it?" If you think like that, it is a defeat of the purpose of democracy. There is a danger in the understanding of the subtlety behind the democratic administration. People do not understand what it actually means. Sometimes it appears that everyone's responsibility is no-one's responsibility. It may look like that. If everybody is concerned with a matter, it means no one is concerned. Suppose a government's water scheme is flowing through the road and the tap is open. Will an individual be concerned with the wastage of water or not? If he thinks: "It is the government's water that is flowing, I am not going to be the loser, let the water flow!", then he is untrue to his citizenship in the country. He thinks that the government is outside him. He is a very foolish man indeed. The government is not outside the constituents of the nation. What is a government? It is only an ideological force that the entire set-up of citizens has created for its own good. The government is not outside you and you cannot see it anywhere else. If you go on looking around, where is the government? You cannot see it. It is only in the minds of the people. It is a power that you have created by thought. So, ultimately, the government is in the minds of the people, it is not physically visible. You go anywhere throughout the length and breadth of India, but you will not see the government; yet it is present everywhere. It is like God existing. God is everywhere, and yet nowhere. So, this is an analogy to explain to you that every citizen is a small unit of responsibility, and government is nothing but a name for the total responsibility of the entire nation; and what is totality if the individuals are not there! If the part is absent, the whole cannot be there. So, there can be no government if each individual is irresponsible. So, this is the philosophical background, we may say, behind the governmental system, democracy and life as a citizen.

Ultimately, perfection, security, prosperity and happiness will be ensured to us only if we are in harmony with the forces that govern life. These forces, which are not merely social, are the determining factors of human happiness, for man is not merely a social unit. When you are at home, you have a personality of your own. When you go to bed and sleep, you do not sleep as a collector sleeping. You have got an individuality and a personal status of your own. You forget all your associations and you begin to realise yourself as an independent person, a unit of reality and that has some relationship with similar such units constituting the whole world. So, the inner essence of man has also to be attuned to the inner essences of all people. We are not merely political people like the M.L.As., M.L.Cs., etc.; we are not merely social units, we are also physical bodies, we are minds, we are intellects, we are also spirits, and all these have to be set in tune. So there is a necessity to bring about a vertical as well as a horizontal harmony. Horizontal harmony may be said to be harmony in family, harmony in society, harmony in the community, harmony in the nation, harmony in the international set-up. This is a kind of horizontal harmony. But vertically, there has to be harmony in the physical body, harmony in the vital breath, harmony in the mind, harmony in the intellect, harmony in the Spirit.

If the internal harmony is not there, the external harmony will not work. Suppose a man is mad, is out of his brain and his physical health is breaking and his consciousness is aberrant, what is the use of his social association? Individuals should be healthy in order that the group may be healthy. The group is nothing but a totality of individuals and so no international organisation can succeed, not even the UNO, if the individuals are not complete in themselves. They must be perfect individuals, representatives of total responsibility. We are citizens, not merely of India, but of the whole cosmos. We belong to an international set-up, no doubt, but also we belong to a universal set-up—God's creation. So you are a child of God, a citizen of the universe, and so if you are not in harmony with the natural forces and the divine laws operating, you will be overcome in the end. You may be apparently successful in your efforts in the beginning, but finally it will collapse as did the Roman Empire. The Roman Empire was politically very strong, perhaps it was an ideal Empire manifesting tremendous organising capacity, but it lacked the spiritual note! The soul was absent while the body was perfectly healthy. It appeared to be healthy. Suppose you take away the soul of a man and the whole skeleton is left, what happens? It falls down. The Roman Empire did not fall on account of the invasion of the

Huns, as historians tell you. Even microbes cannot ask you if your body is perfectly in balance. Even tuberculer germs cannot enter your body, if your body is perfectly maintained. But if you are susceptible to invasion, they attack you. The susceptibility to invasion of any kind should be avoided. People make themselves vulnerable on account of certain inner lacunae.

Together with the strength of the defence forces of the country, there must also be the strength of internal maintenance and security, by which I do not mean merely economic security, but also intellectual, moral, ethical and spiritual acumen, and you are representatives of that aim and ideal. By God's grace you have been placed in such a position that you can instruct people, and so you must be very friendly with people. I began by saying you are human beings like anybody else. So when you are the heads of an organisation or of a jurisdiction, you have to behave as a father behaves in a family. The Collector is the father of the District. And how does the father behave with the members of the family? Great responsibility, and yet great affection. He is strict in the administration of system and discipline, but very affectionate like a mother, a parent like father and mother combined. So this is the way in which we have to envisage things in general, spiritually enlightened within, cosmically harmonious in our thoughts, and politically responsible as units of governmental organisation. This is only a short outline that I have given to you. You can go on enlarging upon it for a lifetime. I pray with an invocation to the Almighty that your adventure in life in every respect may be a total success. May God bless you!

THE COSMOLOGY OF YOGA PRACTICE

You have performed the Yoga physical exercises. But the word 'Yoga' that is attached to these physical exercises should awaken us to a new vision that is behind these physical performances. Why do you call these 'Yoga', when they are only physical exercises? Here comes the meaning of 'Yoga'. This has to be understood before he can derive the benefit that these special exercises are expected to bestow upon us. To understand how a physical exercise like this can become Yoga, you have to know the very background, rather the philosophy, behind these Asanas, the

Yoga exercises. These Yoga-Asanas are based on a cosmology on which the whole Yoga system is rooted. Though you may look just individuals who have performed a few physical feats, there is a relevance of these exercises to certain meanings which go beyond the visible form of the exercises. It would be proper if I mention to you in a few words what this cosmology is, though this is a vast subject on which great experts have written volumes.

Yoga holds that the universe is a complete organism, a wholeness by itself. The so-called parts and isolated units in this universe are, to an extent, comparable to the parts or limbs of the human body, constituting a wholeness never independent of one another. We see varieties in this world making us believe that everything is different from everything else, in the same way as, with a narrow vision of certain parts of the body, we may think that the feet have no connection with the head, if our thought is limited only to the area of the feet and does not extend to the region of the head. If you see the body only through some blinkers, the whole organism of the body cannot become an object of perception. Then, naturally, we cannot see the connection between the legs and the head, for example, and if anyone instructs this narrow-minded individual on there being such a thing called relevance from the feet to the head, that would be a 'philosophy' for him, something which he cannot comprehend. He is instructed about that which he cannot see, and only told theoretically of there being a larger relevance inherent in the visible parts which are the immediate objects of perception. According to the philosophy of Yoga, the universe is not made up of discrete particles, as material science may make out. Even science has now started thinking thrice before pronouncing any judgment on the nature of the universe ultimately. The universe is not constituted of atoms, molecules, etc. It is not connected with a 'transcendent' meaning in the sense of a creator extending beyond the universe of creation. There is no transcendency in the universe; the so-called transcendence is only a word that we use in respect of that which we cannot comprehend or that which has not yet become the object of our consciousness. If our understanding can expand itself adequately, it can visualise the cosmos as a completeness.

Now, cosmology is the doctrine of creation. How is it that you appear to be different from me and everyone appears to be different from everyone else, in spite of the fact that there is an inward structure of the whole of universe? The centre of the universe pulses itself outwardly in a centrifugal manner. There is an urge towards externalisation in space and time. This urge which arises in the centre of the cosmos is usually known as the creative will. Everything is pushed from the centre outwardly to such an extent that the one complete whole gets distracted into particular individualities, as it were, even as our coherent complete waking mind divides itself into many particulars in the dream world that we sometime experience. The centre of our mind is externalised in dream. We see a world of shape, space and time, and we are the cognizers or the observers of this dream world. The vast space-time and cosmos that you see in dream is not outside your mind. The externalisation is only apparent, but the apparent externalisation is so intense that you have desires, loves and hatreds even in dream. You can have hunger and thirst and everything that you see in the waking world even in dream. So, merely because it is an appearance, the experience of its being a reality is not precluded at that time. Likewise, says the Yoga system, this universe of creation is to be explained. What has happened to us today, is precisely what happens to the waking mind in dream. It has dissociated itself into the various objects, and then retains itself as the subject of these visibles. The waking mind cuts itself off into the realm of objectivity and subjectivity. This centrifugal impulse of the universe moves onward and onward until it reaches the climax of creation to an utter particularity and externality, where one becomes totally conscious of the objects only, completely oblivious of the subjective element in such experience. What are we doing in this world? We always look outside, gaze at things externally and judge outward objects and never pass a judgment on our own selves. We are convinced that there is nothing to say about our own selves. Everything is 'Okay' with us. The subject has lost consciousness of itself and has transferred all its values to the objects, so that we live in an object-world. And all evaluation that we make in life in any field of activity is objective not in the sense of impartiality which also goes by the name of objectivity but in the sense of a total transference of value from the conscious subject to the externalised name-and-form-complex, which is known as the object.

Creation does not end merely here. The propulsion to create ends in the manifestation of lifeless material things like stones, bricks, granite, etc. There creation is said to end. When there is a total unconsciousness of everything, creation has achieved its purpose. In the beginning you have the consciousness of all things, and in the end it is an absence of the consciousness of everything. Now, we are in a transitional period. We are individuals being pushed forward, onward, onwardly by the centre of the cosmos, through the impulsion of centrifugality and individualisation. The universe is not an individual, because it comprehends within itself all individuals just as you cannot call the human body as a cell, because all the cells are included within this completeness called the body. But if a particular cell in the physical body were to be capable of asserting its isolation from the other cells of the body, which also go to make up the whole constitution of the body, that would be the predicament in which we are today. We constitute parts of this cosmos, and we are inseparable parts thereof, originally connected with everything. Now your incapacity to see your connection with me or my incapacity to see my relation with anything else outside is due to the interference of space and time in the middle. Space and time are not something existent materially or substantially. They are only conditions of externalisation. A peculiar magic, as it were, has been cast upon us, by which the universal completeness of the universe, to which we originally belonged, is totally lost sight of and we are aware only of the segmentation of the body from the universe of totality. We cannot feel that we have anything within the brick walls, for instance, notwithstanding the fact that there is some connection there, if you go deep into the physics of the objects.

Now, this propulsion to create this centrifugal impulse of creation, which disconnects parts from one another does its work in a very gradual manner. It is not a sudden severing of limbs, but a slow process of self alienation. There is a cosmical awareness originally in the system of things when the parts were not separated from the whole. Thus, the first thing that is to be done in order to make us forget our oneness with the universe is to make us unconscious; this is what they call 'brain-washing' in modern language. Some mysterious power, you may call it by any name, the power of externalisation, brain-washes the parts of their conscious connection with the whole. This unconscious seed of externality is called the causal body in our personality. We have five layers of personality. The causal one is the deeper-most, the inwardmost, the unconscious layer into which we revert when we are fast asleep. This is what they call the unconscious psyche in psycho-analytical language. More outward and external to this causal region or level of our individuality is the rational or the intellectual level. The intellect tells us that everything is outside and that which compells us to see things only in space and time outside is the unconsciousness that is behind the unconsciousness of our connection with the universal completeness. The intellect follows suit here. Lower than the intellect or reason is the mind which is the instrument of thinking. Our judgment which is the function of the reason employs the thinking faculty as the means or the instrument to goad us on into activity in social life. The mind does not directly act upon objects. It moves through the vital energy and the nervous system which pervades throughout the body like electricity. The energy is known as the Prana. The vital force in us which permeates the entire body, the energy as you call it, is the Prana-Sakti which is the externalised form of the mind connecting itself with the physical body.

Now, we have come to the level of the physical body. Here you are at the level of the Yoga-Asanas. You may now know how far you have come down from the original reality of things. And the physical exercises that you perform become a 'Yoga' when you understand the history of your descent from the cosmic total. These physical exercises are a systematisation and organisation of the functions of the body in such a way that the energy pervading the body is inwardised and the centrifugal impulse is forced to move back towards the centripetal aspiration for the higher realisation of realities beyond us. The centripetal is the inward urge moving towards the centre, and the centrifugal is the opposite, moving away from the centre towards the circumference.

Now, from this little introduction of the cosmological basis of the Yoga system, you will know why these exercises become a Yoga. They are not like football and tennis, or some such game, for they are a wholeness by themselves. Though these Asanas appear to be different from one another, they have a common purpose, just as the various dishes or items of food that you eat may be variegated and different one from another, yet the purpose of eating is common, which is the appeasement of hunger, and it is the same in every person. The satisfaction that comes out of the consumption of food is the same, notwithstanding the fact that the items of food are different, one from the other. Likewise are these Yoga-Asanas. There is the Padmasana, there is the Sirshasana and there is every other kind of Asana. All these are like items of dishes served before you but aiming at a common purpose of uniting the powers of the body into a focus of concentration and attention so that they are forced to go inward into the Prana-level from the merely physical, the intention finally being to go further on from the Prana-level to the mental level, from the mental level to the rational or the intellectual level, and then pierce through this dark curtain of oblivion, ignorance, which has made us forget our connection with our Parent, which is the universe. The purpose of Yoga is to make you complete beings, to make you hale and healthy in your personality, to make you total individuals and not distracted psyches, not persons harassed by worries and feelings of insecurity and annoyance, but persons who can stand on their own legs with a power that comes not merely from the meal that you take, the food that you consume, but from the power that descends from the universe. Where from is the strength of the legs that walk? They do not eat any food, you do not give them tea and coffee, the feet eat nothing, but how are they so strong? The strength comes from their organic connection with the total system of the body. Just imagine, the feet which do not consume any diet are strengthened merely by their organic relatedness to the whole system of the body. Likewise, your strength does not merely depend upon the food that you eat, the money that you have, the social status that you may occupy,—nothing of these. None of these things is the source of your power. Your strength lies in your inward relationship with the power that is transcendence and that is the universal. The more you are able to feel your relation with the wider creation outside, the more are you also able to approximate your individual existence with the larger dimension of the universe; then the more is your strength. This fixing of the consciousness upon the larger dimensions of the Reality beyond the mere physical location of the body is the art of meditation, that people speak of so much. You must have heard that there is such a thing called meditation which gives energy, strength, power, etc. How does it bring energy? It brings energy because you draw sustenance from the five elements,—from earth, water, fire, air, ether; from even the trees;

from the solar system. The solar system is full of energy and we do not feel its presence on account of our isolatedness from it even as the law of the government cannot sustain a person, protect him or guard him when he becomes a renegade and cuts himself off from the organisation.

So does this universe of force, including the solar energy etc., not appear to help us in any manner whatsoever, because we have deliberately isolated ourselves from the whole. We have become what they call 'prodigal sons', who have run away from their parents with the false notion that they can live independently by themselves. And you know when any limb of the body assumes independence, it is called a paralytic stroke, and the limb cannot function afterwards. It is strengthened and vitalised only when it is organically related to the body. The moment it assumes independence, it is there no more. We are weaklings, so called, psychically, physically and socially on account of an inward severing of the values from the Cosmic Value. These physical exercises or the Asanas are the beginning, the initial stages of your movement towards the larger realities that are ahead of you, finally your aim being to unite your being to become as vast as possible in your comprehension. This inclusion of the larger dimensions within your vision and field of activity is what is called human consideration, love, affection, sympathy, and the like. Your feeling for others is an outer indication of your inward connection with things. Do you not work for human solidarity? Do you not feel that there should be one humanity, that mankind should be in peace? How does this idea arise in your head, if you have no inward relation with mankind as a whole? Don't you wish that the whole universe should be in peace? Why should this idea occur to your mind at all, if you are not going to be inwardly related to the whole cosmical set-up of things? Your wish for immortal existence and long life and your desire for infinite possessions are indications of your being something more than what you are today in this little body. Your originality, the archetypal existence of yours, is in the heavens, as the philosophers like Plato tell us. You are like reflections of these originals. The originals are in the higher realms of existence which are deeper than the physical. We have spoken about various levels or planes of existence. They say there are seven planes at least, the physical being the lowermost. There is then the astral, the causal and the universal. We have descended too low to the physical, materially isolated bodily level, from which we have to rise up to the original Reality which is our true stature. This art of unifying your being with the Being of the universe by graduated stages begins with the performance of these physical exercises called the Asanas and ends in cosmic Meditation. Then you become a source of Power and competency in every work that you perform. You are administrators, and you become master-administrators because of the knowledge that you have of the set-up of things in their organic connectedness. You do not then treat people as if they are objects or tools or implements who have to be utilised for ulterior purposes. You treat them as brothers, and there lies your success,—when you treat people as you treat yourselves. Here is the way to success. If you look down on people as nobodies and if there is even a little inkling of exploitation of any sort, in respect of others, then the law of the universe will react and tell upon your system. The law of the universe is cooperation and not competition. It is not warfare. That is the law of the universe, the total solidarity for which the prayers of the ancient sages were directed in such scriptures as the Vedas, the Rigveda concluding with a prayer for universal cooperation, collaboration not merely in a social manner, but even in the field of thinking, in collective aspiration and all activity. Yoga, therefore, is not a system of religious thinking, it is a science of living in a manner that shall make you perfect in every way. Perfection is the watchword of Yoga, it is neither an 'ism', nor a religion, a cult, a creed, nor a faith,—nothing of the type. It has no difference of caste, creed or colour, East, West, North, South, etc. It is perfectly scientific and impersonal as the law of gravitation, as the laws that operate in mathematics or logic. I have tried to place before you, in outline, the tremendous significance that is behind the performance of Yoga exercises, placing you in a universal context of things and making you feel a satisfaction that belongs to the whole cosmos, and whoever the Creator of this cosmos be, He shall protect you.

YOGA—THE SCIENCE OF LIFE

I am quite sure that by this time you are all fairly acquainted with the bearing of Yoga exercises on the personal life of the individual,—the anatomical, the physiological, and perhaps, even the medical side of the practice. Today, I would prefer to touch upon another important aspect of the system of Yoga, which is usually missed by adherents and enthusiasts, due to which the practice of Yoga and the propagation of the system known as Yoga does not seem to have brought to the notice of the human public the requisite advantage accruing thereby. Often it appears that Yoga is a personal affair, a private conduct of the individual in respect of oneself, for one's own physical health and physiological balance of the system, which no doubt Yoga is. But there is something else about it, without a knowledge of which the emphasis laid on the individual may not bring the real benefit which would be expected by anyone from the practice. Here we come to the crux of the subject.

We are not merely individuals. This is a very important truth that we have to learn when we study anything. If we are, in fact, isolated individuals, speaking strictly from the point of view of the logical definition of the word 'individual', there would be no communication between one individual and another. The scientific definition of the term 'individual' implies self-affirmation and a segregation of the selfhood of the person to such an extent that there is a complete demarcation of one individual from the other. If such a difference of such a marked nature were to be present in the individuality of the human being, you could very well imagine the consequence. There would be no communication between individuals, merely because of the fact that they are 'individuals'. The isolation that is implied in the affirmation of the self is a bar to any kind of amiable relationship among persons. But what is it that we are aiming at in public life, if not social harmony, peace as we call it, in public life and in our existence as units of society as well as the international system. Thus, it would come to light that Yoga is not merely a personal affair, it is not the business of the individual as a self-centred something, but it has a connotation with a wider dimension, with its connections extending through its tentacles to the far reaches of all creation, as it were. The practice of Yoga is, really, the practice of the art of living. It is not any mystical doctrine of any section of people, it is not a creed or a cult but a system of living, a system which is of such a universal character that no one can afford to forgo it. It is the science of the basic structure of the human individual in its relationships with all that exists, whether in Society or in Nature outside; and from this point of view we may say that the practice of Yoga is the practice of the art or the science of public living in its principal sense. For our purpose we may classify human life into four broad aspects, though there can be minor details of this classification.

The four main sections or facets of human life are the social, the psychological, the natural and the universal. We are units of human society and all our activity seems to be towards the achievement of social good. The enterprises of humanity through governmental systems or social welfare organisations or family units, etc. do all seem to be tending towards a single goal of achievement, namely, welfare of mankind, humanity in its entirety,—social good, well-being, happiness; the greatest happiness of the greatest number, as some people put it. We may say that we are aiming at this much; nothing more and nothing less. We would like to have the intensive form of happiness both in private and public life, in the largest quantity possible. If we carefully analyse the character of our activities and the structure of our enterprises in any field of life, we will realise that there is nothing but this much in our intentions inside while we engage ourselves in any kind of work outside. But what is the measure, or the yardstick, that we are going to employ in the judgment of social values? How are we going to discover that such and such a thing is going to pave the way for social peace? What is our concept of social well-being, what is the meaning of international good? What is it that we are actually aiming at, finally?

The aim behind this total enterprise of mankind's mind has to be measured by a standard that is set by the individual himself. What we call commonweal or social peace is the happiness or the peace that the individual aspires for. And what is society if there are no individuals, though it is true that, from the point of view of a certain branch of psychology, society has an abstract character of its own independent of the individuals that constitute it? We may, from the practical angle of vision at least, conclude that there is no society if there are no individuals. Thus, the pattern of social existence is set by the individual himself. What is good for the individual is good for the society, because the society is an enlarged form of the individual. It is a miniature *Visvarupa* of human nature. I myself become the standard of the judgment of social welfare. It comes to that, finally. What I regard as good for me must be good for all. I feel that a certain type of satisfaction is my requirement and I hold that it is the requirement of everybody else, also. If this were not to be the standard of judgment of values, how else would people work in this world? Here we come to a very interesting secret behind social life: the psychology of human nature, which seems to be the determining factor of all social activity.

Our enterprises in social life, in public life or in political life, are ultimately guided by the standard set by the individual. Psychology becomes the guideline for public activity. So we move perforce from the social outlook to a study of the psychology of human nature. This is the second aspect of the study of human life. The social is the most obvious, visible side of human existence. But the strings which are behind this apparent picture of human society, controlling the movement of society as a whole, are the patterns of human nature. So, unless you are a good student of psychology, acquainted with the nature of the structure of the individual, to a satisfactory extent, there would be no tangible success, perhaps, in your public existence. If you cannot understand human beings, you cannot make them happy, and you cannot also be yourself happy. But you have to go deeper still. Psychology is not everything, though it seems to be a very important aspect of study. What is it that determines the character of the individual? While we have concluded tentatively that human nature as a psychological unit determines social patterns of existence, we have now to understand how it is that the human mind thinks in the way it thinks. There must be something determining the very way of thinking itself. We have an idea of what is good for us. How does this idea arise in our mind? Who put this idea into our heads? How are these ideas implanted in our being? Now we go deeper into a field which is not visible to the eyes, perhaps not included even in the field of the study of psychology. We go to a section of study, a field of analysis and research which usually goes by the name of philosophy, a poor word, indeed, which cannot connote all that we are intending to convey, but which points to a necessity to study human nature in a perspective which is wider than what is comprehended in psychological studies. Here begins the role of Yoga.

Why is Yoga so necessary for us? It tells us where we stand,

and the answer to the 'why' of a thing comes from the system of Yoga. While science can tell you how things work it cannot tell you why things work in the way they work. The 'why' is a difficult thing for us to comprehend and answer, but Yoga has the answer. If we are thinking in a particular pattern say, in the three-dimensional pattern in thinking to which we are all shackled, unfortunately for us, it is because we are planted in a world of space, time and causal relationships. We are now placing our feet on an almost forbidden land, not accessible to science and not visible to the naked eye of the human individual. We think in the way we think merely because of the set-up which can be called spatio-temporal. This is a familiar term, but it is difficult to understand correctly the meaning behind it.

What is this spatio-temporal structure in which the individual seems to be placed? The spatial context is the three-dimensional context. We can think only in terms of length, breadth and height. There is no other way of thinking. Even with the farthest stretch of our imagination we can think nothing else but length, breadth and height. This is what we call the three-dimensional way of thinking. But Yoga tells us that this is not the only way of thinking possible, though perhaps it is the only way available to us, limited as we are to the space-time set-up. It will be very interesting indeed to go a little deeper into this subject. You know, this space-time complex weighs so heavily upon our minds that we are almost its slaves, we are not masters as we imagine ourselves to be. We are forced to think only in a particular manner. We may say, we are brain-washed by space-time which compels us to think only in this way, and no other way.

Everything is quantitative. This is one way of thinking. You may think anything, and you think it in terms of a quantity. It is a measure with length, breadth and height, Even if you think of a minute particle, as small as an electron, you cannot think of it in your mind except as a very little dust which has a small dimension, unthinkable though. This is thinking in terms of quantity. The second aspect is the thinking in terms of quality. Every quantity has a quality. It has a character. There is a way of defining it. It has an attribute. This is how we think of a quantitative substance, whether it is large or small. The third way of thinking is relation. Everything is related to something else. Either it is positively connected or negatively related. You cannot define any object without relating it to something else. When I say that grass is green I mean that this particular thing I call grass is of a colour which is different from what is not green. If non-green things do not exist, green things cannot be seen. A cow cannot be seen unless there are non-cows, and so on. This is only to give you a broad idea of what our definition of relation is, ultimately. Every definition is qualitative, and this definition is given through abstraction of character by relationship with other objects, and if something external does not exist, definition is impossible. So this is a third limitation on our mind. Everything is caught in terms of relationship, definition, abstraction from the external. The fourth limitation on our mind is what is called thinking in terms of conditions or modes. Everything is in some state. You are in one condition, I am in another condition, and X, Y, or Z is in some other condition. Everything is in a particular state, susceptible to change into another state, etc.

These are the only four ways of thinking: thinking in terms of quantity, quality, relation and mode. Now, this limitation is imposed on our minds by the peculiar set-up of space and time. It means that we are conditioned by the laws of Nature,—the Universe. This is the third aspect of life which Yoga studies, apart from the aspect of human society, and human nature as a psychological unit, that is, the relationship of the human individual to Nature as a whole. You are a part of Nature, not merely a part of your family or of human society in this world.

We do not pay sufficient attention to this aspect, unfortunately. We always think in terms of our little family, our mother, father, brother, sister, husband, wife, etc., and if we are a little more generous, we think of the community or the nation. And the best thinking possible for us is what we call the international way of thinking. But what is international thinking? It is just human way of thinking only, quantitatively enlarged. We do not include animals, etc., in our idea of world-solidarity. We think of people only. We are not concerned with anything else than human nature, human beings, and even when we think of the U.N.O., for instance, or the greatest thing conceivable, we as human beings think only of human beings. But the world does not contain only human beings, and it is doubtful if the human being is the best of *all* items available in the world. There may be things better than the human unit, not visible to us, not intelligible to our minds, yet conditioning our very existence, like the cosmic rays emanating from imponderable space, for instance. The destiny of man is not necessarily in human hands. That complacence would be futile vanity with no substance.

Today our modern thinkers tell us of such things as cosmic rays and other subtle forces jetting forth from stellar systems and the regions of nebulae, etc. whose existence is only a name for us. But to what extent they determine our existence here, nobody can understand. Perhaps we could be blown out of existence in one second, if these forces were to begin working actively. With all our efforts, we would then land ourselves in nothing. There is a universal set-up of things beyond the natural forces definable in terms of science. What is mankind, what is man, what is human individual in this vast controlling organisation? First of all, we thought man was one drop in the ocean of human society. Then we came to the conclusion that this drop was very important because it was the totality of the drops that made the whole called society. Then we were led to the more advanced conclusion that even the human individual could not be a self-determining item, because the human individual was controlled by forces which are spatio-temporal, far beyond the reach of human thought, understanding or power. The last step that we have to take is towards the understanding of a universal principle latent in the individual.

Our restlessness, the insecurity that we feel in life, the unhappiness to which we are subject, whatever be the nature of that unhappiness,—all this is due to the working of the universal in us as particulars. There is something in us telling us that there is something wrong with us;—"All is not well, my dear friend!" You are pursuing a will-o'-the-wisp, a phantasmagoria under the impression that you are all-in-all. You are not. You have sides and aspects in you which reach beyond yourself, and the call of the universal in you is the restlessness that is felt in your mind. If you cannot sleep happily at night, if you do not know what will happen to you tomorrow and if you are anxious about your future, all this is because of the working of a secret transcendent power within you from which you are not really separate. You are a particularised unit of a universal organisation in a more real sense than the fact of your being a unit in human society or in any other conceivable whole to which you may empirically belong. Here comes the great clarion call of Yoga. You are not a perishable mortal physical body merely, though in your ignorance you may think that you are such. The law of the conservation of energy, with which you may be acquainted, tells us that nothing can be ultimately destroyed. There can be transformation of nature or character but annihilation is unthinkable. Death is a misnomer, finally, for Yoga. What you call death or destruction is merely the subject becoming aware of a field beyond its local measure, to which also it belongs, and where also it has a duty of its own. Every change, every transformation or mutation, physical or otherwise, is the tendency of the individual to transcend itself into a higher order of reality to which it belongs and which it is essentially. The only word we can use to define this reality, which the individual ultimately is, is the universal.

What do you mean by the universal, may be a question. It is that something indescribable which is the common denominator behind all individuals. This is the reason why we are urged by the impulse to do good to people. Otherwise, wherefrom does this impulse come? Why should I work for the welfare of people if that universal element is not present in me? There is a common principle working in all creation, not merely in human nature but even in the sub-human species, and all that you call the panorama of Nature is guided by a single law, and that law is the reason behind the feeling of oneself for another, the affection that you evince, the love that you express, the connection that you wish to establish with others, and the infinitude that you wish to achieve in your personal as well as public life. There is an endlessness before us. If you need something, you want it endlessly. Suppose you have a little requirement, you would prefer to have it as much as possible, whether it is happiness, or a salary or a status, or even long life. You want to live in this world as long as possible; even if it be for ten thousand years, that would be very good. You would like to live for crores of years. There is no limit to these desires. Everything that you require ultimately hangs on a limitlessness because of the fact that limitless being is behind you working, of which you are only a phenomenon. Thus, the call of Yoga is the call of the universe and the Yoga practice beginning with the physical exercises that you have beautifully performed just now is nothing but an adjustment of your *personality* to the requirements of the universal law which operates in every field of life, including the physical, the body. Thus it is that we are placed in a very happy atmosphere by the Creator of this universe. We have to be happy in our minds that there is something great beckoning us from behind as well as from before. The ultimate goal of all of us is, therefore, success and not failure. We are never going to fail. We are always after victory. *Jaya* is our motto. Triumph is our heritage. Defeat should be unknown to us. Nature never gets defeated, it always succeeds. And if you are inseparable from Nature, victory is your birthright. There is no question of defeat or set-back. Positivity is the law of life. Unhappiness is unknown to us. Sorrow, unhappiness, the sense of defeatism is born of the ignorance of these values, and a subscribing of oneself to the lower values of life, the selfish centres which begin to operate sometimes due to the limitation of our outlook to the physical body and its physical needs merely. Yoga takes us beyond the limits of human perception and tells us that our human outlook and aspirations are only an insignia of an omniscience that is our ultimate heritage, we being immortal units of the Reality which is the centre and the heart of all creation. We belong to all and everything belongs to us. Perhaps the universe is a tremendous democratic set-up where each is for everyone else and everyone is for all. Everything is yours and you are everyone else's. Everything is your duty. It is a duty because it is your right. The two are not separable from you. When the law of Nature begins to work, when the principle of universality begins to guide our life, rights and duties commingle and become one single act, while in our ordinary life they appear to be two different things, where rights are not the same as duties. But there, in that true achievement, they are identical. There is no difference. Because, here, you do not stand outside the law of creation. When the law operates from outside, it looks like a limiting force, sometimes annoying us and making us unhappy. But when we are set in tune with the law, we become the determiners of the law, and we 'will' the law. Obedience to law is happiness. Violation of law is sorrow. And why should you violate the law when you are inseparable from the workings of the law, when the very law is working through you and your very existence is due to the existence of the law? Thus, Yoga makes us beautiful citizens, good administrators and most unselfish individuals, not working for our own personal self, for one's own self does not exist in the scheme of creation. Such a thing is a myth. There is no such thing as 'I'. What exists is a universal purpose, a common good. When this is the great Reality to which we are awakened by the system of Yoga, why should not humanity live in peace? Why should not international solidarity be a reality? Why should not God descend into this world?

This is to give you a short outline of the great heritage before us, the legacy that has been handed down to us by our ancient Masters, the great Seers, who could see through things and not merely see things, as we see. We must be happy, because we are blessed, and a great fortune of positive victory is ahead of us. God bless you all.

THE ORGANISM OF ADMINISTRATION

In the art of administration, the role of Yoga is significant. The chief principle of the system of Yoga can be summed up in a single word: 'Organism'. The term, organism, has deep implications and it is this significant implication behind the principle of Yoga that makes it a novel feature in the conduct of human life.

You have witnessed just now a demonstration of the Yoga-Asanas. The intention behind this practice of the physical exercises in the system of Yoga is to maintain the organic character of the psycho-physical constitution. The body is not merely a machine, and here it differs from organisations of a mechanical character, though the body itself may be regarded as an organisation in a way. There are limbs in the body, just as there are parts in a machine. The physical body is constituted of minute cells. The anatomists and physiologists know very well the structural pattern of the physical body. It has many characteristics that can be compared with the structure of a machine,—for instance, the parts make the whole. But, how does the human system differ from an inorganic machine, notwithstanding the fact that the body also is constituted of parts like a machine? The difference lies here: in a machine, which is inorganic, lifeless, a part can be removed and replaced without detriment to the structural pattern of the machine. But we cannot remove a limb of the body as we remove a part of the machine. We can remove one part of the machine and study it independently. It retains its originality, even if it is wrested out of the whole, which is the machine. But if we remove the heart of a person, take it out of the body and examine it, it will not retain its originality. A heart that is taken out of its relevance to the whole, which is the system of the body, and examined independently outside, will not be a human heart,—it would be a physical substance. But, the physical body is not merely a physical substance. Here comes the role of what we mean by an organism.

There is something in the physical body which distinguishes it from organisations of a mechanical character. The vitality or the life-principle, the *Prana* as we usually call it, is the distinguishing feature. Why do you perform these Asanas? How does the system of physical exercises in Yoga differ from ordinary out-door games, like cricket, foot-ball, tennis, etc? In the usual system of games of the western type, especially, there is a depletion of energy. You feel exhausted after you play the game. You wish to take rest. Prana is diverted spatio-temporally, outwardly: The energy flows out of the body. But in the practice of the Yoga-Asanas, there is an inwardisation of the *Shakti*, the power, the energy, the *Prana*. There is a tendency to the conservation of force and not a spending of energy in the practice of the Asanas.

You heard, just now, the script that was read in connection with the practice of the Yoga-Asanas. Mention was made of the endocrine glands. The endocrine glands are a subtle arrangement in our physical body, which controls the harmonious working of the whole system. The endocrine glands are not like the other glands with ducts. The secretion of these ductless glands is of a different type altogether. It is these glands that maintain us, keep us alive. Whenever there is an exhaustion of energy, a depletion of *Prana*, there is diminution of the activity of the endocrine glands, whereas in the practice of the Yoga-Asanas, the process is quite a different one. There is, as mentioned, a total conservation of force. You not only do not exhaust energy, but increase the output of energy in the body. The endocrine glands begin to function more vigorously here, else they get stifled and there is sluggishness of the function due to a maladjustment of the various parts of this organism, called the body.

Now, I am coming to the point, again, of the organism. The purpose of the practice of the Yoga-Asanas is to keep the balance in the working of the system of the parts of the body. There should not be any kind of over-emphasis or neglect in respect of any part of the body. Suppose a person walks and walks for miles, every day, there is an extra work given to the legs and the other limbs of the body have to contribute their parts, also, for the purpose of the working of the legs, the blood stream moving more towards the legs. There is an unhealthy repurcussion following this over-activity of the particular part of the system. There can also be neglect of the other parts of the body, similarly, the breathing system, the circulatory system, etc. The purpose of the Yoga-Asana practice, is to give the due to every part of the body, and in as much as the mind is intimately and inseparably connected with the body, it influences even the thinking process, the mind becomes perspicuous, there is clarity of thought, you feel buoyant and elastic, a kind of satisfaction automatically follows, a satisfaction that is not the outcome of the possession of material goods, but a spontaneous efflorescence of the vitality of your personality is the cause of the satisfaction that you feel within yourself. You feel happy, relaxed after this routine of practice, merely because of the release of tension in the system. By bringing into force of the principle of the organism in the body, you live a total life, instead of a partial life.

Satisfaction of any kind is nothing but the result of a totality of outlook, a completeness in living, whatever be the field of activity in which one may be engage. Now, I would like to divert to the point with which I began at the very outset. I had occasion to mention that a very significant role is played by Yoga in the art of administration. It is for this purpose that I endeavoured to give this short introduction in regard to the meaning of Yoga. In as much as Yoga is the art of bringing about a sense of organism in life, it applies to social and political organisations also. An organism does not mean merely a physical body. The physical body is one organism, no doubt, but there are other organisms, also, which are larger in dimension. It is precisely the purpose of Yoga to introduce the system of organism to our outward life, too. You must all have heard of the term 'Karma Yoga', the technique of unselfish activity. This art of unselfishly working in human society is nothing but the implementation of the system of Yoga in human life. Just as we have to look to our own physical personality for the purpose of maintenance of health, the physical personality not being an independent unit completely outside human society, it becomes imperative on our part to live this very same kind of Yogic life in our outer social relationships, also.

There are various gradations of organisation. When we enter into the study of the secret of life, we may be said to enter into the region of philosophy. We do not believe, usually, that human society also is an organic structure, merely because of the fact that we are not able to understand the relationship that obtains among people in a social set-up. We have not been able to be secure in human society. We are insecure, as you very well know, and there is anxiety of various types in our social existence. You know, we have no anxiety about the way in which the limbs of the body work in relation to one another. You do not go to bed at night with a feeling of insecurity as to whether the legs will co-operate with the thinking of the brain tomorrow, whether the eyes or the ears may not set-up a strike in respect of the stomach which swallows all the food and gives nothing to the eyes or the ears! You have no fear that, perhaps, tomorrow there may be a battle between the right hand and the left hand. With great composure and satisfaction and security in respect of all the functions of the limbs of the body, you sleep well at night. But we cannot sleep in peace with respect of our attitude to human society. We do not know what will happen tomorrow, what our next door neighbour will do the next moment. We do not live a life of harmonious organic relationship in our outer life. Unfortunately, we seem to be living a mechanical life. Human society is taken to be a machine. Each part is independent and it has no organic connection with another part, and if each human being is to think that he is only a disconnected part and he has no real connection with the other parts, which seems to be the fate of people today, there cannot be any social organisation. There can only be a machine of human society. And if human society is going to be a machine, then we would be like parts of a machine, and I do not think that anyone would like to live in that fashion. There cannot be sympathy then, there would be no altruistic feeling, no love, no affection, no sense of service, no feeling for another, if we are to be only parts of a machine. What feeling does a part have in respect of the other parts of a machine? It works, apparently, in harmony with the other parts on account of their juxtaposition and their arrangement in a certain way by the mechanic.

Likewise, if we are to live in a state of an apparent co-ordination among ourselves, on account of an external pressure exerted upon us by the government, or a social mandate, or by some kind of mechanical rule which has been enforced upon us from outside, then when that force is lifted, we will fly in different directions with no connection among ourselves. Yoga is the recipe and the remedy for this difficulty that we are facing in life today. Yoga is not meant merely for the monastics. It is not a mystical doctrine. It is not a 'spiritual' science. It is, to put it precisely, the system of living in perfect consonance with the law of Nature. And I am coming to a new point now, 'The law of Nature'.

If we are to be in harmony with the system that is operating in Nature as a whole, we can be regarded as healthy persons, physically, psychologically and socially. Scientists,—many of you perhaps are,—and psychologists, too, would be acquainted with the fact that Nature cannot be equated with a machine. It is not a machine but an organism. Only serious biologists, psychologists and philosophers would be able to appreciate this truth. The parts of Nature work in spontaneous harmony amongst themselves. The astronomical system which conditions the movements of planets round the Sun, the so-called rising and setting of the Sun, the changing of the seasons and the various types of phenomena which we observe in Nature, are all motivated by a central organising power which does not stand outside Nature, but works inside it as an inseparable vitality that is immanent.

An administrator, a chief in an organisation, in order to be successful in his vocation, has to behave in the same way as the motivating force behind Nature works in Nature, or that mysterious principle which keeps the body alive, in a relationship among the parts of the body. No one can say why it is that the heart is working so systematically right from the beginning to the end of one's life. Who is controlling this system? We know that we do not have to play any part in the working of the heart, for instance. We can say nothing about it. There is a controlling system immanent in the physical body, in the psychological organism. The word *immanent* is very important, and has to be underlined. It is implicit and it is hidden, it cannot be detected by physical observations. You cannot know the presence of that integrating principle within the psychological organism, which keeps us alive, by any amount of microscopic observation. The principle which keeps the administration in order is inside the set-up of the administration, is a part of the administration itself. I will recite to you a small anecdote which is of a very instructive character and also may appear a little humorous.

It appears that during the reign of the king Raja Bhoja (in the early mediaeval times of India), who was a great patron of Sanskrit learning, a poet sought entry into his court. All learned men at that time were patronised by this king. One great Sanskrit poet wanted to get admission into the court of this king. He was standing at the gate outside and told the watchman, "May I have an interview with His Highness? I want to be one of the court-poets, if possible." The person incharge went and conveyed the message to the king: "There is a learned man, evidently, he seeks admission to the court." The king said nothing. He asked someone to bring one tumbler of milk filled to the brim, and told the assistant, "Take this cup full of milk, and give it to the poet standing there, and say nothing." The tumblerful of milk was handed over. The poet said, "What is the order from the king?" The gentleman said, "There is no order, he has said nothing. He has only given you this milk,—that's all." "Oh, I see, this is the reply. Please listen," he said. The poet took a handful of sugar, poured the sugar very slowly, carefully, into the milk which was to the full, and told the assistant, "Please take this milk back to the king." The milk was brought back. When the king asked, "What is this? How is it that the milk is returned," it was told to the king that the poet said nothing, just as he himself said nothing, that the poet had only poured sugar gradually and slowly into the tumbler full of milk, and there it was. The king seems to have said: "Very good, here is the man. I want him." The poet was admitted. No one knew the secret, what the mystery was of this milk this sugar business.

The idea was this. The king wanted to convey the message that the court was full. There was no vacancy. That was the meaning of the milk filled to the brim in the tumbler. "I have no place." But the poets' answer was: "Even if there is no place, I can find a place, just as sugar can find a place in the milk, though full to the brim." And not only that; the sugar has been so effective that it has sweetened the whole of the milk. "My presence in the court will sweeten your court in the same way as the sugar has sweetened the whole of the milk. Secondly, my presence in the court will not be felt and I will not be an unwanted man, or an extra person, even as one cannot see the presence of sugar in the milk."

This is an anecdote which should give illustration to the ways of a good administrator. Every person who can be regarded as a real leader, a true administrator, is not to be outside the set-up of the administration. He is not just one individual among the many, rather he is a super-individual power. Are we not more than a physical system or disconnected parts? We have an impersonal significance in us, beyond the bodily limbs. This is something which the Yoga will tell you. We are not persons but vehicles of impersonality. The more you are able to develop this impersonal character in your personality, the more will you be a successful leader of people, because impersonality is nothing but the capacity to enter into the personality of other people. But, if you are also to be merely one of the personalities, you cannot enter into others' hearts. Your dimension of outlook is to be wider than the dimension of the outlooks of other people. You are to be a power, rather than a person. You have a significance as a force rather than as an individual, and when you become a true administrator, you become a super-individual element, unknowingly.

Yoga is not a difficult technique, though it appears a difficult one in the beginning. It is an art of expanding the area of your outlook and conduct, so that you learn to live a larger life in your own personal career and private aspirations, as well as be an incentive to others to whom you owe a responsibility, so that when you become the most efficient leader of people, you become a superman, almost.

The lesser the vehemence of your personality or individuality, the greater is the capacity in you for positive achievement. But when one's individuality protrudes itself or becomes an ostensible feature in the organisation, it sets itself, at times, in opposition to other individuals. A true leader of people ceases to be one individual among other individuals and rises above the totality of individualities of others. That is the meaning of the impersonality that the leading individual develops. He may appear to be an individual from the point of view of his physical body, but from the standpoint of his inner outlook, he is not just that much. He is a vibration of an impersonal type, of a super-individual nature. Well, I cannot say that all of us can become supermen.

It is a far-fetched ideal. But we have to try to approximate our lives one step at least, in the direction of the superhuman expectation. Nature is a vast infinite organisation, and we are tending towards the realisation of this infinitude in our lives. That is why endless things are what we seek economically, physically, temporally. Vast possessions are our desire. A very long life is our desire, and anything that we seek seems to have no end. We seek happiness. To what extent? You may say, "Well, there is no limit,—as much as is possible." This urge within us for an endless satisfaction, an infinitude of possession in our quest is an indication of what we are essentially. Nature seems to speak to us in the language of *Dharma*, and infinity, and to the extent we are able to rise to the expectations of this infinity in our working, to that extent we shall be perfect in our life. But if we assert our egoism, if we are too ostentatious in our behaviour, if our conduct in life, in society, is repugnant to the equal affirmations of other people, then we would be a failure in our vocations. We may be factory-workers, office-goers, army-men, whatever we are,—we may be sweepers on the road,—whatever work we do, the spirit behind this work should be of uniformity. When you look to the spirit behind the work, you will find there is no difference between the work of a Prime Minister or a low-paid labourer as far as their contributions to the well-being of the Nation are concerned. There is an organising spirit that is working behind every kind of activity, and when there is harmony among the various types of the manifestation of this central principle of working, we are said to have a national conduct. We should generally speak of a national character. It is the character of the consciousness developed in ourselves in respect of the total ideal of the entire Nation. Dharma is the ideal towards which the Nation is moving and working. If our daily conduct and the little work that we do even in the lowest capacity contributes, directly or indirectly, to the fulfilment of the ideal that is before the Nation, then we have a national character, whatever be the work that we do,—that would make no difference. If we worked only for a parochial purpose, then we would lose the national character. Today we have come to a stage of life where it is not enough if we are merely national units. We are also international citizens. We all know it very well. We are not merely this. There is something more true. We are citizens of the Universe.

You are not merely members of a small family. You are not fathers or mothers, brothers or sisters. You are conscious, significant, responsible units which contribute and ought to contribute to the welfare of the whole country, to the fulfilment of the ideal of the whole Nation, which keep in view the ideal of the whole world towards which human society is moving.

I conclude with a word of caution, you may say, that even an international ideal is not the goal of life. Our ideal is a universal one, and we are not moving merely towards the fulfilment of a national ideal or an international purpose, but a universal realisation. The universe is beckoning us from inside, it is not outside us. The universe is in our hearts. That is the great principle finally, you call the universe, of which you are an integral part When you are summoned by it, you become restless until you get it, until you attain it, until you become one with it. Organisations are degrees of the Universe. There is the physical organisation, the psychological organisation, the social organisation, the moral organisation, the intellectual organisation, all feelers of the Universal Organisation.

HUMANITY AS YAJNA OR SACRIFICE FOR PERFECTION

I am supposed to be here to introduce to you, under the auspices of 'The Yoga Society' of this Academy, a way of the assessment of values, which we may regard as a little removed from the usual manner of the human outlook of life, a system of living whose physical expression is the Yoga-Asanas.

We are here to bestow a little thought upon the impact that Yoga can have on human life as a whole and the relevance it has to the objectives of human existence. There is a need for a re-orientation of the assessment of values, at least from the point of view of Yoga, and this necessity for re-orientation arises on account of the very nature of Yoga itself. Literally, or grammatically, Yoga means 'Union'. The definition or the explanation of the word does not go beyond this simple implication, 'Union is Yoga'. But union with what? And who is to be united, with what?

This is not easily explained, and it is left to us to go into the depth of the suggestiveness of this term, 'Yoga'.

The objectives of life are also the purposes of life. Our culture regards the central aims of existence as the *Arthas*, or the *Purusharthas*, to be pursued by every human being. We live in the world for a purpose, and the activities of life are nothing but implementations of various methods for the fulfilment of the objectives of human life. We are after the fructification of our ideas and the fulfilment of our desires. The object is counterposed with the subject. The object, in its general perspective, is the whole world before us. We are facing the world, in front of us, every day, as an object of our consciousness. Matter is there staring at Spirit, and the Spirit within us envisages the movement and the structure of Matter, which is the world in front of us. Human activity or endeavour, in all its phases, may be said to be an act of Consciousness, struggling to establish an adjustment of itself with the structural patterns of Matter. We are daily trying to adapt ourselves to circumstances, physically, socially, politically and in all the fields or vocations of life. The adjustment of Consciousness is the principal motive, the guiding factor behind the various vocations of life in general. This is the *Artha* which we speak of in philosophical language,—the purpose of existence. We pursue the objective of life and try to make it a part and parcel of our experience. And experience is nothing but the union of the object with the subject. The desire of the Spirit or Consciousness gets fulfilled, when it is united with its object, and a desire is nothing but the movement of Consciousness in the direction of the object. The impulsion of Consciousness towards the object that it has set before itself is the aspiration, the longing, the desire, the craving, whatever you may call it. The intention behind this desire is the cessation of the desire itseif, and we are supposed to be happy, when the desire is fulfilled. We are in a state of anguish when the desire is not fulfilled. The unhappiness that follows from the propulsion of a desire from our Consciousness can be explained psychologically as a result of a self-aberration of Consciousness itself. We go out of ourselves in the act of desiring an object. I move away from myself, as it were, in the direction of something other than myself, and this is what we mean by desiring anything. The subject alienates itself into the object. The *Seer* moves towards the *Seen*. I try to behold myself in something other than my own self, with the basic intention or aspiration to come in union with that which is the so-called object of desire.

There is something interesting about all this movement of Consciousness in the direction of the object. It is not easy to understand why this movement takes place at all. Why should we desire anything, is a simple question that we can pose for ourselves. Why is it that we should be perpetually asking for one thing or the other? How is it that we never remain contented with what we have or what we are? This is a question which takes us beyond the empirical structure or feature of human society. A mere perception of the existent conditions of life will not enable us to give an answer to this question. The phenomena of ordinary human life cannot provide an answer. This question arises from a realm of values which transcends the perceptional ken of our sense-organs. The world that we perceive is the object of our senses. Whatever the senses can cognise or perceive, is the world around us. But the senses are only the external instruments of this propelling force, the desire of Consciousness. There is something deeper and more implicit behind the activities of the senses, which is the reason behind these activities themselves. This basic or fundamental urge, being precedent to the activities of the senses, cannot be explained by the senses themselves. Why we should ask for anything, is a question that the senses cannot answer: well, our mind or the reason may be able to answer. Not so, is the position. Even our reason is incapable of delving into the depths of this mystery. Because, unfortunately, our mind, and even the so-called reason, seems to be working like a hand-maid of the senses and doing merely the function of collecting the evidences given by the senses sifting them into a pattern and arranging them in some sort of an order, passing a judgment on the nature of the various reports received through the senses. Though there is a co-ordinating and synthesising activity exercised by the reason subsequent to the reports given by the senses, the quality of the judgment does not much differ. It does not mean that our reason gives a superior judgment in respect of the world of perception, quite different in every way from what the senses themselves are able to perceive. The mind and the reason seem merely to agree with the basic structure of the evaluation of values envisaged by the senses. We cannot, therefore, understand what is happening to us by the exercise of the phenomenal reason. We are conditioned by the factors which are at the back of the operation of the reason itself. I had occasion, sometimes back, when I had visited this Academy in this very context, to speak on the other aspects of the subject: how the mind is conditioned by the structure of the universe itself. The universe that is perceived by the mind, the reason and the senses, seems to be weighing heavy upon the mind and the reason in such a manner that the mind cannot think independently of the way in which the world is made. The phenomenal character of the world impinges upon the mind in such a manner that the mind can think only phenomenally. The so-called noumenal implications behind the phenomenal perceptions remain untouched by the exercise of the phenomenal reason. We think in terms of the laws that operate in the physical universe so that we are compelled to be satisfied with being physical entities. But you know very well, physical satisfactions are not real satisfactions. People who are physically comfortable are not necessarily happy people in the world. Which person can say that he is really happy in spite of material possessions that he may have, the social status which he may occupy? Why is it that we are always kept on tenter-hooks and we always go on hoping for a better future even when not knowing what that future would be like? How is it that we are always impelled by an urge whose nature is not clear even to our own minds? Is it not true that we are perhaps beckoned by some transcendental meaning in our own selves? Transcendental, because we seem to have no access to that realm. Well, it comes to this, that we do not know our own selves, a very uncomfortable conclusion though. If that is the case, how can I understand anybody else? If the very instrument of action, which is my own personality, is beyond my own self, how could I use this instrument as a tool in the understanding of the world-structure outside? We are unhappy today, as intensely, as people were two thousand years ago. It is a futile patting ourselves on our backs to imagine that we are advancing in civilisation. Where are we advancing, we do not know. Well, it is true, that we are moving, but it is uncertain, in what direction it is. If we are sincere and honest in the investigation of the world situation today, and the psychological condition of people anywhere in the world, we would be in a state of discomfiture, and we should be really sorry to learn that, basically, we have not advanced a whit culturally, beyond what people had to experience and pass through in the ages that are gone by. We are as insecure and unhappy today as the people in the past were. The reason is something that appears to be beyond the investigating capacity of the psychological apparatus with which we are endowed today; and our education has not helped us. Our certificates, our degrees from colleges and universities have not taken us far. We have doubts, the very same misgivings that people had centuries back, and we do not sleep with a satisfied heart. We go to bed with a doubt, get up with a doubt and live our day with a doubt, and at the back of it there is a sense of insecurity gnawing into our vitals. The reason is not far to seek. We have been moving in the wrong direction, under the impressicn that we are advancing in civilisation, technology etc. We are fond of technological development and industrial revolution and scientific advancement. Very good, all this is well. But where does it take us? What is the objective? What is the *Artha*? What is it that we are pursuing, and for what aim or end, is a question that we have not posed before ourselves and we have not been able to answer.

We have in one grand hymn of the Vedas, a point given to us, enabling us to contemplate in the right direction. The ancient seers of the Vedas, in their grand contemplation of the cosmos as a unitary structure, visualised the human being as an inseparable part of the cosmos. They viewed the individual as inextricably involved in the purposes of the cosmos. The involvement of the individual in the structural pattern and the purpose of the cosmos implies a sort of obligation on the part of the individual in respect of the cosmos. We have a duty towards the world, towards the universe, in its entirety. This obligation that we are expected to perform in respect of the world outside, is what goes by the name of *Dharma*. We may translate this term, for the time being, as the law that operates in the world. Any kind of law is 'Dharma'. The essential nature, intrinsic to the substance of a particular thing or object is the 'Dharma' of that object. It is the 'Dharma' of the 'fire' to burn, to give an example; it is the 'Dharma' of the 'wind' to move in a direction, to blow; it is the 'Dharma' of the body, to evolve, to grow, decay and to move towards its cause. The intrinsic nature of anything is the 'Dharma' of that particular thing. The ancient seers emphasised this obligation on the part of every individual, which they designated as 'Dharma'. Now, I must, at the very outset, tell you that 'Dharma' does not mean religion in the commonsense meaning of the term. It is not a belief in God; it is not a worship that you perform in the temple; it is the necessary obedience which you owe to the very nature of things. It has nothing to do with religion in the sense of piety as a super-phenomenal or extra-cosmic attitude in life. It is a scientific truth or principle which has to be accepted on the part of the individual. There is a 'Dharma' of the body, for example. The legs have to walk and the brain has to think. The various limbs of the body have to perform their coordinating functions. Every limb of the body has a 'Dharma' in respect of every other limb of the body. There is a cooperating *Yajna*, or a sacrifice, being performed by every limb of the body.

This term 'Yajna' comes into high relief in this context of the great hymn to the Vedas, I made reference to. The central culture of Bharatavarsha, India, may be summed up in one term, 'Yajna'. You have heard this word uttered many a time. People perform 'Yajna'. They perform 'Havan'; they offer sacrifice, pour sacred ghee in the fire. But, this is only an outward expression, a symbol of the intention behind what is known as 'Yajna'. The performance of a ritual is a spatio-temporal shape given to the inner idea expectation which is the 'Yajna'. I am coming to the point, again. Your obligation to the world, as a whole, is the 'Yajna'. You may ask me, why do you call it a Yajna? Why do you call it a sacrifice? Why do you say that my duty towards my nation is a 'Yajna'? It is a 'Yajna' because of an important factor involved in this process of the fulfilment of duty. In the discharge of duty, whatever be the nature of that duty, we diminish ourselves in one way and enlarge ourselves in another way. The diminution of the assertive or the individuating factor in ourselves is the 'Yajna' or the sacrifice that we perform for the sake of the enhancement of the larger dimension of our personality. Human society, in the Vedic hymn I mentioned, is envisaged as one single organism. We owe an obligation mutually among ourselves, merely on account of the fact that we live a single life of immanent relationships which obliges us to manifest this inner communion in outward activity, conduct, behaviour etc. Our conduct or behaviour, externally, in human society, is an outward manifestation of the internal bond that is perpetually maintained among ourselves, even without our knowing the very existence of this relationship. We are called phenomenal beings merely because of this fact,—phenomenal, because we do not know the 'noumenal' implication of our existence. Yoga is the technique, the art, the science of bringing you into union with the 'noumenal' implication of your own self. The phenomenal individuality of yours is brought into coordination with the 'noumenal' universality of your existence. This is something very profound for us to contemplate. Phenomenally, we are cut off from the world. On an outward observation through the perceptional faculties of the senses, we may regard ourselves as men and women, people belonging to different nationalities, age groups, different levels in economic existence, etc. This is not our real nature. Our unhappiness, to reiterate, is our inability to recognise the fact that we belong to a different order of existence altogether, raised above the one in which we seem to be involved today in this world of diversities. Yoga tells you of the great implication of the Vedic hymn which proclaims that, ultimately, finally, basically, we are neither men nor women. We are not even human beings as we understand ourselves to be. We are bits of universal force. We are eddies, waves as it were, in the ocean of Cosmic Power and it is this deeper reality of ours that keeps us ever restless. That is why we cannot sleep a single night with composure in our hearts, because we have lost our mother, our parent as it were. We have been cut off from our own very source. We are sundered completely from our own self. This is 'Atmaghata', that has taken place, as the Isavasya Upanishad puts it. These people who have lost the consciousness of the Self, are the killers of the Self, and they go to regions which are Sun-less, dark and torturous, says the Upanishad. This is a way of putting the condition that awaits a person who takes appearance for reality and completely misconstrues the relation of himself empirically with this basic Reality of all things. We have a reality in our ownselves which is commensurate with the Reality of everyone else. The *Artha* that we are pursuing, the objective of our life, the *Kama*, or the desire that we are evincing in respect of objects of sense, are nothing but the phenomenal expressions of the beckoning of the noumenal Reality within us. It is calling us. The mother is calling the child, "You come". The universal call is the pull that is exerted upon us in the form of a desire for things in the world. This is the metaphysical meaning, the philosophical explanation behind even ordinary desires or any kind of impulsion from within us to do anything whatsoever, personally or socially, or in any other capacity.

So, Yoga gives us a great message: the message not of any scripture, not of any religion, but the message of the Cosmos, the message that comes from the distant stars, like the cosmic rays, as the modern scientists tell you, which come and impinge on us without our knowing that they are on our heads. The Universe is speaking to us in the language of desire and it tells us that our destination, our central goal of life, is a graduated attunement of our personality with the various degrees of manifestation of this ultimate Reality. The necessity to tune ourselves with the requirements of political administration, the needs of human society, the requirements of even a family or the demands of our own physical personality,—all these are the various degrees of the expression of the law of the one Universal Existence. The various duties that we are called upon to perform in the different vocations of life are the obligations that we owe to this one Reality in its various facets. So, 'Dharma' is Universal. It is not a religious term. It is a scientific expression. It is the 'Law' that binds you to the Whole. It is the principle by which the part is coordinated to the completeness of the structure of the universe. Here is the message of Yoga for you, and difficult as it is to contemplate the further implications of this wonderful message, it is imperative at the same time to bear this in our mind every moment of our life, if we are to breathe a breath of satisfaction, if we are not merely to go on cursing our fate, finding fault with things and getting dissatisfied with anything and everything in life. If it is given us to be happy at least for a moment in our life, if this is a practicable proposition at all, I would tell you that this cannot be, if you are not to be in union with Reality.

Satyameva jayate, is a great motto with which you are all familiar. And what is this Satyam, the Truth? *Satyatvam badharahityam* said a great master. That which is 'uncontradictable', is the Truth, and if 'Truth alone triumphs', it is another way of saying that the 'Uncontradictable' alone triumphs. My dear friends, can I put you a question? Have you seen anything in this world which is uncontradictable? Everything is contradicted by everything else. There is supersession of values. Everything is transcended by something else. There is nothing in this world which cannot be negated by a subsequent occurrence or historical procession. It is because of this fact that it is said that there is no Reality in the appearance of this world. The appearance carries Reality, no doubt, the appearance of the world is a vehicle of Reality, but the structure itself is not Reality. We may make a distinction between *Nama-Rupa-Prapancha* (the world of names and forms) and *Vastu-Tattva* (essential Reality). The vehicle is the outer, phenomenal, transient expression of a particular degree of Reality and not the whole of Reality, so that at no occasion in the process of human history can you discover the whole of Reality. By a study of human history the entirety of Reality cannot be known because at every moment of human history there is only a partial expression of it and the reason behind the procession of human history can only be said to be the universal impulse within everything to effloresce into the realisation of the destiny of history. The rivers will not be quiet until they reach the ocean. There is roaring and rushing and moving and meandering of the rivers and rivulets. All this noise continues until they reach the sea. So is human history supposed to cease moving when the destiny of the cosmos is reached. This destiny is known as *Moksha*, a term with which, I believe, you are familiar, again. *Moksha* is the 'Infinite Value' or the ultimate determining factor of the principles that govern the fulfilment of all objectives,—of *Artha* or material gain, and the achievement of *Kama* or desire both conditioned by a tremendously restrictive discipline, the rule of 'Dharma'. 'Dharma', 'Artha', 'Kama' and 'Moksha',—these four aims are so comprehensive that they mean the total Integral Life of all.

Moksha is the Infinite Value. It is not the last value, or one of the four ends of life. It is the Infinite itself. You cannot say that the Infinite is the last end in the long chain of development. It is Infinitude and, therefore, it subsumes within itself all other values. The temporal values, the objects of the world, the desires of life, the various vocations which we pursue, are all subsidiary to our allegiance to this ultimate call of life in its totality which we designate as 'Moksha', or liberation of the Spirit. The activities in life, in the various fields, and the various aspirations of mankind, whatever be its movements, whatever be the directions they take, all these are the gradual growth of the human personality towards this attainment.

This is the message of Yoga. It is, thus, impossible for a person not to be a 'Yogi'. *Tasmat Yogi Bhava*, (therefore, become a Yogi), says the *Bhagavat Gita*. This is the message of the Eternal to the temporal. It is not Krishna speaking to Arjuna; it is the Absolute admonishing the relative. *Tasmat*,—therefore, because of the fact that it is impossible even to exist maintaining one's integrity without relationship with Reality. Just as, without life-breath, we cannot live, without contact with Reality we cannot exist. The values that we seem to be admiring in life, are assertions of this Universal Spirit, and it is the battle between the Spirit within and the material universe without that we call history. It ceases, it fulfils itself, it finds its consummation, when Matter emerges into Spirit, and Spirit unites itself with Matter, so that the subject and the object cease to be two contending parties. They stand as one integrated Principle,—the Absolute.

This is the goal of life towards which everyone is moving. 'You' and 'I', and everyone else, not merely human but even the other levels of existence are all tending towards this mysterious culmination of the values of all life, and what can be a greater 'call', what can be a more solacing message than this wondrous word that we hear from the adepts who have trodden this path, seen through the vicissitudes of life, and plumbed the depths of existence.

At this auspicious moment, I invoke the blessings of the Almighty upon you all, that, in the words of the great *Mantra* called the *Gayatri*, we have our understandings properly directed. We have no other prayer except this,—that our understandings move in the direction of Reality. We need understanding and nothing else. Understanding itself is satisfaction. *Chit* (Consciousness) is *Ananda* (Bliss). The more you understand, the more do you become happy. It is wisdom that gives you satisfaction and not material possessions. The more you know, the more do you commingle with Reality. The goal of life is wisdom of existence, the knowledge of Reality, union with the cosmos, and this is the ultimate aim of Yoga. It is not merely the ultimate aim, it is also the immediate aim. It is that which is under our very nose, just new, and the step that we have to take now is the step in the direction of Yoga. Life is Yoga.

Talk broadcast from the Ahmedabad Radio Station August 27, 1980

The principles of education are based on the concept of life and the aim of existence directed by the nature of its structure and the prevailing conditions of the environment in which we live It is taken for granted, usually, on the basis of observation and experiment conducted through the methods of empirical science, that the universe is formed of physical, biological and psychological units, called things, entities and persons, in which, when selected and studied in their isolated capacity are known as individuals, and, when taken in groups with kindred characters, go by the name of society. The educational process has normally been a series of techniques in studying and gathering information on the objects of sensory perception and mental cognition, which are supposed to constitute the environment of man.

On the supposition that the units forming the human environment are outside the subject of perception and cognition, educational institutions have been including in the curriculum of studies such subjects as mathematics, astronomy and physics; chemistry, biology and psychology, sociology, civics and economics, geography, history, and politics. To these primary subjects of study were dovetailed certain accepted doctrines of ethics, philosophy, religion and aesthetics, founded on the assumption that persons and things are independent units contained in the cup of the universe, almost like pebbles filled in a bottle, heaped together in mechanical contacts with one another but individually enjoying absolute independence, each for itself. This vision of the universe is practically the basis of modern educational philosophy and psychology and its implementation in the teaching field of institutions. We, thus, hear students being asked to choose a group of subjects among the several enumerated above, and they obtain a pass or a degree after a course of learning how to add, subtract, multiply or divide factors of computation in arithmetic, algebra and geometry, how things behave on observation of their bodies, how they act and react among one another—in short, what is the result on an empirical investigation of the visible structure and behaviour of perceived objects.

The whole system of present day education may be called mechanistic in the sense that it takes the relationship of things among themselves as one of physical contact or of permutation and combination of essentially dissimilar characters brought together into action by change movements of things or by a pressure exerted by factors which are wholly external to their individual wake of constitution. All this naturally implies that we do not live in a world of any inner bond of friendly relationships but are basically formed of elements, characters and aims foreign to one another, which cannot ultimately be united into a real, vital fraternity of mutual relationship. We seem to be living in a billiard ball universe where things are scattered at random in space and they appear to be working in reciprocal contact, collaboration or cooperation either by mere accident or due to sheer selfishness which needs a certain kind of assistance from others for the fulfilment of their objectives. Whether the world is ruled by chance or by the selfishness of its essential nature, it does not, on this supposition, appear to be anything more than a medley of soulless activities of ultimately purposeless motions of mindless forces with an unintelligible intention that seems to be lurking and struggling behind the deepest core of each individual unit, whether inorganic or organic, physical, biological or psychological.

This would naturally be the picture of the universe with which modern science provides us, and an educational system rooted in the perspective of such a scientific analysis and deduction would obviously be mechanistic, soulless, non-purposive, and an altruistic camouflage of a basically selfish intention of every individual. To put it more plainly, this form of educational career can carry with it no other purpose in the end than to perpetuate a physically and egoistically comfortable existence,—to wit, the acquisition of food, clothing and shelter, physically; of sex-satisfaction, vitally; gain of name, fame and power, psychologically; these being the manifest pattern of the psycho-physical organism,—and where the purpose of education has been recognised to cover such fields, as the welfare and protection of other persons than one's own self, it could be easily discovered that it is only a tactful extension of these aims of the psycho-physical individual, for an interest in others is seen to be conducive to an intensification of the satisfaction of these urges as well as to furnish better chances of their fulfilment, as they cannot be fulfilled adequately if there is no cooperation from others and from external factors of various kinds, which fact the personal ego knows well by a subtle insight deeper than sensory or intellectual apprehension.

This is really the unpleasant secret that comes to the surface of one's observation behind the so-called noble efforts of man, based on this educational wisdom, born of this view of the universe. This should also explain why man has always been feeling insecure in an unfriendly environment, irrespective of a love for others and a sense of brotherhood which he has been demonstrating and apparently working for externally, for these otherwise noble virtues are based on false values and cannot hold water for long. An outward form of cooperation and friendly relationship founded on an essentially self-assertive and unfriendly attitude cannot be regarded as having any meaning, ultimately. The truth, when it is bluntly put, would appear to be that we live in a world of love and cooperation which arise from an internal dislike for and irreconcilability with others! Such is the world, such is life, and such is man's fate, when such is the structure and aim of our general attitude and our education, one cannot expect students and teachers to behave in a way which is not demanded by the essential nature of things. This is modern education in its plain colour.

As genuine interest, love and cooperation are characteristics of the soul, these qualities cannot be expected from any soulless system of education based merely on the mechanics of a physical observation and study of inorganic matter, even if it be the study of the solar and stellar system and the electro-magnetic core of atoms, which, science tells us, are the building bricks of the cosmos. If science is right in its proclamation of such results as the ultimate fact of creation, man can never hope for peace, or gain freedom, worth the name.

But is this true? The untiring hopes and aspirations of man are a standing refutation of these deductions devolving from a reliance on materialistic science and behaviourist psychology. Human longing has always been for the achievement of absolute freedom and perpetual peace, with a consciousness of this achievement which implies that consciousness must be capable of reaching a state of absoluteness, which must at once be one of immortality and non-exclusive universality. Minus these profounder implications of the aims of life, which are amply manifested by every man in his everyday life, human endeavour would be a blatant futility, at best a perpetual self-deception, heading towards one's own doom. That a unitive, non-mechanistic, universal purpose is at work behind the mechanised urges and relations of men and things is proved by the very existence and irrepressibility of aspiration. And, that the educational process has to be reoriented and transformed into a process of the vital evolution of a soulful subjective aim of every individual comes naturally to high relief. There is in life a divine core of a basically spiritual reality, hiddenly present in all things.

That the universe is primarily a 'kingdom of ends', wherein every individual or unit is an essence of selfhood rather than a means of exploitation by other individuals; that this aim of a collective organisation of 'ends' and 'selves' is the basic ideal of all pursuit of knowledge; that education is a systematised process of unfolding gradually this eternal fact of all life; that it calls for a parallel advancement along the lines of greater and greater unselfishness and inclusive consciousness of existence tending towards the realisation of a universal Selfhood; that material amenities and economic needs (Artha) and the satisfaction of one's emotional side (Kama) are permissible only so long as this law (Dharma) of this eternal truth of the liberation of the self in universality of being (Moksha) regulates its fulfilment, and that, thus, the whole of the life of an individual is one of studentship and learning in the light of broader and broader outlooks of life which lie ahead of oneself at every stage, are to constitute the vitality and meaning of the educational process. Education is the creative evolution of the total man towards the realisation of his cosmic significance, passing through his personality, the society and the world.

FOUNDATIONS FOR AN EDUCATIONAL CAREER

Education is the process of the gradual and systematic summoning of the tendency in the human being to the realisation of perfection. As the concept of perfection is unclear in the initial stages, the approach to the mind of the public, in this direction, has to be initiated with immense patience and care. When we deal with persons, we are really concerned with minds, and hence all successful approach in life is *psychological.*

We have, first of all, to place ourselves in a position where we can appreciate sympathetic thoughts and feelings of people. For this purpose, we may classify society into three categories: (1) the student, who includes the child and the adolescent; (2) the man of the world or active society, including the youth and the middle-aged man; (3) the retired person, including all those who do not lead an active life but are in the evening of their age. Social regeneration has to keep in view all these stages of life and provide for their respective inner demands.

For the present we may confine ourselves to the minds of the budding generation, viz. the student population, for we have to begin the work of reformation and the regeneration of society at the stage of the student, when the mind is flexible and amenable to the educational process. Here we have to start from the standpoint of the *taught* and not merely of the *teacher*. Education is not a process of merely emptying out the mind of the teacher by pouring its knowledge into the minds of students, but a feeling of their needs and supplying them with the proper thing, at the proper time, in the proper manner. A teacher, thus, has to be a good psychologist and should not regard teaching as a kind of business with the students. The teacher should have the capacity to make himself liked by the minds which need teaching. This pleasant process of the imparting of knowledge is education.

In these days, neither the students nor the teachers are happy with the educational process, because it has been forgotten by the authorities concerned that education has to be physical, intellectual, emotional, moral, active and spiritual, all at once, in a way beautifully fitted to the conditions in which one is placed. The technique of education should take into consideration the average of the intelligence-quotient, health, social conditions, etc. of the students. It should also concentrate itself on methods for bringing about and effecting (1) the development of personality, (2) an adequate knowledge of the world, (3) an adjustment of self with society, and (4) a realisation of the permanent values of life.

By development of personality what is meant is the wholesome building up of the individual, not only with reference to the internal states of body, mind and intellect, but also in relation to the external world reaching upto the individual through the different levels of society. In this sense, true education is both a *diving inward* and a *spreading outward*. Knowledge of the world is not merely a collection of facts or gathering information regarding the contents of the physical world but forms a kind of insight into its inner workings as well, at least in so far as one's inner and outer life is inextricably wound up with them. With this knowledge it becomes easy for one to discover the art of adjusting oneself with society. This adjustment is not possible in any appreciable degree for one who has not acquired some amount of knowledge of the spiritual implications of the structure of human society. The aim of the education of the individual in society is the realisation of life's values,—personal, social, civic and even universal,—all mutually related and determined by a common goal to which these are directed.

Above all, we cannot start teaching students without our understanding the purpose of education. Many a Hindu, for example, has allowed himself or herself to be proselytised for different reasons. One such reason consists in the prospects of economic upliftment and raising of social status which the converters promise to these poor souls who have been unfortunately relegated to the unwanted section of Hindu society, by somehow depriving them of the facilities to improve themselves economically. The second reason is the baneful practice of untouchability and pollution by touch, which certain orthodox groups cultivated for a long time and which has not completely died out even today. Now the question arises: Why should have these things happened? Why should there be suppression and untouchability etc. in human circles? The answer is: lack of *proper education*.

But what is proper education? Bearing in mind the essentials of the process enumerated above, it should be added that though education should be an immensely practicable affair, we should not think that the practicability of a thing consists in what is called 'succeeding' in life in any political sense of the term, because one may manoeuvre to succeed for some time, as one does in business, for instance, but be extremely unhappy within, in spite of the so-called 'practical' success. This happens because here we have only a soulless practicality of affairs, bereft of the sap of life which sustains it. Though, when we occupy a house, we are not always conscious of its foundation, nor is the foundation visible to the eyes, it goes without saying that the whole edifice stands on the foundation. Likewise, human success in life may look beautiful like a decorated and furnished building, but it cannot stand if it is not firmly fixed on a strong base. Our purpose here would be to have some idea as to what could this foundation of life's education be.

Education is for living life and not to suffer it. It is a wrong concept of the basis of life that has led to the defective structure of the present educational system. It is not necessary that religion in the orthodox sense or *Dharma* as the conservatives understand it should be proclaimed in the schools. The right type of education should have a very broad outlook and exceed the limits of parochial religions or the cult of any class of society and should be free from the prejudices of caste, creed and colour. The present-day system of education is thoroughly unsatisfactory, for, while it rejects all religion in the name of secularism, it rejects also the essentials of human aspiration and makes education a dead mechanism which has to be operated by a living being from outside. Education is not a machine to be driven by an external impulse but constitutes a vital process which has life in it and grows of its own accord when soul is poured into it. The bread-earning education has to become a life-earning education, for the latter, in addition to supplying bread, shall also supply man with a soul to live by.

The erroneous construction of the educational basis is, then, grounded on a mistaken concept of life's values. The world we live in is believed to be a solid mass of matter. Even our own bodies are seen to be parts of the physical Nature governed by mechanistic laws, which alone appears to be all that is real. It has become a commonplace today, especially in the universe of science, that life is strictly determined by the law of causality which rules over the entire scheme of the world. We are told that distinctions that are supposed to obtain between such realms of being as matter, life and mind are superficial and are accounted for by the grades of subtlety in the manifestation and spreading of particles of matter. Even the organism of the human body which appears to defy the laws of the machine of the universe as envisaged by science is explained away as only one of the many forms of the workings of the forces of matter which is the ultimate stuff of all things. It is said that even mind is only a subtle, ethereal exudation of forces of matter. The human being is reduced to a speck in the gigantic structure of the cosmos. Behaviourist psychology with its materialistic implications gives a finishing touch this to doctrine of the mechanistic view of life.

The fact that man is not merely a humble cog in the deterministic machine of a relentless world and that the essence of man is a spiritual principle, co-extensive with the Universal Spirit, was easily discovered in the course of human evolution. Those in India, educated under the scheme of Macaulay, however, continued to move along the ruts of a so-called modernism of thinking, a rationality of approach and a scientific attitude of life, so much spoken of in these days. People began gradually to shed their spiritual legacy and started to strut proudly under the unseen yoke of a culture wedded to a secret achievement of suzerainty over them. It is this fatal tendency of thought that has to be counteracted by right means of education today.

A correct appreciation of human values is essential before introducing any suitable method of education. It is impossible to solve the problem of the educational method so long as the authorities feel satisfied that the body of man is the final word about him. The mistake seems to be not so much with the students as with those concerned with the act of teaching, for the students, under the current which flows before them, move with it from an early age. We have to observe with regret that one of the reasons why, for example, some Hindus are willing to change their religion is because they are dissatisfied with the promises of their own religion and the way in which their religion treats them. Apart from the pernicious practice of physical segregation in the form of untouchability and the intellectual assumption of superiority on the part of a few of the classes of society, a sort of false and inadequate values in religion have been responsible to a great extent in causing a schism between man and man in the country. There is the natural instinct to visualise the better in an unknown promise of the future and, like the calf which moves from one place to another in search of the distant greens which it sees with unclear eyes, one is tempted to undergo a conversion of faith. Essentially, what is needed in religion is its understanding by its followers. Often the cry 'save us from our friends', seems to have a meaning. The foolish friend is worse than a knowledgeable enemy. The *Pundits* of the Hindu religion and the scholars who do research in its fields have been both moving in blind alleys, the one clinging to rigid tradition and blind faith and the other to an arid rationality, though untenable. It is not true that we have nothing to learn from the West, as some conservative Hindus may hold, for we have to respect the change of times and the need for a revaluation of values. Indian culture has survived due to its flexibility, when other ancient cultures have died out due to their rigidity. It is also not true that Indian religion is mere superstition, myth and fable, as some modern scientific thinkers in oriental learning seem to think. The good is to be taken from wherever it is found, for knowledge is the aim of education, and not dogmatic clinging to unsound conservatism.

It is necessary to write a small text-book on the constitution of man in the Universe in such a simple way that it could be understood even by children of a primary school. It may begin with simple questions and answers, stories and even small plays which can be enacted on the stage. The book should contain information on the structure of the human personality in relation to outer Creation in a readable and intelligible manner. It should also deal with the fundamentals of human conduct on the basis of this relation of man to Creation. Not only this; some knowledge should be provided of the aim of such conduct on the part of human beings. These things should be said without saying things like philosophy, ethics, teleology and such phrases which are the jargons of the schools of thought. No stereotyped phrases or technical terms should ever be used in such a book. In fact, these should be avoided, because now one is concerned with the primary standard of education where technicality of any kind is to be carefully set aside. The lessons may abound in apt stories and simple plays intelligible to beginners. This may form the background of a preliminary booklet on the fundamentals of life.

There should be three or four text-books in a graded series of this nature, suitable to the primary, elementary, high school and college standard of education. The books should be written in such a way that students should be able to take interest in the subjects and cherish a faith that they are going to be benefited by the study. The high school and college levels should gradually introduce advanced learning.

In the text-books for higher classes, which will outgrow the elementary teachings, stories, etc. of the early stages, the student may be introduced to the great heritage of India in the form of its deep culture. The spiritual-cum-temporal import of the hymns of the Vedas, such as the Purusha-Sukta, the Mandukya Upanishad, the conversation between Yajnavalkya and Maitreyi in the Brihadaranyaka Upanishad the suggestiveness of the Creation theories of revelations like the Aitereya Upanishad, the epics of the Ramayana and the Mahabharata and the basic gospel of the Bhagavad Gita should find a proper place in the higher stages of education. An acquaintance of the student with the immortal heroes of India, like Rama and Krishna; sages like Nara-Narayana, Vasishtha, Vyasa, Suka, Dattatreya, Jadabharata, Vamadeva, Uddalaka, Yajnavalkya, Parasara, etc.; India's great rulers like Prithu, Marutta, Ambarisha, Mandhata, Sibi, Harischandra, Dilipa, Bhagiratha, Raghu, Aja, Dasaratha, Janaka, Rama, Yayati, Bharata, Yudhishthira, Vikramaditya, Asoka and the like, is essential at a particular stage. Short life-sketches of teachers like Sankara, Ramanuja and Madhva, and saints like Gauranga, Nanak, Tukaram, Jnanesvar, Mirabai, Surdas, Tulasidas, Kabirdas, Purandaradas, etc., should be provided in suitable places. The contributions to India's cultural revival by Swami Vivekananda, Swami Ramatirtha, Swami Dayananda, Swami Sivananda, Annie Besant, Rabindranath Tagore, Aurobindo and S. Radhakrishnan should be brought home to the minds of students, particularly in the college level. To give a broader vision of culture in general and to point out the unity underlying human aspirations, a separate section may be devoted to the lives and teachings of Buddha, Mahavira, Christ, Mohamed, the Sufi saints and the Sikh Gurus.

Teachers should, at the background of their minds, keep behind education the fourfold aim of human existence,—Righteousness in all its stages and forms (*Dharma*), economic independence (*Artha*), emotional satisfaction (*Kama*) and spiritual realisation (*Moksha*), as the principal incentive to all human activity. This viewpoint should be constantly maintained at the teaching level, so that the purpose of education may not be missed on the way to the achievement of tangible results. It is also necessary to remember that without some standard of self-control (*Yama-Niyama*), which has to be properly defined at any given situation, the curriculum of studies is not going to be flawless. This is a rule to be observed both by the teacher and the taught. The educational career is a holy pursuit. Its sacredness should never be profaned by indulgences of the subhuman urges. The intellectual, volitional, emotional and active sides of human nature should all receive adequate attention. No one side should be stressed at the expense of the others. Else, there is likely to be a revolt of the neglected aspects at some later stage. The relation between the inner and the outer realities, the psychic nature of man and the physical and social nature of the world, should be harmoniously maintained at every stage of teaching. Let not the teacher think that the student is an instrument that can be operated merely by external pressure. This would be a gross blunder. For the student is a living being, a human individual, with outer desires and inner aspirations not yet properly articulated. Ignorance of this fact has led to the grievous condition of the present-day educational institutions. The individual (*Vyashti*) and the universal (*Samashti*) are organically related and not mechanically dovetailed.

The mechanistic view of education held by Western educationists and imitated almost everywhere nowadays forgets the life-element present in the bodily structure of man and his environment. Education has concern with life, mind and intellect and the theory that these are exudations from the bodily mechanism is the erroneous knowledge imported from Western psychologists. The individual, family, community, nation and the world at large are quantitative extensions of the set-up of the individual's bodily existence, but it is to be remembered that these outer forms have their inner being hidden from the physical eye but asserting themselves perennially as a universal spirit which speaks out in various languages of mind and intellect the same message of the integral value of the entire existence The law of action and reaction, called Karma, the laws of physics, chemistry, biology, psychology and sociology of the moral urge and of political history, are all different affirmations of this eternal truth. Holding this in view, the ancient teachers in India instituted the order of the four classes of society (*Varnas*), to harness wisdom, power, material and labour into a single force of progressive human society. This institution had also the advantage of preventing class rivalry and competition, and substituting it with cooperation and mutual respect of values. The institution of the stages (*Asramas*) of life revealed the ultimate purpose of all existence pressing itself forward in every stage of life,—of the student, the man of the world, the mature philosopher and the one who has attained insight into universal life. The last stage is the culmination of human endeavour and its needs have to be reflected in everyone of the preceding steps. This is India's grand vision of perfection.

The Western yoke on India has left an impact which always insists that whatever modern science says alone is right. Unfortunately, this is not true, for the field of science is sensory, on which are founded experiment and logic, and today the boasts of science are slowly getting exploded as false and vainglorious. One is told that man comes from the ape, that one's ancestors were untutored tribes, that the past history of one's land is the story of animal-men roaming wildly in jungles, that life began with fungi which grew on earth millions of years ago, and that hunger and sex exhaust the psychic urges of humanity. Contrast with this the sublime wisdom of the masters who proclaimed that the world was originally involved in the universal being of God, that life, mind and reason are evolutes which spring back to God in a gradual self-realisation, that history also records the lives of mighty sovereigns and great sages whose personalities manifested the cosmic order of justice, truth and knowledge, that our life is a faint pointer to the latent potentialities for a vaster life in eternity and infinity and that our aspirations are indicators of what we are in ourselves essentially. There is no reason why spiritual intuitions should be mere fancies and only scientific findings be correct. We are already in an age where the very foundations on which science is based are being doubted and are regarded as questionable hypotheses. Sense, reason and intuition are three stages of knowledge, the succeeding one being more inclusive and nearer to reality than the preceding.

Care has, however, to be taken in ensuring that in our enthusiasm, the relative merits of the Eastern and Western cultures are not missed but duly recognised. Neither should a total abrogation of the foreign nor a lowering of the dignity of the indigenous culture be resorted to even by mistake. Cultures stand or fall in accordance with their ability to meet the needs of human nature in the changes of time. Physical education and instruction in the sciences is a necessity, especially in this century, and this knowledge should be imparted in the regular modern manner of educational discipline in the institution, coupled with a touch of the personal element in teaching. This latter aspect is more important in the educational process than the way in which it is likely to be appreciated by many.

Teaching is a more difficult task than learning, for the student has mostly to imitate the teacher and do what he says, while the teacher has to take the original initiative and the trouble of understanding the mind of the student. But we should not imagine that the role of the student is one of mere submission, for the faculty of judgment is present in everyone, though it is incipient in the student Teaching is a process in psychology and calls forth not only superhuman patience but also infinite understanding on the part of the teacher.

Apart from the curriculum of teaching in the arts and sciences, there should be provision for recreation, excursion, pleasant exercise and open-air living. Contact with Nature is as important as lessons in the classroom. A student should not, if possible, be allowed to mingle with persons who are likely to disturb the educational career. A screening away of the student from communal or political movements is essential. Hostel arrangements in the schools would help much in isolating students from undesirable contacts. A distinction may be drawn, if necessary, between residential scholars and day scholars, as it is done even now in certain Christian colleges. Residential education would come near the system of *Gurukulavasa*, where students are not allowed to contact even their parents and relatives during the period of education. All these things may be a little difficult where poverty is rampant and facilities for living are scanty, particularly in our country. It is here that the well-to-do should come forward and help the implementation of true education. The premises and the atmosphere of the school should be clean and attractive so that the mind receives a subtle impact of an elevated mood while one is in it. The dignity of the behaviour of the teachers, the restriction of their conduct purely to educational work, and their unselfishness of motive, add much to the perfection of the course of education. As far as possible, the school should be away from cities and not in the thick of the crowd, which may have an undesirable effect on the minds of students. They must have pure air to breathe both, physically and psychologically.

It is difficult to control the emotions of the younger generation. Regimen and discipline should be mollified by adequate entertainment. Educational and cultural film shows may form a part of occasional programmes. Music and dance of an elevated nature, as also familiarity with the arts of sculpture and painting exert a good influence on the emotion and give it a mild satisfaction. It is to be seen that the emotions are not allowed to grow wild either by too much restriction or by too much enjoyment. Emotions have to be canalised towards the culture of the spirit which seeks its manifestation in the form of life in the world. A satisfactory training in noble living cannot be given in a few years alone. The basement has to be laid at the first standard of education and the work of construction should continue at least upto the Higher Secondary School level, which would ensure training for about twelve years, the minimum period fixed in the tradition of *Gurukulavasa*. Charging of high fees from students may deter large sections of people from availing themselves of such benefit. Poverty is a great hindrance to progress everywhere. The richer classes should come forward and help the working of this system, for the country is not going to be freed from mental slavery and ignorance of culture by educating merely the sons and daughters of a few aristocrats in its different corners. To enable this method of education reach at least the majority, funds are obviously necessary, for the teachers have to be paid well to prevent them from falling into indifference and corruption. More important still is to find proper teachers. Much spade work has to be done in the beginning, and adequate funds invested for the purpose. It is a question of the blending of the intellectual, economic, moral and spiritual powers. All these have to be combined into a single force, as it was done in ancient India by a loving co-operation between the sages and rules.

Summing up, certain features may be reiterated, which go to make for success in the educational process. Firstly, the building of the school or the college should be architecturally attractive and stately, catching one's spirits and elevating them spontaneously. Unclean, slovenly and ill-maintained sheds have a depressing effect on the mind, even without one's knowing it consciously. Secondly, the premises of the institution should be perfectly clean and one should be able to breathe an air of health when one steps into it. Thirdly, the institution should be away from the atmosphere of the city and be in natural surroundings, untouched by the busy, community life and also the communal and political atmosphere of urban areas. Fourthly, the authorities should manage to enshrine an atmosphere of seriousness, solemnity and sublimity in the premises of the institution. Fifthly, there should be a neatness of conduct between teachers or professors and students and a mutual sense of affection and trust between them has to be established, so that the whole institution becomes a fraternity dedicated to a common purpose. Sixthly, there should be a comprehensive and methodical layout of the curriculum of studies in different classes. Seventhly, suitable text-books have to be prepared embodying the subjects of the curriculum. Eighthly, as obedience to the principal of the institution is compulsory in every case, it should be seen that he sets a practical example to others by his ideal personal demeanour, impartiality of treatment and devotion to the ideal of the institution. Ninthly it should be a rule that trainees cannot go out of the premises of the institution during the 'spread-out' of the school or college hours, without permission of the concerned authority. Tenthly, attempt should be made to run as many residential schools as possible, so that the ancient system of *Gurukulavasa* may once again be revived, and students are not allowed to contact outsiders during the whole period of their educational career. Finally, the authorities of the institution should succeed in infusing confidence in the students as to the genuineness of the interest which they have in the welfare of the latter.

All this work is a difficult aim, but it can be achieved with effort.

APPENDIX

A FEW OF SWAMI KRISHNANANDA'S MAJOR WORKS [PUBLISHED BY THE DIVINE LIFE SOCIETY, RISHIKESH (U.P.) UPTO 1980]

1. The Essence of the Brihadaranyaka Upanishad
2. The Realisation of the Absolute
3. The Ascent of the Spirit
4. Resurgent Culture
5. The Secret of the Katho-Upanishad
6. A Short History of Religious and Philosophic Thought in India
7. The Philosophy of Bhagavadgita
8. The Yoga of Meditation
9. The Yoga System
10. An Introduction to the Philosophy of Yoga
11. Mundakopanishad (Reprint: First Print prior to 1954) (11-13 are Diamond Jubilee Numbers)
12. The Essence of Aitareya and Taittiriya Upanishad (Reprint: First Print prior to 1954)
13. Isavasyopanishad (Reprint: First Print 1976 re-edited by Swami Krishnananda)
14. Moksha Gita—Commentary (Reprint: First Print prior to 1954)
15. Vaishvanara Vidya (From Chandokyopanishad)
16. Interior Pilgrimage (A handwritten booklet of 60 pages written at the personal request of Sri Swami Chidananda Maharaj to commemorate the 60 years of life completed on Swami Krishnanandaji's 61st Birthday, contains 60 headings)
17. Studies in Comparative Philosophy
18. Panchadasi
19. The Spiritual Import of Religious Festivals
20. Yoga the Universal Science
21. The Struggle for Perfection
22. Hanuman (A poem which tells of an 'incident' in the studies of Swamiji. A certain author had written the holy scripture, the original Valmiki Ramayana in English verse and it was a good piece well rendered. Unfortunately the author of this English version had omitted the highly important and significant portion, *viz.*, the Sundarakanda—the saving of Sita's life at a most crucial moment by Sri. Hanuman, Lord Rama's dedicated messenger to Sita. This omission hurt Swami Krishnananda who decided to write this portion himself. He chose the very same metre in which the rest of the verses had been written by the said author, thus enhancing the value of the original and restoring the omission in this great work)
23. Chandokya Upanishad
24. Philosophy of Religion
25. Mandukya Upanishad